THE
NEW YORK
MUSICALS
OF
COMDEN
& GREEN

THE NEW YORK MUSICALS OF COMDEN & GREEN

ON THE TOWN

•

WONDERFUL TOWN

•

BELLS ARE RINGING

APPLAUSE

NEW YORK • LONDON

AN APPLAUSE ORIGINAL

THE NEW YORK MUSICALS OF COMDEN & GREEN

Design and production by Sue Knopf

Library of Congress Cataloging-In-Publication Data

    The New York Musicals of Comden & Green.
        p. cm.
    Contains the librettos of 3 musicals with lyrics by Comden and Green.
    The music for the 1st-2nd works is by Leonard Bernstein; the music for the 3rd work is by Julie Styne.
    Contents: On The Town -- Wonderful Town -- Bells Are Ringing.
    ISBN 1-55783-242-0
    1. Musicals--Librettos. I. Comden, Betty. II. Green, Adolph.
    III. Bernstein, Leonard, 1918- On The Town. Libretto.
    IV. Bernstein, Leonard, 1918- Wonderful Town. Libretto.
    V. Styne, Julie, 1905- Bells Are Ringing. Libretto.
ML48.N49   1996
782.1'4'0268--dc20

                                                            96-32626
                                                              CIP
                                                              MN

British Library Catalogue in Publication Data
A catalogue record for this book is avaible from the British Library

APPLAUSE BOOKS   **A&C BLACK**
211 West 71st Street   Howard Road, Eaton Socon
New York, NY 10023   Huntington, Cambs PE19 3EZ
Phone (212) 496-7511   Phone 0171-242 0946
Fax: (212) 721-2856   Fax 0171-831 8478

Distributed in the U.K. and European Union by A&C Black

CONTENTS

Photograph by Thomas Palumbo

Foreword

When my partner Elaine May and I got to New York to perform in a nightclub, the very first people back to see us were Betty and Adolph, and they were the most generous, and the kindest. Betty Comden and Adolph Green became, to me, the very center of everything that's funny and vital about New York, and the theater in New York.

Betty and Adolph live and write in a place where dreams are born and plans are never made. It's not on any chart; you can find it with your heart. I've always thought that when we all get to heaven that for state occasions they will probably play John Phillip Sousa, Irving Berlin, but at the party afterwards, God will say, "Do you think we could get Betty and Adolph to do something?"

—Mike Nichols

Dedication

This book
is dedicated to
George Abbott

On the Town

Music by Leonard Bernstein
Book and Lyrics
by Betty Comden and Adolph Green

BASED ON AN IDEA BY **JEROME ROBBINS**
CHOREOGRAPHY BY **JEROME ROBBINS**
ORIGINAL DIRECTION BY **GEORGE ABBOTT**

On the Town

$\mathcal{N}$ew York is the ongoing background of our lives—Brooklyn girl, Bronx boy—and whether we have been conscious of it or not, it is the background of much of our work in the theater.

These shows abound in the absurdities of life in the "Big City," thorny blends of adventure and loneliness, indifference and danger at every corner suddenly illuminated by unexpected rays of warmth and love.

On the Town, the first show for which we wrote the book and lyrics, was also the first for composer Leonard Bernstein and choreographer Jerome Robbins. In the spring of 1944, Leonard, one of our oldest friends, and Jerry, whom we were about to meet, had just burst upon the scene with their first ballet, "Fancy Free," and were approached by two young producers, Oliver Smith, the distinguished scene designer, and Paul Feigay, to create a Broadway show. We, at the time, were the desperate remnants of our old nightclub group, "The Revuers," and were hanging on by our still God-given teeth as a duo at the Blue Angel. At Leonard's insistence, they all came to see us and we wound up miraculously as the bookwriters and lyricists of this projected show.

We also wrote ourselves two meaty parts in it (Ozzie and Claire), the only way we could hope to get on the Broadway stage. Wartime, three sailors on a 24-hour leave in New York. Lots of adventure, lots of loneliness, laughter, improbable romance against the relentless ticking-away of time, and the poignancy of parting—a lifetime in just one day. The show was written, rehearsed, and opened on Broadway within a period of six months. We had only ten days out of town. This miracle was accomplished by George Abbott, then a youngster of about 60, who came in as director and so came into our lives and changed them forever.

Although *On the Town* is largely about contemporary young people, and is lighthearted and fanciful, even at times surreal, its score has a symphonic texture unlike that of any musical comedy before or since.

"We ... wrote ourselves two meaty parts in it (Ozzie and Claire), the only way we could hope to get on the Broadway stage."

Upper left, left to right: Leonard Bernstein, Jerome Robbins, Betty Comden, Adolph Green

Upper right, left to right: Adolph Green, Betty Comden, Leonard Bernstein

Middle, left to right: Betty Comden, Adolph Green., Leonard Bernstein

Lower, left to right: Leonard Bernstein, Betty Comden, Adolph Green

Cast of Characters

IN
ORDER
OF
APPEARANCE

The stars of the original cast.

Top row, left to right: Betty Comden,
John Battles, Chris Alexander
Bottom row, left to right: Adolph
Green, Sono Osato, Nancy Walter

WORKMEN:	
SINGING QUARTET	
FIRST WORKMAN	Martin Sameth
SECOND WORKMAN	Frank Milton
THIRD WORKMAN	Herbert Greene
•	
OZZIE	Adolph Green
CHIP	Chris Alexander
A SAILOR	Lyle Clark
GABEY	John Battles
ANDY, A SAILOR	Frank Westbrook
TOM, ANOTHER SAILOR	Richard D'Arcy
FLOSSIE	Florence McMichael
FLOSSIE'S GIRL FRIEND	Lula King
SUBWAY BILL POSTER	Charles Rhyner
LITTLE OLD LADY	Maxine Arnold
MISS TURNSTILES' ANNOUNCER	Frank Milton
IVY SMITH	Sono Osato
A POLICEMAN	Lonny Jackson
MR. S. UPERMAN	Milton Taubman
HILDY ESTERHAZY	Nancy Walker
ANOTHER POLICEMAN	Roger Treat
WALDO FIGMENT	Remy Bufano
CLAIRE DE LOONE	Betty Comden
AN ACTOR	Martin Sameth
FIRST MUSICIAN	Sam Adams
SECOND MUSICIAN	Herbert Green
BALLET GIRL	Cyprienne Gablemans
BALLET BOY	Ben Piazza
FIRST GIRL DANCER	Barbara Gaye
SECOND GIRL DANCER	Allyn Ann McClerie
MADAME MAUDE P. DILLY	Susan Steele
PITKIN W. BRIDGEWORK	Robert Chisholm
LUCY SCHMEELER	Alice Pearce
FIRST WAITER	Herbert Greene
SECOND WAITER	Ben Piazza
MASTER OF CEREMONIES	Frank Milton
A GIRL	Nelle Fisher
FIRST DANCING GIRL	Allyn Ann McClearie
DIANA DREAM	Frances Cassard
DOLORES DOLORES	Jeanne Gordon
RAJAH BIMMY	Sam Adams
THREE SAILORS	Lyle Clark, Frank Milton, Don Weissmuller

PREHISTORIC MEN, BIRD GIRLS
SINGING TEACHERS
DIAMOND EDDIE'S GIRLS
NIGHTCLUB PATRONS

1. Overture   Orchestra

Act One

SCENE 1: THE BROOKLYN NAVY YARD

2.	I Feel Like I'm Not Out of Bed Yet	Three Workmen and Men's Quartet
2a.	New York, New York	Gabey, Chip, and Ozzie

SCENE 2: A SUBWAY TRAIN IN MOTION

2b.	Chase Music	Orchestra

SCENE 3: A NEW YORK STREET

3.	Gabey's Comin'	Ozzie, Chip, Gabey, Women's Chorus

SCENE 4: PRESENTATION OF MISS TURNSTILES

4.	Presentation of Miss Turnstiles	Announcer and Ivy Smith
4a.	Chase Music	Orchestra

SCENE 5: A TAXICAB

5.	Come Up to My Place	Hildy and Chip
5a.	Chase Music	Orchestra

SCENE 6: THE MUSEUM OF NATURAL HISTORY

6.	Carried Away	Claire and Ozzie
6a.	Carried Away Encore	Claire and Ozzie
6b.	Chase Music	Orchestra

SCENE 7: A BUSY NEW YORK CITY STREET

7.	Lonely Town	Gabey
7a.	High School Girls	Orchestra
7b.	Lonely Town Pas de Deux	Orchestra
7c.	Lonely Town Choral	Gabey and Chorus

SCENE 8: A CORRIDOR AND STUDIO IN CARNEGIE HALL

8.	Carnegie Hall Pavane	Ivy, Madame Dilly, Women's Chorus

SCENE 9: CLAIRE'S APARTMENT

9.	I Understand (one verse)	Pitkin
9a.	Carried Away Tag	Claire and Ozzie

SCENE 10: HILDY'S APARTMENT

10.	I Can Cook Too	Hildy
10a.	I Can Cook Too Encore	Hildy

SCENE 11: TIMES SQUARE

11.	Lucky To Be Me	Gabey and Chorus
11a.	Lucky To Be Me Incidental	Orchestra (Underscore)
12.	Times Square Ballet	Orchestra
13.	Entr'acte	Orchestra

Act Two

SCENE 1A: DIAMOND EDDIE'S NIGHTCLUB

14.	So Long, Baby	Diamond Eddie's Girls (Women's Chorus)
15.	I Wish I Was Dead	Diana Dream
15a.	I Understand (*recit.*)	Pitkin

SCENE 1B: THE CONGACABANA

16.	Conga Cabana	Orchestra
17.	I Wish I Was Dead (Spanish)	Dolores Dolores
18.	Ya Got Me	Hildy, Claire, Ozzie, Chip
18a.	Ya Got Me Encore	Hildy, Claire, Ozzie, Chip
18b.	I Understand (*recit.*)	Pitkin

SCENE 1C: THE SLAM BANG CLUB

19.	Slam Bang Blues (Dixieland)	Orchestra
20.	I Understand (Pitkin's Song)	Pitkin
20a.	Chase Music	Orchestra

SCENE 2: THE SUBWAY TRAIN TO CONEY ISLAND

21.	Subway Ride and Imaginary Coney Island	Orchestra

SCENE 3: THE DREAM CONEY ISLAND

21a.	The Great Lover Displays Himself	Orchestra
21b.	Pas de Deux	Orchestra

SCENE 4: ANOTHER SUBWAY TRAIN TO CONEY ISLAND

22.	Some Other Time	Claire, Hildy, Ozzie, Chip

SCENE 5: THE REAL CONEY ISLAND

23.	The Real Coney Island	Rajah Bimmy

SCENE 6: THE BROOKLYN NAVY YARD

24.	Finale, Act II Claire, Ivy, Three Sailors	Ozzie, Gabey, Chip, Hildy, and Entire Company

Act
One

Act One

SCENE 1

SCENE 1

After a short orchestra prelude, the curtain goes up on a street just outside the Brooklyn Navy Yard—with the entrance to the Yard itself on one side of the stage. It is early morning—just before six o'clock. It is quiet—the light is just beginning to seep through—and gets brighter and brighter as the scene progresses. WORKMEN are standing about in various states—some come with GIRLS whom they kiss goodbye during this first song—sung by the WORKMEN. The movement is all slow and quiet—but there is an air of expectancy—of a day about to begin.

FIRST WORKMAN
> I feel like I'm not out of bed yet.
> *(yawns)*
> A-a-a-a-a-a-h
> Oh, the sun is warm,
> But my blanket's warmer.
> Sleep, sleep in your lady's arms,

QUARTET OF WORKMEN
> Sleep in your lady's arms.

SECOND WORKMAN (*To THIRD WORKMAN, who is absorbed in reading a paper. Spoken against last line of song*) Ya got the time, bud?

THIRD WORKMAN (*Annoyed*) Uh—three minutes to six.

FIRST WORKMAN
> I left my old woman still sleeping.
> M-m-m-m-m-m-m-
> Oh, the air is sweet,
> But my woman's sweeter.
> Sleep, sleep in your lady's arms.

QUARTET OF WORKMEN
> Sleep in your lady's arms.

SECOND WORKMAN Hey, what time is it?

THIRD WORKMAN One minute to six.

FIRST WORKMAN
> All night I was walking the baby:
> Wa-a-a-a-a-a-h.
> Oh, his eyes are blue,
> But her eyes are bluer.
> Sleep, sleep in your lady's arms.

QUARTET OF WORKMEN
> Sleep in your lady's arms.

SECOND WORKMAN What time is it now, bud?

THIRD WORKMAN (*Yelling furiously*) Aw, six o'clock, will ya!?

> *(The whistle blows—to the accompaniment of noisy, frantic chords in the music. WORKMEN dash busily into the Yard. SAILORS and WORKMEN emerge from the entrance. There is great activity and hurry. On top of this, the three principal sailors enter—all in exuberant state of excitement. CHIP and OZZIE lead, GABEY following, all looking about eagerly.)*

OZZIE Come on Gabey, hurry up!

CHIP Twenty-four hours!!!

(*GABEY bumps into another SAILOR as he looks around.*)

SAILOR Hey, why don'tcha look where ya goin'? You'd think it was your first time in New York!

GABEY It *is!*

(*ALL THREE look about in great excitement.*)

(GABEY, CHIP, OZZIE)
New York, New York!
It's a helluva town!

CHIP
We've got one day here and not another minute
To see the famous sights!

OZZIE
We'll find the romance and danger waiting in it
Beneath the Broadway lights,

GABEY, CHIP, OZZIE
But we've hair on our chest,
So what we like the best
Are the nights!

CHIP
Sights!

OZZIE
Lights!

GABEY
Nights!

GABEY, CHIP, OZZIE
New York, New York, a helluva town,
The Bronx is up and the Battery's down.
The people ride in a hole in the groun'.
New York, New York, it's a helluva town!!

CHIP (*Pointing*) Hey, Gabey! (*CHIP consults his guide book with reverence and excitement*) It says here, "There are 20,000 streets in New York City, not counting MacDougall Alley in the heart of Green-witch Village, a charming thoroughfare filled with . . ."

OZZIE Here we go again!

CHIP (*With a threatening gesture at OZZIE*)
The famous places to visit are so many,
Or so the guide books say.
I promised daddy I wouldn't miss on any,
And we have just one day.
Gotta see the whole town
Right from Yonkers on down to the bay,

GABEY, CHIP, OZZIE
In just one day!
New York, New York, a visitor's place,
Where no one lives on account of the pace,
But seven millions are screaming for space.
New York, New York, it's a visitor's place!

(TWO SAILORS enter, weaving and weary-looking, one happy, the other very glum.)

GABEY Hey! Look who's coming back! Tom and Andy!

GABEY, CHIP, OZZIE Hullo, Tom! Hullo, Andy!

ANDY *(Happily)* 'Lo, guys!

TOM *(Sadly)* Hullo.

OZZIE Hey, fellas, how are the New York dames?

ANDY *(Brightly)* Wonderful—I don't remember a thing!

TOM Awful! I remember everything.

(TOM and ANDY exit.)

OZZIE *(Laughs)*
Manhattan women are dressed in silk and satin,
Or so the fellas say,
There's just one thing that's important in Manhattan,
When you have just one day
Gotta pick up a date—

CHIP
Maybe seven . . .

OZZIE
Or eight
On your way.

GABEY, CHIP, OZZIE
In just one day!
New York, New York, a helluva town.
The Bronx is up and the Battery's down.
The people ride in a hole in the groun'.
New York, New York, it's a helluva town!!

(Scene segues to a stylized version, set to music, of a New York City street and its CROWDS, with GABEY, OZZIE and CHIP vainly trying to make their way. The tempo increases until the curtain parts on the next scene. The CROWDS, frenziedly crossing, suddenly turn facing upstage, and as the music ends they are in their subway places: some sitting, some standing, hanging onto straps, forming a tableau as the SUBWAY SCENE comes in behind them. End of music, ACTORS' poses, and placement of subway happen at the same moment.)

SCENE 2

*A subway train in motion. Typical NEW YORKERS seated and standing. LIT-
TLE OLD LADY is seated. FLOSSIE and her GIRL FRIEND are hanging on straps.*

FLOSSIE So I said to him, "Listen, Mr. Gadolphin, Betty Hutton herself in
person would look like a dead zombie after my day's work in this office."

FRIEND So what did he say?

FLOSSIE So I said, "After all, a girl hasn't got fourteen arms."

FRIEND For Heaven's sake.

> *(TWO PEOPLE get up and the GIRLS get the seats. CHIP, GABEY and
> OZZIE enter through crowd. FLOSSIE and her GIRL FRIEND talk together.)*

CHIP Now, I've got our whole tour organized . . .

> *(He thumbs through his guide book.)*

OZZIE A-a-a-a-h!

CHIP Holy smoke, Oz, I wanna see New York. I've never been anywhere bigger
than Peoria, and I'm not gonna miss any of the famous landmarks. Now, I
got our whole day figured out: 10:30 Bronx Park; 10:40 Statue of Liberty . . .

OZZIE I wanna see the beauties of the city, too, but I mean the kind with legs!

> *(CHIP turns away in disgust.)*

Back home in Scranton, everybody's covered with coal dust. I want one of
those New York City glamour girls, the kind you see in the movies. How
about it, Gabe?

GABEY I want one special girl. I—I had a wonderful girl once. She lived on a
farm right next to ours, 'bout five miles away.

OZZIE (*Turns to GABEY*) Y-a-a-a, we know! Minnie Frenchley, in the 7th grade!!
Forget your purple past, kid. Think of New York! Chip and I'll show you all
the sights. The most crowded place you've ever been in is a cornfield . . .

GABEY (*Grabs OZZIE and twists his arm*) I told you about that! Say "uncle"!

OZZIE O.K., Uncle! Uncle!

FLOSSIE So I said to him, "Listen, Mr. Gadolphin, I will not work overtime, no
matter what. Whether it's handling the Snodgrass-Rumshinsky account—
or you."

FRIEND So what did he say?

FLOSSIE So I said, "One more crack out of you, Mr. G., and the Grand Illusion
Brassiere Company is looking for another yours truly."

> *(BILL POSTER enters through CROWD. He is carrying a bag of subway
> advertising cards.)*

FRIEND So what did he say?

BILL POSTER Pardon me, boys, gotta little art work to do . . .

> *(He puts bag down on floor in front of LITTLE OLD LADY, picks out a
> card and gives the BOYS a quick glance at it.)*

Well, they sure picked a nifty this month.

GABEY What's that?

BILL POSTER It's "Miss Turnstiles for the Month."

> *(He turns and steps up on the seat.)*

LITTLE OLD LADY Watch what you're doing, Mister.

BILL POSTER Take it easy, lady, take it easy. "Meet exotic Ivy Smith . . ."

(He places the card in space over the door.)

OZZIE Oh boy, I'd love to meet her.

CHIP Obviously an upper class society girl.

GABEY Fellas, she reminds me of Minnie Frenchley.

(BILL POSTER gets down, picks up another card from his bag.)

BILL POSTER *(Reading)* Now look at that for an all-round creature: "Ivy's a home-loving type who likes to go out night-clubbing . . ."

GABEY *(Reading)* Gee, she loves the Navy.

BILL POSTER Yeah, but her heart belongs to the Army.

(Their faces fall.)

"She's not a career girl, but she is studying singing and ballet at Carnegie Hall and painting at the Museum. She is a frail and flowerlike girl—who's a champion at polo, tennis and shotput."

(OZZIE whistles.)

Got it all over last month's Miss Turnstiles.

GABEY She's wonderful!

BILL POSTER *(Leaving)* Why don'tcha date her up? Well, so long, fellas. Drop in again sometime.

(Exits.)

GABEY That's the girl for me, fellas. I'd like to meet her today.

"That's the girl for me, fellows."

Center: GABEY (John Battles), CHIP (Chris Alexander), OZZIE (Adolph Green)

CHIP There are two million, five hundred thousand women in New York—and—it's impractical.

OZZIE If Gabe wants her, he can have her. He's a Naval hero. He deserves a girl like that!

> *(GABEY has climbed on the seat and is taking the picture down.)*

LITTLE OLD LADY (*Rises, protesting*) Young man, that's vandalism!

CHIP Hey, Gabe, what are ya doing?

OZZIE Put it back, Gabe . . .

GABEY (*Staring at it*) Why? I like her . . .

LITTLE OLD LADY Destroying public property! You're liable to a fine of $500. I'll get a policeman!

OZZIE Hey, I think she means it.

LITTLE OLD LADY (*Screaming*) Conductor! Conductor! Police!!

OZZIE Hey, come on, let's get out of here!

LITTLE OLD LADY Put that back!!

CHIP Come on, Gabe! Come on!!

OZZIE (*Grabs GABEY bodily, forces him through crowd*) Gangway, folks!!

LITTLE OLD LADY Vandals! Vandals! Police!

> *(She tries to follow them, but the BOYS push through the CROWD and exit. The subway disappears, and the LITTLE OLD LADY brandishes her umbrella and runs back and forth looking for a policeman, jumps up and down in the spirit of a silent movie chase, and runs off to chase music.)*

SCENE 3

A New York Street.GABEY, CHIP and OZZIE enter. GABEY is still engrossed in IVY's picture.

CHIP But Gabe, be reasonable. There are twenty thousand streets in this town— and you'll never find her in one day.

GABEY So that's my hard luck. (*He looks at the picture*)

CHIP Well, I'm not gonna waste any more time on this. I'm way behind on my schedule already. Bronx Park is a dead issue. (*Crosses it off his guidebook*)

OZZIE Hey, Chip. If Gabe hadn't pulled us out of the drink, we wouldn't *be* here in New York! We'd be just a couple of pleasant memories.

GABEY (*He doesn't want to hear it*) Oh, the hell with that. (*He moves away and continues to stare at the picture*)

OZZIE (*Getting an idea*) Chip, you and me are gonna help him find her.

CHIP WHAT!?

OZZIE We're going to help him find Ivy Smith.

CHIP Help him find her? (*Waves guidebook excitedly*) That's crazy, I gotta . . .

OZZIE What's the matter with you? Haven't you got any gratitude? What kind of people come from Peoria, anyway? I'll give up all my girls till tonight to help Gabe—If you'll promise to give up your sightseeing.

CHIP All right. But how're we gonna do it?

OZZIE That's your department. You're the guy with the systems! 10:30—Yellow-stone Park; 10:45—Opium Dens—

CHIP Let's see the card, kid.

> (*CHIP grabs the picture from GABEY and holds it away from him.*)

GABEY (*Trying to get it back*) Hey!

CHIP Uh . . . I got it. We'll break up and follow all the clues on this poster . . . and . . . and we'll meet. At Times Square, at Nedick's . . . at . . . eleven . . .

OZZIE Swell! One of us'll find her. And then, Gabe, she's all yours.

GABEY Aw, that'll never work.

CHIP It might work. It's all down there in black and white. She's got to be one of those places.

OZZIE Now look, Gabe, if you do happen to run into her, without me there to advise you, just remember: the whole secret is be a bigshot. You're impor-tant, see. You're a hero.

> (*Dusts off GABEY's ribbons*)

Just keep saying to yourself, "Gabey's coming." Get it?

GABEY Gabey's coming.

OZZIE Yeah. Gabey's coming.

OZZIE AND CHIP
> Gabey's comin',
> Gabey's comin' to town!

He's on the town.
With a day to burn,
You're gonna turn
New York City upside down!

GABEY, CHIP, OZZIE
    Gabey's comin' to town!

(A number of GIRLS enter and pose.)

OZZIE Here's the way you do it!

(To the GIRLS, for GABEY'S instruction:)

    Hello, baby, gosh you're pretty;
    I'm so tall and strong and witty;
    God's great gift to New York City.
    How's about a date tonight?

CHIP

    When a guy is feeling tender
    He don't want no solo bender,
    What he craves is sweet surrender.
    How's about a date tonight?

GIRLS *(Excited)*

    Date tonight? Date tonight? Love it!

    Gabey's comin',
    Gabey's comin' to town!
    He's on the town!

"Hello, babe, you look delicious."
Center: OZZIE
(Adolph Green)

Gonna brush my teeth
Down underneath,
Slip into my sheerest gown
Gabey's comin' to town!

OZZIE

Hello, babe, you look delicious
You're the answer to my wishes.
Let's start buying breakfast dishes.
How's about a date tonight?

CHIP

Aren't we having lovely weather?
We're two birdies of a feather;
We could make such tunes together.
How's about a date tonight?

GIRLS

Date tonight? Date tonight? Love it!

Gabey's comin',
Gabey's comin' to town!
He's on the town!

Gonna take a dive
In Chanel Five,
For that lover,

GIRLS & GABEY

For that lover,

GIRLS, GABEY, CHIP & OZZIE

For that lover of renown!
Gabey's comin' to town!

(*The GIRLS exit.*)

CHIP Gabey, you go to Carnegie Hall. And Ozzie, you go to the Modern
Museum.

OZZIE (*Disgusted*) Museum?

CHIP It's at 79th Street and Central Park. And I'll investigate through the
subway people.

GABEY & OZZIE Huh?

CHIP The underground authorities.

GABEY But what about your dames?

OZZIE A-a-h, we can pick up somebody later on. That's easy. After all, the girls
we're willing to date aren't fancy contest winners.

CHIP Yes. Can you imagine what that Miss Turnstiles must be like?

GABEY To win such a title—Miss Turnstiles for June!

(*THEY exit.*)

"Gotta pick up a date—"
From the MGM film On The Town
Left to right:

Jules Munshin, Frank Sinatra, Gene Kelly

Act
One
SCENE 4

SCENE 4

Presentation of Miss Turnstiles. There is a fanfare, and the ANNOUNCER *steps on.*

ANNOUNCER Miss Turnstiles for June!

> *(A line of* GIRLS *sways in, backs to audience.)*

Every month some lucky little New York miss is chosen Miss Turnstiles for the month. She's got to be beautiful, she's got to be just an average girl, and most important of all, she's got to ride the subway. There are 3,000,000 women who ride the subway every day. And which fortunate lassie will be picked this month for the signal honor? Beautiful, brilliant, average, a typical New Yorker—

> *(A spotlight which has been roving up and down the line of* GIRLS *as it sways across the stage suddenly stops on one of the* GIRLS. *The line stops, and the girl,* IVY SMITH, *turns around with a happy "Who, me?" expression.)*

YES, YOU!! Ivy Smith!

> *(*IVY *runs forward and the other girls disappear. A* REPORTER, *a* PHOTOGRAPHER *and* ASSISTANT, *a* DRESS DESIGNER *and* ASSISTANT *gather around to glamourize and publicize* MISS TURNSTILES. *During this, the* ANNOUNCER *sings. A large blowup of the Miss Turnstiles poster flies in.)*

She's a home-loving girl,
But she loves high society's whirl.
She adores the Army, the Navy as well,
At poetry and polo she's swell.

> *(The* PHOTOGRAPHER, *the* REPORTER, *the* DESIGNER *and* ASSISTANT *back off, and* IVY *and A* SERIES OF MALE ADMIRERS *as delineated in the lyric [*HOME-LOVING TYPE, PLAYBOY, SOLDIER, SAILOR, AESTHETE, ATHLETE*] do a satiric dance based on the contradictory attributes that Miss Turnstiles seems to possess:* IVY *does a brief pas-de-deux with each of them and a final dance with them* ALL. *At the end of the dance, the voice of the* ANNOUNCER *is heard.)*

ANNOUNCER But, of course, at the end of each month, a *new* Miss Turnstiles is chosen, and when that happens . . .

> *(The* ADMIRERS *all disappear.* IVY *waves a sad farewell to them. Her picture, an enlargement of the subway advertisement, which has been on display at the rear of the stage, disappears. She waves goodbye to that. The same line of* GIRLS *appears again, sidling on with their backs to the audience.* IVY *disconsolately resumes her place in line and sidles off with the rest as the Curtain closes.)*

> *(Second Chase Interlude. The* LITTLE OLD LADY *finds a* POLICEMAN, *tells him about the vandalism, and they run off.)*

SCENE 5

A taxicab. Inside the cab is a young tough GIRL CABBIE, who is asleep. A MAN wearing a jacket, on the back of which is printed "S. UPERMAN," awakens her roughly.

UPERMAN Hey—hey, you!

HILDY (*Hardly awake*) Taxi?

UPERMAN Wake up, Esterhazy, it's me—your boss—Uperman.

HILDY (*Trying to look alert*) Oh, Mr. Uperman, good morning.

UPERMAN (*Very sarcastic*) Good morning to you. I just dropped by to tell you this is the last time I'm catching you asleep. You're fired.

HILDY But Mr. Uper—

UPERMAN And if that cab ain't back in the garage in an hour, I'll turn you in to the cops.

> (*He exits.*)

HILDY (*Philosophically*) Well, a civilian again! Might as well make this last fare a good one.

> (*She looks around. A MAN rushes up to the cab.*)

MAN Taxi. Grand Central Station—quick.

HILDY (*Looking at him disapprovingly*) Uh-uh. Too small.

> (*He rushes off in a huff.*)

ANOTHER MAN Taxi!

HILDY (*Turning him down*) Too big!

> (*He withdraws. CHIP enters. A GIRL approaches; HILDY shouts at her.*)

AND NO GIRLS!!

> (*GIRL runs away. CHIP, consulting his guidebook, tries to get his bearings. HILDY sees him and her face lights up. She shouts at him*)

Hey, you!

CHIP (*Looking up, startled*) Who? Who, me?

HILDY Yes, you. Get in.

CHIP (*Coming over to her*) Oh, maybe you can take me to the subway people.

HILDY (*Does a take*) The what?

CHIP The subway people . . .

HILDY (*As if she knows all about it*) Oh, sure—sure—and when we get through with them, we'll go see the Cat People. Only get in.

> (*He starts getting into the back of the cab.*)

No. Up front! This ride's on me!!

CHIP But lady, I . . .

> (*She pulls him into the front seat.*)

HILDY What's your name?

CHIP Uh—John Offenblock—but the fellas call me Chip.

HILDY (*Coquettishly*) Chip, huh. Betcha can't guess my name.

CHIP Guess it? Oh, that's ridiculous. Why, the law of averages . . .

HILDY O.K. You win! The name's Esterhazy. Brunhilde Esterhazy. (*Slight pause*) Kiss me!

> (*He doesn't. She grabs him. They disappear in a clinch behind the steering wheel, and come up after a moment, he, all flustered, and she all aglow.*)

Well! Let's go to my place!!

CHIP I—I'd like to, lady,—but I have to . . .

HILDY Aw, what's the matter with me, Chip, why won't you come? I'm young, I'm free, I'm highly attainable.

CHIP (*Leaning against the door*) Look, Miss, I got a promise to stick to . . .

"I'm young, I'm free, I'm highly attainable."

CHIP (Chris Alexander), HILDY (Nancy Walker)

HILDY You stick to me instead, kid. I've been waiting for you all my life. Knew you the minute I saw you. You're for me. I like your face. It's open, ya know what I mean? Nothing in it. The kind of a face I can fall into. Kiss me!

> *(She grabs him, pulls him down in the seat, and kisses him. He breaks away and gets up.)*

CHIP Listen, lady . . .

HILDY Just call me Hildy.

CHIP Look, Miss—I got something important to do today. Just lemme outta here.

> *(He starts out of the cab.)*

HILDY (*Moves over and grabs his sleeve*) A-a-a-h, no you don't. You're going with me while I turn in my cab. After that, we'll go up to my place.

CHIP Now, look, miss, I've got to find this Miss Turnstiles for my pal . . .

HILDY (*Hits her forehead with hand, then turns and looks out window*) Miss Turnstiles for your pal! Well, I thought I'd heard 'em all. You're not going to get rid of me that easy, kid.

> *(She turns to him.)*

CHIP Oh, no, it's true. If I didn't have to help my buddy, I'd be out seeing the famous sights my father told me about. He was here in 1934, and gave me this guidebook, and . . .

HILDY (*Grabs the guidebook*) I'll take you any place you want to go. Get in.

CHIP I shouldn't do this.

HILDY Come on, Chip.

CHIP (*Guiltily*) O.K., a quick tour of the city.

HILDY (*Triumphantly*) Then up to my place!

> *(She pats his knee.)*

CHIP No—to help find Gabe's girl.

HILDY No—up to my place!

CHIP But . . .

HILDY It's all settled. Where d'ya wanna go first? (*She starts the cab with a lurch. Yells at unseen passerby*) Ah, the same to you!

CHIP
> My father told me, "Chip, my boy,
> There'll come a time when you leave home;
> If you should ever hit New York,
> Be sure to see the Hippodrome."

HILDY
> The Hippodrome?

CHIP
> The Hippodrome.

HILDY
> Did I hear right?
> Did you say the Hippodrome?

CHIP

Yes, you heard right.
Yes, I said the Hip . . .

(She brakes suddenly. He is shaken up.)

Hey, what did you stop for?

HILDY

It ain't there anymore.
Aida sang an "A" and blew the place away!

CHIP Aw, I wanted to see the Hippodrome!

HILDY Give me a chance, kid. I haven't got 5,000 seats, but the one I have is a honey! Come up to my place.

CHIP Oh, no, lady; I'd rather see the Forrest Theatre.

(She reluctantly puts the cab in gear and starts off.)

When I was home I saw the plays
The ladies' drama circle showed.
Now I'm here, I want to get
Some tickets for "Tobacco Road."

HILDY

"Tobacco Road?"

CHIP

"Tobacco Road."

HILDY

Did I dig that?
Did you say "Tobacco Road?"

CHIP

Yes, you dug that.
Yes, I said "Tobac" . . .

(She brakes again. He somehow recovers from the braking.)

Hey, what for did you stop?

HILDY

That show has closed up shop.
The actors washed their feet
And called it "Angel Street."

CHIP I wanted to see "Tobacco Road."

HILDY Stick with me, kid, and I'll show you the road to ruin. Come up to my place!

CHIP No, could we go to Battery Park.

(She puts the cab back in gear again.)

Back home I dreamt of catching fish
So big I couldn't carry 'em.
They told me that they have my size
Right here in the aquarium.

HILDY

Aquarium?

CHIP

Aquarium.

HILDY

     Hold the phone, Joe,
     Did you say aquarium?

CHIP

     I'm still ringing.
     Yes, I said aquar . . .

     (She brakes. He has the same reaction as before.)

     Did you stop for what, hey?

HILDY

     The fish have flown away;
     They're in the Bronx instead,
     They might as well be dead!

  Come up to my place!

CHIP No, let's go to Chambers Street.

     (Once more she puts the cab in gear)

     They told me I could see New York
     In all its spreading strength and power
     From the city's highest spot,
     Atop the famous Woolworth Tower.

HILDY

     The Woolworth Tower?

CHIP

     The Woolworth Tower.

HILDY

     Beat me, daddy.
     Did you say the Woolworth Tower?

CHIP

     I won't beat you,
     But I said the Wool . . .

     (She brakes. He is thrown onto the floor of the cab.)

     Did you stop for hey what?

HILDY

     That ain't the highest spot.
     You're just a little late,
     We've got the Empire State!

     (She begins driving furiously.)

     Let's go to my place!

CHIP

     Let's go to Cleopatra's Needle.

HILDY

     Let's go to my place!

CHIP

     Let's see Wanamaker's store.

HILDY

     Let's go to my place!

CHIP

Let's go to Lindy's, go to Luchow's.

HILDY

Go to my place!

CHIP

Let's see Radio City and Herald Square.

HILDY

Let's go to my place!

CHIP

Go to Reuben's!

HILDY

Go to my place!

CHIP

Go to Macy's!

HILDY

Go to my place!

CHIP

To the Roxy!

HILDY

Go to my place!

CHIP

Cloisters!

HILDY

My place!

CHIP

Gimbel's!

HILDY

My place!

CHIP

Flatiron Building!

HILDY

My place!!

CHIP

Hippodrome!!!

HILDY My place!!!!

(*Blackout.*)

(*The Third Chase Interlude. UPERMAN finds a cop, tells him about HILDY's taking the cab. They run off. LITTLE OLD LADY and her cop follow in pursuit.*)

ON THE TOWN

Act One
SCENE 6

SCENE 6

Museum of Natural History. The scene is a large chamber in the Museum of Natural History devoted to prehistoric animals. It's rather an eerie sight, filled with pterodactyls hanging from wires, skeletons of some smallish strange reptiles, and the skeleton of one huge dinosaur, with its shadow projected enormously against the back wall. This figure dominates the scene. A few feet away from it stands a realistic statue of a Pithecanthropus Erectus, an ancestor of present-day man, somewhat more ape than man, who roamed the earth in around 6,000,000 BC. The statue bears a striking resemblance, enough to be startling, to OZZIE, *who is at this moment part of a small group of people gathered in front of the dinosaur skeleton listening to a lecture. The* SPEAKER *is a fussy little professorial type,* WALDO FIGMENT, *and* OZZIE, *looking about for a possible Ivy Smith, isn't paying the strictest attention.*

FIGMENT (*Speaking slowly and painfully*) This unique skeleton—I have reconstructed without any clue whatsoever—except for one tiny bone—found during a picnic in Westchester—in the bushes. Let us consider that these huge beasts might be living today—but they were the victims of over-inflation. They became too goddamned big! Thank you. Let us move on.

> (*The* CROWD *disperses, muttering and generally discussing the dinosaur as they drift away, leaving the stage clear except for* OZZIE, *who stares after them disappointedly, and* PROFESSOR FIGMENT, *who is busily arranging his notes in a briefcase.*)

OZZIE Mr. Bones, maybe you can help me. I'm looking for a girl called Ivy Smith and I thought she might be at the Museum of Modern Art.

"Don't touch that dinosaur!"

Center: OZZIE
(Adolph Green),
PROF. FIGMENT
(Remy Bufano)

FIGMENT (*Testily*) She probably is. This is the Museum of Natural History.

> (*FIGMENT moves to exit. He notices OZZIE start to move up to the dinosaur and turns back.*)

OZZIE Chip and his guide book . . .

FIGMENT And don't touch that dinosaur, or I'll call a policeman. It took me forty hard long years to construct that. (*Looks at dinosaur and sadly shakes his head*) Sometimes I wish I hadn't gone on that picnic.

> (*FIGMENT exits, shaking his head. OZZIE yawns and stretches wildly and freely, unconsciously assuming the pose of the Pithecanthropus statue, which he is standing beside. OZZIE is entirely unaware of his resemblance to the statue. As he is doing this, CLAIRE DE LOONE enters briskly, apparently on her way to look at the dinosaur. She is a handsomely attractive, smartly dressed girl, and seems to be of the cool and poised school. However, upon seeing OZZIE and the statue side by side, both with arms stretched aloft, she stops dead in her tracks and shrieks.*)

CLAIRE A-a-a-a-a-ah-h-!

OZZIE (*Stifles yawn, sees her*) Don't be frightened, lady. They're all dead.

CLAIRE But you!! You're alive. (*She drops handbag on bench*) How wonderful!! (*Takes camera from bag*)

OZZIE (*Surprised—and conscious of being accosted by an attractive girl*) And you're alive, too. Don't we make a lovely couple.

> (*He makes a gesture toward her.*)

CLAIRE Yes, you do. (*Referring to him and statue, of course*) It's fantastic. I've got to get the two of you together. Hold it, please.

> (*She draws back and snaps photo. Included in her equipment are a notebook and pencil and tape measure in her handbag. OZZIE freezes in pose.*)

Incredible. A Pithecanthropus Erectus—in a sailor suit! Dear, you're priceless!

OZZIE (*Taking all this as flattery*) Really, well, how about some cheesecake.

> (*He drapes himself in a Dietrich pose, pulling up his trouser leg.*)

CLAIRE (*Beside herself*) That leg! How extraordinary! In all my studies, I've never seen one like it. (*Snaps another photo*) This is wonderful. What a lucky girl I am. Now—your measurements.

> (*CLAIRE approaches him, taking out her tape measure. OZZIE is more and more suprised and pleased. He continues posing.*)

OZZIE Well, I'm a Junior Miss size 11—That's about all I can remember.

CLAIRE Gorgeous!!

> (*She puts the tape measure over her arm and starts to make a note in her notebook. She turns away from OZZIE, and he takes the tape from her arm playfully.*)

OZZIE (*From behind her*) Now it's my turn.

> (*He measures her bust, humming.*)

New York, New York—a helluva town!!

CLAIRE (*Taken completely off guard*) How dare you!

> (*She turns and grabs the tape measure. He thinks he's being wooed.*)

OZZIE Two can play the same game as well as one, you know!

CLAIRE (*Backing away*) Now look here!

> (*OZZIE chases her around the Pithecanthropus Erectus.*)

Just what I should have expected from a Pithecanthropus Erectus—No breeding! What's the idea?

> (*OZZIE bumps into the Pithecanthropus Erectus.*)

OZZIE Owww! Out of my way, Quasimodo!! (*He resumes the chase*)

CLAIRE (*Angrily*) Quasimodo is right! The spittin' image of you.

OZZIE (*Standing still abruptly*) Huh? (*He looks at the statue, does a terrific take as he realizes*) You mean I look like that?

CLAIRE (*Surprised he doesn't know*) Look like?! Well, what on earth did you think I was taking your picture for?

OZZIE (*Deflated, realizing she wasn't chasing him*) You mean . . .

CLAIRE (*Getting the misunderstanding, realizing he thought she was on the make*) Oh, I see, you thought I was carried away by your irresistible charms. I'm sorry—

> (*She is cool, amused, but keeps looking at him. He gets gloomier and gloomier.*)

I'll clear the whole thing up. I'm just a cold-blooded scientist. An anthropologist. The name is Claire de Loone.

OZZIE An anthropologist! (*Completely deflated*) Pleased to meetcha.

CLAIRE (*She looks him up and down. Writes in her book*) I'm writing a book for this Museum—an anthropological study called "Modern Man—What Is It?"

> (*He sniffs.*)

And that's my only interest in modern man. You bear an extraordinary resemblance to this Pithecanthropus Erectus, a man extinct since six million B.C. And that's why I need your picture—and your measurements. Now then—

> (*She goes over to him with tape measure and notebook.*)

OZZIE Aaah, I'm just wasting my time. Look, lady, I'm looking for a girl named Ivy Smith. She was chosen Miss Turnstiles for the month of June. Do you know her?

CLAIRE No, I don't. But you might ask at the information desk on your way out.

> (*Measuring his arm, looking at him.*)

Now don't be moody—

> (*Measures his chest from under-arm to waist.*)

You made an understandable mistake. Now the head—

> (*Takes his hat off, hands it to him, measures his head.*)

Ah! That sub-super-dolico cephalic head! Sailor, I love you for having that. *(Makes a note admiringly)*

OZZIE Gee, all my life I wanted someone to love me for my sakidophalic head.

CLAIRE Now don't be bitter.

> *(She pushes his hat forward, measures the back of his head between the ears. She holds the tape measure out and is surprised to find about only two inches. She looks at him and then makes another note. OZZIE pushes his hat to the back of his head.)*

"Now—your measurements."

CLAIRE (Betty Comden), OZZIE (Adolph Green)

*"Ah! That sub-
super-dolico-
cephalic head!"*

CLAIRE (Betty
Comden), OZZIE
(Adolph Green)

OZZIE There aren't so many of us left. We had a sakidocephalic class reunion last year. Not many of the old faces around.

CLAIRE (*Rolling up tape measure with finality*) Thank you . . . I'm finished now. (*She goes to bench*) You may go now. Ask at the information desk on your way out for your friend. (*She sits and makes a note in her book*)

OZZIE I can go now!—I can go now!! You use me as a guinea pig, take my measurements, then you tell me I can go. All right, I'll go.

    (*CLAIRE looks at him.*)

I've been neglecting my duty anyhow.

CLAIRE Goodbye.

OZZIE G'bye.

    (*Turns back to CLAIRE.*)

Hey, look—

    (*Approaches her.*)

Seeing as how you're not interested in modern man, then you probably haven't got a date tonight.

(CLAIRE looks up, surprised.)

Uh—(*He sits*) You gonna be busy later?

CLAIRE Very busy. I'll be busy for the rest of my life. I'm engaged to be married.

OZZIE Uh-huh. Well, in that case, I'll be going—

(OZZIE rises, starts to go, then turns to CLAIRE.)

CLAIRE Goodbye.

OZZIE G'bye. Who's the lucky man?

CLAIRE I'm engaged to be married to the famous Judge Pitkin W. Bridgework. We're celebrating our engagement tonight.

OZZIE Is he hot stuff?

CLAIRE (*Rises and approaches him angrily*) Hot stuff! Of all the loathsome phrases. Pitkin is the finest man I've ever known. He understands me completely. We have a purely intellectual relationship. It was Pitkin who made me study anthropology. I made a clean breast to him of all my past and he understood. He said, "Claire, I understand. Just make a scientific study of man and know them objectively, and you'll get them out of your system."

OZZIE Well, did it work?

"I'm engaged to be married ..."

CLAIRE (Betty Comden); OZZIE (Adolph Green)

CLAIRE (*Staring at him*) Almost completely.

> (*She makes a lunge for him. She grabs him in her arms and bends him over her knee in a passionate kiss. His hat falls off. They come out of it.*)

Of course, sometimes I get carried away.

OZZIE (*Retrieving his hat*) You too?

CLAIRE I'm afraid so.

OZZIE Gee, that's just my trouble.

CLAIRE Claire—another demerit. (*She tosses notebook away*)

> Modern man, what is it?
> Just a collection of complexes and neurotic impulses
> That occasionally break through.

OZZIE You mean sometimes you blow your top like me?

CLAIRE

> I do.
>
> I try hard to stay controlled
> But I get carried away,
> Try to act aloof and cold,
> But I get carried away.

"Carried away!"
OZZIE (Adolph Green), CLAIRE (Betty Comden)

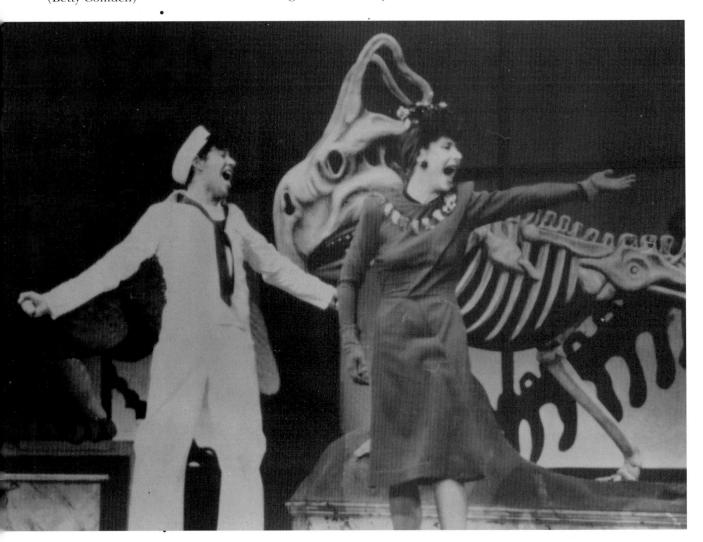

ON THE TOWN

CLAIRE & OZZIE

Carried away, carried away,
I get / she gets carried, just carried away!

CLAIRE

When I sit and listen to a symphony,
Why can't I just say the music's grand?
Why must I leap upon the stage hysterically?
They're playing pizzicato,
And everything goes blotto,
I grab the maestro's stick and start in leading the band!

CLAIRE & OZZIE *(As she conducts)*

Carried away, carried away,
I get / she gets carried, just carried away!

OZZIE

And when I go to see a moving picture show,
And I'm watching actors in a scene,

(Gesture of a picture screen.)

I start to think what's happening is really so.
The girl, I must protect her.
The villain don't respect her.
I leap to her defense and punch a hole right through the screen!

(He punches his left hand forward.)

CLAIRE & OZZIE

Carried away, carried away,
He gets / I get carried, just carried away!

(They pat each other, commiserating.)

OZZIE

I try hard to keep detached,
But I get carried away.
Try to act less booby-hatched,
But I get carried away.

CLAIRE & OZZIE

Carried away, carried away,
He gets / I get carried, just carried away!

OZZIE

When shopping, I'm a sucker for a bargain sale.
If something is marked down upon a shelf,
My sense of what is practical begins to fail;
I buy one, then another,
Another and another,

(He reaches for things on shelves.)

I buy the whole store out and I'm in business for myself!

CLAIRE & OZZIE

Carried away, carried away,
He gets / I get carried, just carried away!

CLAIRE

And when I go to see my friends off on a train,
Golly, how I hate to see them go,

For then my love of traveling I can't restrain.
The time has come for parting,
The train's already starting,
I hop a freight and in a flash I'm off to Buffalo!

(She does "Off to Buffalo" step.)

CLAIRE & OZZIE
Carried away, carried away,
We get carried, just carried a————way!

(End of number—then encore.)

CLAIRE
I'm the scientific kind,
Yet I get carried away.
Ancient man is on my mind
And I get carried away.

CLAIRE & OZZIE
Carried away, carried away,
I get carried, just carried away!

CLAIRE
I take anthropology so literally,
That these modern days are not for me.
Right now, I feel we're living prehistorically;
To us the past has beckoned,
We're going back this second
To happy days we knew in six million BC!

CLAIRE & OZZIE *(As a drum beat starts)*
Carried away, carried away,
He gets / I get carried—

(The drum becomes a slow tom-tom beat. THREE PREHISTORIC MEN come on. THREE BIRD GIRLS enter. The THREE MEN circle the stage. The LAST ONE motions to OZZIE to join them. He assumes the "Apeman" walk and falls in line. CLAIRE begins to scratch and walk like the BIRD GIRLS. ONE MAN comes down and picks up CLAIRE, sets her on the bench. ANOTHER MAN picks up a club and hits a THIRD MAN who is dancing with a BIRD GIRL. The THIRD MAN bows deeply, relinquishes his GIRL to the "CUTTER-IN" MAN, picks up the club and starts to hit OZZIE in the same manner, indicating that he wants to dance with OZZIE's BIRD GIRL. CLAIRE watches in horror.)

CLAIRE *(As OZZIE is about to be clubbed, she leaps from the bench)* Oh, no—no—oh, no, oh, no, no!

(But she is too late. OZZIE is clubbed and staggers back into her arms.)

OZZIE No cutting in!

(The GROUP now forms a semi-circle, with OZZIE and CLAIRE in the center. The FIRST MAN starts to pick one of them by the "eenie-meenie-miney-mo" system. He goes around the circle, and OZZIE is "it." CLAIRE, delightedly, picks up the club and prepares to hit him. She makes a mighty swing and hits, instead, the skeleton of the dinosaur. It falls to pieces, as the prehistoric characters scurry away with much chirping. CLAIRE and OZZIE are once more back in the museum. They look at the wreckage of the dinosaur and sing:)

OZZIE & CLAIRE
We got carried, just carried a————

(They break off as FIGMENT enters. He sees the wreckage and starts after CLAIRE and OZZIE.)

OZZIE Come on! Let's get outta here!

(They pick up CLAIRE's handbag, notebook and pencil, and dash off, with FIGMENT in full chase after them.)

(The Fourth Chase Interlude begins. The previous characters in the chase are now joined by FIGMENT, who demands that the POLICEMAN run after OZZIE and CLAIRE, who have destroyed his dinosaur. Then the LITTLE OLD LADY and UPER-MAN stream by in hot pursuit.)

"To happy days we knew in six million B.C.!"

Center: CLAIRE (Betty Comden), OZZIE (Adolph Green)

SCENE 7

A busy New York City street. GABEY enters, looking around lost. PEOPLE are passing on the street. A MAN is seated on a bench reading a newspaper.

GABEY (*To* MAN) I beg your pardon, can you tell me where Carnegie Hall is?

> (*MAN shakes his head "No." TWO GIRLS enter, crossing the stage. GABEY speaks to them.*)

I beg your pardon . . .

> (*They don't answer, still giggling on their way out. GABEY is alone.*)

> Gabey's comin',
> Gabey's comin' to town.
> So what? Who cares?
> Back on the ship
> It seemed such a snap;
> You'd tap a girl on the shoulder,
> She'd turn around,
> And she'd say "I love you."

> But once on shore,
> It's not such a snap.
> You get the cold shoulder,
> The old run-around,
> You're left with no one but you.
> Gabey's comin', Gabey's comin' to town.

> A town's a lonely town,
> When you pass through
> And there is no one waiting there for you,
> Then it's a lonely town.

> You wander up and down,
> The crowds rush by,
> A million faces pass before your eye,
> Still it's a lonely town.

> Unless there's love,
> A love that's shining like a harbor light,
> You're lost in the night;
> Unless there's love,
> The world's an empty place
> And every town's a lonely town.

> (*GABEY sits on bench. A GROUP OF HIGH SCHOOL GIRLS enters. Behind them comes A GROUP OF SAILORS. They're talking among themselves, see the GIRLS, follow them off.*

> *ONE SAILOR remains. A GIRL starts to leave, sees GABEY, who makes a gesture toward her. She turns from him in embarrassment, almost bumps into the remaining SAILOR. She recoils from him, goes and sits on bench opposite the SAILOR. The SAILOR follows, they go into a* pas de deux *after which they exit.*

> *GABEY watches forlornly. After they exit—*)

PASSERSBY

> A town's a lonely town,
> When you pass through
> And there is no one waiting there for you.

GABEY

> Then it's a lonely town.

PASSERSBY	GABEY
You wander up,	
	You wander up
You wander down.	And down.
The crowds rush by,	The crowds rush by,
A million faces pass	A million faces pass
Before your eye.	Before your eye,
	Still it's a lonely town.
Unless there's	
	Love,
	A love that's shining like a
a harbor light,	harbor light
	You're lost in the
Like a harbor light,	night,
Unless there's love,	Unless there's love,
The world's an empty place	
	And every town's
And every town's	
A lonely town.	A lonely town.

Lonely Town pas de deux

A GIRL (Nelle Fisher), TOM (Richard D'Arcy)

SCENE 8

A corridor in Carnegie Hall. A SOPRANO is singing "The Bell Song" from Lakme in a nearby studio. An ACTOR strolls on.

ACTOR (*Reciting as he walks, using many gestures*) "Down, down, I come like glist'ring Phaeton wanting the manage of unruly jades. In the base court—come down? Down court— Down King!"

(*As he reaches center stage, about to come off, a WAGNERIAN SOPRANO enters opposite, crossing stage, engrossed in singing Brunnhilde's "Call of the Walkyrie." TWO MUSICIANS enter carrying instrument cases, arguing.*)

FIRST MUSICIAN You call him a conductor? He used the baton like a meat cleaver.

SECOND MUSICIAN You know that fourth bar after H—They ought to let me conduct the orchestra. I'd show them how to do it.

(*As they exit, a LITTLE MAN, very dejected, holding a wilted flower, enters and crosses. As he exits, a BALLET GIRL in rehearsal clothes enters, talking over her shoulder.*)

BALLET GIRL Are you going to the auditions for "Hold Your Britches"?

BALLET BOY (*Enters fussily, tying ribbon around his head*) No! I'm only interested in ballet.

(*He exits. IVY enters. THREE DANCERS come on, TWO GIRLS, ONE BOY. BOY picks up GIRL and lifts her in attitude, lowers her to floor with a jar.*)

FIRST GIRL DANCER (*Still worried by the bad return to the floor, bawls out her partner*) That stinks! Come here.

SECOND GIRL DANCER Now watch!

(*She pirouettes, unwatched, across the stage. The TWO DANCERS try it again and soar offstage. As they hit the wings, the SECOND GIRL DANCER gets to her toes*)

Look! I'm Swan Lake.

(*SECOND GIRL DANCER "points" offstage. The LITTLE MAN, no longer dejected, returns across stage, carrying a triumphantly erect flower. He is smiling happily. As he exits, the CARNEGIE HALL DROP reveals the studio of MADAME MAUDE P. DILLY. She is practicing scales at her piano, punctuating notes with copious swigs from a whiskey bottle.*)

MADAME DILLY Do do re do do re mi do . . .

(*She takes a drink. IVY enters, pretty, her hair in ribbons as in the poster.*)

Hel-l-o-o, Miss Smith.

IVY Good morning, Madame Dilly.

MADAME DILLY No, no, sing your greeting, always s-i-i-n-g your greeting.

IVY (*Singing*) Good morning, Madame Dilly.

MADAME DILLY You've got your diaphragm wrapped around your spinal column. We haven't been practicing, have we?

IVY I have been practicing, Madame Dilly. I practice every minute I'm not working. There's been complaints. But I'm determined to move onwards and upwards. That's why I'm studying singing and ballet like it says on my poster picture. But sometimes I feel I'd like to quit that crummy job.

MADAME DILLY (*Firmly*) No, no, don't do that. There is nothing wrong with . . . being an actress.

IVY Oh, what's the use of saying that. I'm not an actress. I'm a cooch dancer. And it's so inartistic.

MADAME DILLY It pays well. And the money you earn at Coney Island goes for your singing lessons. You are already in arrears about fifty dollars. So, keep working—working.

IVY But Madame Dilly, what if the people who picked me Miss Turnstiles find out? They'll expose me as a phoney—and I'm not. Those are all the things I really want to do some day.

MADAME DILLY And you can make them all come true by studying with me, the best teacher on this side of the corridor. Now, to the grindstone. Place your feet wide apart.

(*IVY does so.*)

Nothing helps like a firm grip on the floor. (*DILLY returns to the piano, strikes a note and sings*) Now curl your toes and say: "I'm singing. I'm singing."

IVY I'm singing. I'm singing.

MADAME DILLY Now, again—in the relaxed position—over!

(*IVY bends over. When she starts to sing, DILLY sneaks a drink.*)

IVY I'm singing. I'm singing.

MADAME DILLY Good! Now—up through the toes—through the diaphragm—and out the front.

IVY (*As she straightens up, concentrating*) I'm singing. I'm singing.

MADAME DILLY Now—quiver my fingers with those lovely high tones.

(*DILLY places two fingers on IVY's upper lip and turns her head.*)

IVY (*In a high soprano*) I'm singing. I'm singing.

MADAME DILLY No, no, no. Try to think of your mouth as a triumphal arch through which passes a procession of pear-shaped tones—like pearls on a rope. Again, please.

(*DILLY returns to the piano and strikes a chord.*)

IVY I'm singing. I'm singing.

(*This is worse than before. DILLY wheels from the piano in a fury, thundering and pounding her bosom vigorously.*)

MADAME DILLY The RESONATORS!!!

IVY (*Discouraged*) Oh, Madame Dilly, occasionally I feel I'm not making any progress . . .

MADAME DILLY (*Suddenly anxious*) Now, none of that. You've a splendid voice—Magnificent—and I'm giving you priceless vocal secrets! Now: position eight.

ON THE TOWN

(IVY goes to piano.)

Your vocalise.

(IVY does a handstand, with feet resting on the piano. DILLY sits, strikes a chord.)

IVY Do—do re do—do re mi do—

MADAME DILLY Good. Good placement. *(And she sneaks another drink)*

IVY Do—re—mi—fa—do.

(GABEY wanders through the corridor outside. Simultaneously, MADAME DILLY holds her bottle up to the light, finds it really is empty, rises, and puts it in her bosom.)

MADAME DILLY I must go now, just for a moment. You must stay here and practice your scales. *(She goes to the door)* I'll be back before you can say Jack Daniels—Jack Robinson.

(She bumps into GABEY at the door. He backs into the room.)

Oh, you clumsy! Really!

GABEY I beg your pardon.

(IVY is continuing her scales. GABEY notices her, takes a quick look at her picture which he has, bends down to take an upside-down look to see if it is the same girl.)

IVY Do—do re mi—do.

GABEY Hey!

IVY *(Coming out of her handstand, kneels on floor hastily pulling skirt over her knees)* A gentleman should always knock.

GABEY Oh—uh . . . *(He looks at picture)* Are—are you—could you be—is your name—by any chance—is your name Ivy Smith?

IVY *(Rises)* And what if it is?

GABEY *(To himself, for courage)* Gabey's comin'. Gabey's comin'. *(Starting with great bravado)* The name's Gabey. I'm pretty hot stuff in the Navy. I'm in town for one day, and I'm gonna do this old burg up brown. I'm a pretty special guy and I need a pretty special girl, and you're a pretty special girl, and we're gonna step out tonight, and *(Collapsing)* . . . goodbye.

(He rushes to the door in a panic. Her voice stops him.)

IVY Wait a minute, sailor.

(He turns, she moves toward him.)

How did you know who I am?

GABEY I saw your picture in the subway.

IVY *(Moves toward him in excitement)* You mean you saw my picture and—*(Quickly assumes an air of indifference)* Oh—that.

GABEY Yeah, and it said how you were studying singing at Carnegie Hall, and so I thought I'd like to—like to look you up—and—and hear you sing.

IVY That's the most peculiar line I ever heard.

ON THE TOWN

41

GABEY Well—to hear you sing—and—maybe to try to make a date with you for tonight.

IVY (*Quickly, as she looks at him, then away*) I gotta be somewhere. (*Fake sophisticated tone*) I'm afraid a date is quite out of the question.

GABEY Sure. Who do I think I am, anyway? You probably get society guys, rich fellas pestering you all day long.

IVY Oh, yes, by the drove. The social whirl occasionally takes its toll.

GABEY Yes, I guess it does. Well, I'll be going now.

(*He turns away, then back. She turns to face him. Sincerely:*)

But all I wanted to say is—I'm glad to meet the famous Miss Turnstiles. You know, that really makes my day complete. I—I liked your picture first because I thought you looked like Minnie Frenchley—but you—don't look anything like her. You're much more beautiful. And to look like that and do all those things—opera, sports, and—oh, gee—you're wonderful. G'bye.

(*He goes out the door and starts off. She follows him outside the studio door.*)

IVY Don't go. That's a much nicer speech. Wouldn't you like me to affix my signature to that picture you have?

GABEY Would you?

(*He takes out his pen, she comes over to him.*)

That's wonderful.

(*Gives her the fountain pen, she signs the picture.*)

Gee, the guys on the ship will be jealous of me.

(*IVY gives him the picture.*)

"Best regards"—Gee, thanks.

IVY And I mean it.

GABEY (*Takes the fountain pen back*) Gee, I found you. I found Ivy Smith. Uh, Miss Smith, do you think maybe you could make it tonight?

IVY Oh, I couldn't. I'm much too occupied. But how long are you going to be in town?

GABEY Only twenty-four hours.

IVY (*Sudden decision*) Gabey, I'd love to go out with you.

GABEY My gosh, you will?

IVY Uh-huh.

GABEY You're going out with me? Well, uh . . . uh . . . shall I come and get you?

IVY No, I'll meet you. Where are you going to be?

GABEY Nedick's. Times Square, at 11 o'clock.

MADAME DILLY (*Entering*) Well! What's going on here?

IVY Madame Dilly.

GABEY I beg your pardon.

MADAME DILLY Really, Miss Smith, you should be practicing every minute. You mustn't waste my precious time. Not if you're so anxious to better your position.

IVY Please, Madame Dilly.

MADAME DILLY Is this tar a friend of yours?

IVY Well, no, but . . .

MADAME DILLY Then leave at once, young man.

GABEY Well, goodbye.

IVY G'bye—Nedicks.

MADAME DILLY On your way, bellbottom.

> *(He exits.)*

Just what were you saying to him?

IVY Oh, Madame Dilly, he's such a nice boy.

MADAME DILLY They're all alike.

IVY Oh, no.

MADAME DILLY Sex and art don't mix. If they did, I'd have gone straight to the top. If you want to go onward and upward, keep your mind on your work. I see I'll have to watch you. Now, your vocalise.

IVY

Do-do-re-do.

MADAME DILLY

Do-re-mi-do.
Mustn't be discouraged if the going is slow.

IVY

Do-do-re-do.

MADAME DILLY

Love life must go,
If you'd be a nightingale instead of a crow.
Sing high and low.

IVY

Do-ti-la-do.

MADAME DILLY

Any voice can grow
If you'll sing your do-re-do.

IVY

Onwards!

MADAME DILLY

Do-do-re-do.

IVY

Onwards! Upwards!

MADAME DILLY
> Sex has to go.

IVY AND MADAME DILLY
> Sing high and low, do-ti-la-do,
> And you soon will know
> Anyone can go
> From the lowest low
> To the very highest high
> If they will only sing their
> Do-do-re-do
> Do-re-mi-do.

(A CHORUS of SINGING TEACHERS enters and joins IVY and DILLY.)

SINGING TEACHERS
> Onwards!
> Do-do-re-do.
>
> Onwards! Upwards!
> Sex has to go.
> Do-re-do, do-re-do, do-re-do,
> Upwards and on!
>
> Do-do-re-do.
> Your little voice will grow,
> You'll be a nightingale instead of a crow.
>
> Do-do-re-do.
> Don't be discouraged, babe.
> Don't be discouraged if the going is slow.
>
> Do-do-do-do-re-mi-do.
> Sex is out.
> Sing it high and low,
> Sing it high and low,
> Sing it high and low.
>
> You will be a nightingale
> If you will sing your
> Do-do-re-do.
> Do-re-mi-do.
> Do-do-re-do.
> Do-re-mi-do.

(They march offstage as IVY executes a dance, then return.)

> Sing high and low,
> Do-ti-la-do.
> Anyone can grow
> If you sing your
> Do-re-do.

(IVY leaps offstage and there is a blackout.)

Claire's apartment. This is a double set. On one side is a corner of CLAIRE's apartment, a fairly luxurious place, with an aura of wealth about it, in direct contrast to HILDY's flat, which is opposite. There is a door on the back wall leading to the kitchen, another leading to the bedroom. Through the large window of CLAIRE's apartment the city skyline can be seen. The LIGHTS go on in CLAIRE's apartment. OZZIE and CLAIRE enter.

OZZIE Gee, what a dump!

CLAIRE Thank you for your dimensions. I'll send you a copy of the book.

OZZIE Well, aren't you gonna kiss me goodbye?

CLAIRE A silly tradition. Come here.

> *(She kisses him lightly on the cheek, then suddenly gets him in a terrific clinch. At this point, a suave, stately, portly GENTLEMAN comes from the kitchen, wearing a cocktail apron and carrying a tray on which are two glasses and an opened bottle of champagne. He stares for a moment in polite surprise, then comes down to them. It is PITKIN W. BRIDGEWORK, the Judge, CLAIRE's fiancé.)*

PITKIN (*Jovially*) Hello, darling.

Writing "On The Town"

Leonard Bernstein, Adolph Green, Betty Comden, Jerome Robbins

(OZZIE and CLAIRE break away quickly.)

CLAIRE *(Breathless and surprised)* Why, Pitkin, darling—what are you doing here?

PITKIN Don't you remember? We're celebrating our engagement today.

> *(To OZZIE.)*

Hello!

> *(OZZIE nods.)*

CLAIRE *(Looks at OZZIE, then at PITKIN. A bit flustered)* Oh, of course, darling, how stupid of me. I was supposed to meet you here, wasn't I?

PITKIN Yes, I've been waiting for two hours—

> *(CLAIRE gestures as if to speak.)*

—but don't bother to explain. I understand!

CLAIRE Well, you must forgive my appearance. I was practically raped.

> *(OZZIE looks at PITKIN. There is short pause.)*

PITKIN *(Moves to OZZIE, expansively, warmly extending tray)* Why, how do you do?

> *(OZZIE hides behind CLAIRE.)*

CLAIRE *(A little beside herself)* No, darling, you don't understand. I was collecting material for my book—at the Museum—and I was measuring this man, and . . .

PITKIN *(Extremely good-natured)* No sordid details, Claire. *(Puts tray on table)* I understand.

> When I met you I knew you were obsessed with men.
> Obsessed with men were you!
> But I know that soon you'll cool that fire,
> And lose that primitive desire,
> And throughout it all I'll be at hand
> To tell you, Claire, I understand!

CLAIRE *(Resigned)* Very well, Ozzie, this is my fiancé—Judge Pitkin W. Bridge-work, and darling—this is Ozzie.

> *(She pushes OZZIE toward PITKIN, indicates OZZIE's head.)*

A type Z-3 dolico-cephalic. Very rare specimen.

PITKIN *(Sincerely shakes hands with OZZIE)* Pleased to meet you. Any rare specimen of Claire's is a rare specimen of mine.

OZZIE Well, congratulations. I gotta be going. *(He starts for the door)*

PITKIN No, no, Ozzie, don't go. Stay and drink a toast with us.

CLAIRE Pitkin, is this wise?

PITKIN Love to have him—love to—just one moment—I'll get another glass. *(Exits into kitchen)*

CLAIRE *(To OZZIE)* I think you'd better go.

OZZIE But I've never tasted champagne before.

CLAIRE Oh, very well. But if you say the bubbles tickle your nose I'll brain that dolico-cephalic head.

"And I drink!"

OZZIE (Adolph Green), CLAIRE (Betty Comden), PITKIN (Robert Chisholm)

PITKIN (*Enters with the third glass*) Here we are, darling. (*He pours the champagne*)

CLAIRE (*Takes a glass and hands it to OZZIE*) Do you really think I should drink, dear? You remember the last time.

PITKIN Good for you.

CLAIRE Well—

OZZIE I drink to the happy couple.

PITKIN And I drink to the success of "Modern Man—What Is It?"

CLAIRE And I drink.

> (*They drink. PITKIN splutters.*)

PITKIN O-o-o-h! Bubbles—they tickle my nose.

> (*CLAIRE glares at him, swallows her drink at a gulp.*)

There now, darling, any ill-effects?

CLAIRE (*Moving to OZZIE*) On the contrary—I feel great.

> (*She makes a lunge at him, grabs him around the neck.*)

OZZIE (*Laughs embarrassedly and disengages himself*) I gotta be going.

> (*He makes a move to avoid CLAIRE, but she stops him.*)

PITKIN No, no. Please stay and entertain Claire.

CLAIRE Oh, Pitkin.

PITKIN Don't worry, darling. I have a date with Congressman Bundy. Meet you later at Diamond Eddie's for our engagement party. Just the two of us. Have a good time. Enjoy yourself. (*He goes out the door*) Finish the champagne.

CLAIRE Goodbye, darling.

> (*OZZIE sits on the couch and puts his glass on the floor. CLAIRE has a puzzled look on her face.*)

PITKIN (*Offstage*) Goodbye, sweet.

CLAIRE (*Grabs OZZIE and kisses him*) Pitkin understands.

> (*CLAIRE and OZZIE look at each other and burst into:*)

CLAIRE AND OZZIE
Carried away, carried away,
We get carried, just carried away!!

> (*They rush toward each other.*)

> (*Blackout.*)

Hildy's apartment. The apartment is small, cramped and crowded. There is a couch and a small table on which are a phone and a phone book. HILDY and CHIP enter. CHIP is leading. He carries two grocery bags full of food, including a large chicken. HILDY carries a package which she puts on the floor.

HILDY (*As she enters*) Just put 'em down anywhere, Chip.

CHIP (*Looking around for any empty spot*) But I haven't time to stay for dinner. It'll take you, I should say, roughly four hours to cook all this stuff. Besides, I've got to find Ivy Smith.

HILDY Ivy Smith! Ivy Smith! That's all I hear. Fine friend you've got, falling for a picture. (*She sits on the sofa*)

CHIP Well, she is a remarkable girl. She sings and dances and—and—

HILDY Yeah, yeah, that's swell.

CHIP And besides, she's beautiful.

HILDY Well, stop looking wistful. (*Rises*) You've got a girl who can cook. (*HILDY drags a frying pan from under the sofa, blows dust from inside, then wipes the outside on the seat of her pants as she takes frying pan to the table, and puts it down*) Besides, don't you know all those pictures are touched up? You put ribbons in my hair and photograph me through a wall, and I bet you couldn't tell the difference.

CHIP I'm not so sure, besides, I've got to find the real Ivy Smith.

HILDY O.K. (*On her haunches, thumbing through the phone book*) Here's the phone. We'll call the I.R.T. and find her.

CHIP Just like that?

HILDY Sure.

(*She consults phone book. CHIP looks for a place to put down his package.*)

Put 'em down anywhere.

(*He hesitates, starts to put them on sofa.*)

No, no, on the floor.

(*She dials phone. He places the package at the end of the sofa on the floor.*)

I.R.T.? Hold it, Jack.

(*Hands phone to CHIP. CHIP takes the phone. HILDY lounges on the couch, proceeding to vamp him during the following conversation, pulling her hair over her eye and leering at him.*)

CHIP Er—hello?—I'd like to speak to Miss Turnstiles, please—Miss Ivy Smith— Oh, she's not there? Well, look , I'd like her address, please, and telephone number—Oh, you don't?—Well, look, I'm a sailor and I'm here for one day—Hullo? (*He replaces phone*) Hey, they hung up! They don't give out that information—especially to sailors.

HILDY (*She is still busy vamping him*) Well, ya did your best, kid. (*Coughs, clearing her throat ostentatiously*)

CHIP I tried, didn't I? I did try.

HILDY (*Sitting up, straightening her hair*) Yeah, you were sensational. I cried like a baby! (*Pats the empty space on the couch beside her in invitation*)

CHIP And I'll try them again later.

HILDY Yeah. Much later. (*Pats the couch again*) Let's try this first.

CHIP (*Moves to couch, sits*) Well, as long as I tried . . .

> (*He suddenly makes a lunge at her and smothers her in a bear hug and violent clinch. Suddenly, there is a sneeze outside the bedroom door and LUCY SCHMEELER, a bedraggled figure in a bathrobe, enters. CHIP and HILDY come out of the clinch. LUCY gives a little coo of surprise.*)

HILDY (*Rises, flustered*) Well, what the hell are you doing here?

> (*CHIP rises.*)

LUCY I'm soddy, Hildy, I just couldn't go to work today—got an awful code—and I didn't know . . .

HILDY Of all the days you picked!!!

CHIP Pardon me, Mrs. Esterhazy.

LUCY Oh, I'b not her mother!

HILDY Chip, this is my roommate, Lucy Schmeeler. She's a grand girl.

CHIP How d'ya do.

LUCY Heddo, Chip.

CHIP Well . . . you live here . . . all day?

LUCY I'b soddy. Hildy and I sleep in shifts. She goes out to work at night. I cob home from work at night. She cobs home from work in the morning and I go out to work in the morning.

HILDY All right, he gets it. Thank you.

LUCY I'b soddy—I've gotta inhale. 'Scuse me. (*She puts a towel over her head and kneels down over an inhaler on the shelf.*)

CHIP (*Takes HILDY aside*) Think she'll stay under there long?

HILDY Sure, sure—she'll be under there for days.

> (*They fall into a violent clinch. LUCY sneezes. They come out of the clinch. LUCY comes up from the towel.*)

LUCY I'b sorry—'scuse me . . . Y'know, Hildy, this is just like taking a picture. If I had a camera, I could get the two of you together.

HILDY You could do that by just leaving the room.

> (*LUCY, hurt, picks up the inhaler and exits.*)

CHIP C'mere . . .

> (*He grabs HILDY. They sit on the couch and clinch. There is the noise of LUCY spraying her throat, four times. HILDY raises her head.*)

HILDY (*Coming out of clinch*) Is that *you*, Chip?

CHIP No.

> (*LUCY comes out of the room with an atomizer. They sit and look at her.*)

LUCY I gotta get some gargle.

(She exits into bathroom. They clinch again. In a split second she is back. They break. She proceeds to the bedroom door, then turns back, brightly)

I got the gargle.

HILDY (*Goes to her*) Well, I'm very glad to hear that. Lucy, would you step into the other room for a few minutes?

LUCY What for?

HILDY I'd like to go over some figures with you.

LUCY Figures?

HILDY (*Between her teeth*) The rent, Lucy, the rent.

LUCY But, Hildy, we paid the rent. I don't understand . . .

"I got the gargle."

LUCY (Alice Pearce), CHIP (Chris Alexander), HILDY (Nancy Walker)

ON THE TOWN

(HILDY grabs her into the bedroom. CHIP picks up a bag of groceries, puts them on the shelf. LUCY enters without her bathrobe.)

I'b going out.

(LUCY disappears. HILDY appears in the doorway, leans on the jamb nonchalantly. CHIP grins. LUCY reappears, tying scarf over her head, marches to the outside door.)

CHIP With that cold?

LUCY I'b going to an air-cooled movie. Hildy says—that you and she . . .

HILDY (*Lounging still, interrupts* LUCY) It will do you a world of good, Lucy.

CHIP Yes—yes it will. Well, goodbye, Miss Schmeeler.

LUCY Goodbye, Mr. Chips.

(There is a reaction from LUCY as she realizes what she has said. Then she exits.)

HILDY Well, now what?

CHIP We eat, huh?

HILDY Sure, we can do that first.

CHIP You claim you can cook.

HILDY That's often been considered one of my strongest points.

CHIP Yeah? What's the specialty of the house?

HILDY Me!!

(She throws the chicken to him, he tosses it back and she throws it in the frying pan.)

Oh, I can cook, too, on top of the rest,
My seafood's the best in the town.
And I can cook, too,
My fish can't be beat,
My sugar's the sweetest aroun'.

I'm a man's ideal of a perfect meal
Right down to the demi-tasse.
I'm a pot of joy for a hungry boy,
Baby, I'm cooking with gas!

Oh, I'm a gum drop,
A sweet lollipop,
A brook trout right out of the brook,
And what's more, baby, I can cook!

Some girls make magazine covers,
Some girls keep house on a dime,
Some girls make wonderful lovers,
But what a lucky find I'm.

I'd make a magazine cover,
I do keep house on a dime,
I'd make a wonderful lover,
I should be paid overtime!

'Cause I can bake, too, on top of the lot,
My oven's the hottest you'll find.
Yes, I can roast, too,
My chickens just ooze,
My gravy will lose you your mind.

I'm a brand-new note
On a table d'hôte,
But just try me a la carte.
With a single course,
You can choke a horse.
Baby, you won't know where to start!

Oh, I'm an hors d'oeuvre,
A jelly preserve,
Not in the recipe book,
And what's more, baby, I can cook!

(HILDY goes through a violent pantomime with back to audience, apparently preparing one of her specialties. She finally wheels around, displaying a peeled banana.)

Baby, I'm cooking with gas!
Oh, I'm a gum drop,
A sweet lollipop,
A brook trout right out of the brook.
And what's more, baby, I can cook!

(She rushes at him on the sofa and the lights black out. Lights come back up for the encore.)

Some girls make wonderful jivers,
Some girls can hit a high "C,"
Some girls make good taxi drivers,
But what a genius is me.

I'd make a wonderful jiver,
I even hit a high "C,"
I make the best taxi driver,
I rate a big navy "E"!

'Cause I can fry, too, on top of the heap,
My Crisco's as deep as a pool.
Yes, I can broil, too,
My ribs win applause,
My lamb chops will cause you to drool.

For a candied sweet
Or a pickled beet,
Step up to my smorgasbord.
Walk around until
You get your fill.
Baby, you won't ever be bored!

Oh, I'm a paté,
A marron glacé,
A dish you will wish you had took.
And what's more, baby, I can cook!!

(The lights black out.)

SCENE 11

Times Square. Much excitement, brilliantly lit signs. PEOPLE are strolling back and forth. A NEDICK's stand is on one side. GABEY wanders in, looking for IVY, goes to NEDICK's, doesn't see her, stops A MAN.

GABEY I beg your pardon, sir, can you tell me the correct time?

> *(The MAN indicates a moving sign on a building and GABEY follows his finger.)*

The time is now . . .

MAN Ten thirty-seven.

> *(The MAN goes to NEDICK's.)*

GABEY Oh, thanks.

> *(A GIRL enters, saunters up to GABEY.)*

GIRL Hello.

GABEY Hello.

GIRL What are you doing?

GABEY I'm waiting for my girl. She'll be here in half an hour.

> *(THE GIRL moves away disgustedly.)*

> I used to think it might be fun to be
> Anyone else but me.
> I thought that it would be a pleasant surprise
> To wake up as a couple of other guys.

> But now that I've found you,
> I've changed that point of view,
> And now I wouldn't give a dime to be
> Anyone else but me.

> What a day,
> Fortune smiled and came my way,
> Bringing love I never thought I'd see,
> I'm so lucky to be me.

> What a night,
> Suddenly you came in sight,
> Looking just the way I'd hoped you'd be,
> I'm so lucky to be me.
> I am simply thunderstruck
> At the change in my luck:
> Knew at once I wanted you,
> Never dreamed you'd want me, too.

> I'm so proud
> You chose me from all the crowd,
> There's no other guy I'd rather be,
> I could laugh out loud,
> I'm so lucky to be me.

(During the above, a CROWD has collected around GABEY.)

PASSERSBY

> What a day,
> Fortune smiled and came my way,
> Bringing love I never thought I'd see,
> I'm so lucky to be me.

ON THE TOWN

What a night,
Suddenly you came in sight,
Looking just the way I'd hoped you'd be,
I'm so lucky to be me.

I am simply thunderstruck
At the change in my luck:
Knew at once I wanted you,
Never dreamed you'd want me, too.

GABEY

I'm so proud
You chose me from all the crowd,

PASSERSBY

There's no other guy I'd rather be.

GABEY

I could laugh out loud,

GABEY & PASSERSBY

I'm so lucky to be me.

(*FLOSSIE and her GIRL FRIEND enter.*)

FLOSSIE (*Over music*) So I said to him, "Listen, Mr. Gadolphin, any boss who gives his employees only thirty-five minutes for lunch ought to be drawn and feathered."

FRIEND So what did he say?

FLOSSIE So I said, "After all, an individual needs time to refuel."

FRIEND It stands to reason.

(*FLOSSIE and her GIRL FRIEND have progressed to the NEDICK's stand. IVY enters and looks around for GABEY.*)

FLOSSIE Don't it, though?

IVY (*To NEDICK's MAN*) Do you have the time?

*The Times
Square Ballet*

ON THE TOWN

NEDICK'S ATTENDANT Ten thirty-nine.

> *(She orders a drink and pays for it.)*

FLOSSIE And I said, "Furthermore, Mr. Gadolphin, nylon stockings are not as important as a girl's self-respect."

FRIEND Naturally.

> *(MADAME DILLY enters and sees IVY.)*

MADAME DILLY Well, Miss Smith.

IVY Oh, Madame Dilly.

MADAME DILLY Might I have a word with you?

> *(Takes IVY aside.)*

So you *are* meeting that sailor.

IVY Yes, I am. I called up my boss and told him I was sick.

MADAME DILLY He called back and said if you didn't show up tonight, he'd fire you.

IVY He did? Well, let him.

MADAME DILLY I'd hate to lose that fifty.

IVY But just this once.

MADAME DILLY It's not the money, my dear. After all, I'm known as a patroness of the arts.

IVY But what if . . .

MADAME DILLY (*Threatening*) No. You keep your job. If you should default in your payments, I might be forced to tell the authorities that the glamorous Miss Turnstiles shakes her belly in Coney Island!

IVY Oh, Madame Dilly . . . !

MADAME DILLY (*Haughtily*) No, I don't care to argue about it.

> *(She moves off. IVY reluctantly follows her. They exit.)*

FLOSSIE So I said to him, "Listen, Mr. Gadolphin, I'm not in the habit of making appointments with married men—no matter how late at night it is."

FRIEND So what did he say?

FLOSSIE So I said, "After all, we've got to consider Mrs. Gadolphin."

> *(They exit. GABEY enters, looking around, spies CHIP offstage.)*

GABEY Hey, Chip!

CHIP (*Entering*) Gabe!

GABEY Chip! Hey, guess what, I found . . .

CHIP Gabey! Gee, I'm glad to see you. O.K.? Right on the dot, eh?

GABEY Sure.

CHIP Well, I suppose you want to know how I made out—in finding Miss Turnstiles. Well, I—(*Calls offstage*) Oh, IVY SMITH!

> *(GABEY is amazed. HILDY enters in hairdress IVY wore on subway ad.)*

HILDY Here I am.

CHIP Miss Smith, uh, this is Gabey.

HILDY (*Moves to him, hand extended in elegant pose*) How do you do? I gave up a concert and a shot-put rally to come and meet you.

GABEY (*Takes her hand*) Thank you.

CHIP Don't look so disappointed, Gabe, uh, these pictures, you know, they're always retouched.

(*HILDY gives him a dirty look. OZZIE enters.*)

The Times Square Ballet

OZZIE Hey, Gabe! (*GABEY turns*) Here she is—IVY SMITH! (*Points offstage*)

    (*CLAIRE enters, also in the same hairdo, and assumes a pose. Then she goes to GABEY and shakes his hand.*)

CLAIRE My dear boy, when this man told me your story, I just had to drop everything and come—

    (*She sees HILDY and stops. EVERYONE looks at EVERYONE ELSE, as they discover what's going on.*)

GABEY (*Laughing*) Now, wait a second, fellas.

OZZIE (*Points to HILDY*) That dame's a phoney.

CHIP (*Indicates* CLAIRE) Who is that woman?

OZZIE (*Shoves* HILDY *aside and goes to* GABEY) Listen, Gabe, Chip's trying to put something over.

CHIP Don't listen to him, Gabe. This girl's the real thing.

GABEY Wait a minute, guys, willya? Listen . . .

OZZIE (*To* CHIP) What are you trying to do to Gabey?

CHIP Whaddaya mean? I spent all day . . .

OZZIE I know what you were doing all day.

HILDY (*Moving between* CHIP *and* OZZIE *and pushing them apart*) O.K., fellows—break it up.

CLAIRE I told him this was a ridiculous idea.

(HILDY *goes to* CLAIRE. *They shake hands and go over to* NEDICK's.)

GABEY Listen! I know you were trying to help me. Thanks! But I found her myself.

CHIP Miss Turnstiles?

OZZIE What?

GABEY Sure, there was nothing to it. I walked into Carnegie Hall, there she was. Made a date. That's all there was to it. Sure, you should have seen me.

OZZIE Aw, don't give us that line, Gabey. It's impossible.

CHIP Why, statistics prove things don't happen like that.

GABEY Well, they did this time.

(*To* HILDY *and* CLAIRE:)

Gee, girls, thanks for dressing up like Ivy Smith. And Oz—thanks for the slogan. It worked.

CHIP Is that how you got her?

OZZIE You mean you followed my advice?

(MADAME DILLY *enters.*)

GABEY Sure. She'll be here any minute.

(*He leaves* NEDICK's *to look around for her.*)

OZZIE (*To the* NEDICK's ATTENDANT) Make that six—and no chasers.

MADAME DILLY (*Spies* GABEY) Hey—Bellbottom!

GABEY Oh! Madame Dilly.

MADAME DILLY (*Takes him aside*) You're just the one I'm looking for. I bear a message from Miss Ivy Smith.

GABEY Ivy!

MADAME DILLY She entrusted me—with her sincerest regrets.

(*She takes a swig from her bottle.*)

GABEY Huh?

MADAME DILLY She can't make it. She said she's going to some . . . some party.

GABEY But she had a date with me.

MADAME DILLY My dear boy, she just can't be bothered. There!

> *(She hands him a note with a flourish and exits.)*

OZZIE (*Laughing, as though finishing a joke*) So she said: "Come in."

> *(General laughter.)*

CHIP (*Referring to his drink of orange juice*) Gee, this is good!

HILDY Well, I'm not staggering yet.

> *(GABEY returns to Nedick's disconsolately, having read IVY's note. To GABEY:)*

Hey, when do we get a glimpse of this Miss Turnstiles?

OZZIE Yeah, it's about time.

GABEY I don't think she'll be here.

OZZIE What? Didja get stood up?

GABEY No, but I never really did meet her.

OZZIE Why, you son-of-a-gun!

CHIP Well, the law of averages . . .

GABEY No, I was just kidding. I went to Carnegie Hall and hung around, but she wasn't there. I never did find her. So, I went to a movie. Like you said, Chip, the town's too big. Things just don't happen that way.

OZZIE Sure—forget about her.

GABEY S'long, fellas. See you on the ship. (*He starts to go.*)

OZZIE Hey, wait a second Gabey, don't go. Claire'll get you a date. Hey, Claire, how about a girl for Gabey?

CLAIRE (*Drinking her orange juice*) I don't know any girls.

HILDY Wait a second—I can get you a date. My roommate, Lucy Schmeeler.

CHIP (*Horrified*) What?!

HILDY A-a-a-h, she's a nice girl, hasn't been out in years. And pretty, too. She's got a page-boy down to here—(*Puts her hand under her nose to indicate the length of it*)

GABEY Sure—swell, why not?

HILDY O.K., I'll call her from the first nightclub we hit.

OZZIE Nightclubs!! Yowie!! (*He does a bell kick*) Kid, we'll show you a great time tonight.

ALL THREE Yes—this town belongs to the Navy!

> *(They lock arms and plunge GABEY into a ballet depicting the teeming night life of the city—DANCE-HALL GIRLS, pinball machines, POLICE, SAILORS AND SOLDIERS on leave—all kinds of people. The FIVE PRINCIPALS walk forward through the CROWDS, celebrating their night on the town.)*

> *Curtain.*

OZZIE (Adolph
Green), CLAIRE
(Betty Comden), A
GIRL (Nelle Fisher),
GABEY (John Bat-
tles), IVY
(Sono Osato),

Act Two

SCENE 1A

Diamond Eddie's Nightclub. This is the first of three scenes depicting different nightclubs. The basic set is the same, but different props, change of personnel and size of set make the change of atmosphere. The curtain opens on DIAMOND EDDIE's. There is loud music, much smoke, much loud talk and laughter. SIX GIRLS are entertaining.

GIRLS

So long, I'm on the loose again.
So long, I counted up to ten.
Bye, bye, baby, I got wise.
Too long you made a fool of me,
Too long you had me up a tree,
Now you get the booby prize.

FIRST GIRL

So you cry: boo hoo hoo,
And you feel oh so blue.
It's no use, now I'm leaving you.

GIRLS

You need a new pal, papa!
So long, I've stood it long enough.
So long, it's my turn to call your bluff.
So long, baby, I've got wise to you!

(The GIRLS do a short dance, during which the HEADWAITER enters and has an altercation with ANOTHER WAITER.)

FIRST WAITER I told you I wanted a table for five—

SECOND WAITER But—

FIRST WAITER *(Exploding)* I don't care what you want! Get a table for five!!

(The SECOND WAITER comes off, gets a table and five chairs, which he sets up. CLAIRE, OZZIE, CHIP and GABEY come on. They are seated with much confusion as the dancing GIRLS are finishing their dance. The GIRLS exit, with much tossing of plumes and flourishes. The MASTER OF CEREMONIES bounces on.)

MASTER OF CEREMONIES *(Clapping the GIRLS off)* Ha-ha-ha-ha! Welcome to Diamond Eddie's. *(Walks rapidly around table)* Well, everybody, take out your little mallets and hit yourselves over the head with 'em. Ha, Ha! *(He emphasizes this last "ha, ha" with a stamp of the foot)* Now, someone's handed me a message. *(Looks in his pocket)* Yes, it's someone's birthday—now—and I want you all to join me in a chorus of Happy Birthday for that man we all know and love—uh—*(Glances at message surreptitiously)* Rodney Smithers, a furniture manufacturer from, uh, Grand Rapids, Mich—

(The ORCHESTRA breaks into "Happy Birthday," ALL sing with MASTER OF CEREMONIES leading. During this, TWO SAILORS with GIRLS enter. A table is set for them. In the confusion, ONE GIRL is pushed against CHIP. She sits on his lap, abruptly, but doesn't seem to be too anxious to leave, as she apologizes after "Happy Birthday" is over.)

ONE GIRL Oh, I'm sorry. I'm so terribly sorry.

(CHIP is amused. HILDY enters, sees what's going on, comes over with murder in her eye. GIRL continues.)

I really didn't mean to sit on your lap. It was an accident, really it was. You see, it was this way . . .

HILDY (*Who has reached the table and puts her hand on GIRL's shoulder*) Scram!

> (*GIRL joins her party in a huff. HILDY puts her arm around CHIP's neck, pats his cheek affectionately, sits and turns to GABEY.*)

Well, Gabe, I just talked to Lucy—told her all about you. She was out of the house before I could hang up.

OZZIE Playing hard to get, huh?

CLAIRE (*Holding up her shot glass*) Oh, just what I wanted. A jigger of solid glass.

CHIP Gee, Gabe, you look unhappy.

GABEY Aw, no, I'm fine.

CHIP Hey, you're not still thinking of that Miss Turnstiles?

GABEY Naw.

> (*FIRST DANCING GIRL has come on with a tray of souvenir dolls.*)

OZZIE (*Seeing GIRL with dolls*) Hey, Girlie! Whatcha got over there?

FIRST DANCING GIRL (*Coming over to him*) Dolls.

OZZIE Dolls! Hey look, dolls! Just what you need.

GABEY (*Protesting*) I don't want a doll.

OZZIE (*Knocking himself out trying to cheer up GABEY*) Ha-ha—take it—ha-ha, Gabe—show it to the fellas on the ship. What fun.

CLAIRE (*Rising*) Cool off, darling, you'll have a stroke.

> (*CLAIRE pushes OZZIE down in his chair. GABEY takes the doll. CLAIRE dismisses the GIRL. As the GIRL leaves, OZZIE pats her on the fanny.*)

GABEY Yeah, take it easy, Oz, I feel great.

MASTER OF CEREMONIES (*Bouncing back onstage*) And now for that treat you've all been waiting for—that star of the networks—Miss Diana Dream!

> (*All applaud as DIANA DREAM enters, bowing regally to the customers.*)

DIANA DREAM (*Singing with stylized gestures*)
I'm blue, my life is through.
I thought I had a date with you,
I guess I just don't rate with you,
I wish I was dead and buried!

> (*GABEY gets progressively lower, until he is sitting with his head between his knees. At the end of the next verse, HILDY notices his condition.*)

I'm blue, a cast-off shoe.
I'll break right down and cry tonight,
'Cause you told me a lie tonight,
I wish I was dead and bur—

> (*HILDY interrupts her.*)

HILDY I'm sorry, I'm very sorry. This is too depressing. I've got a friend over there who's dyin'!

> (*The MASTER OF CEREMONIES comes in, takes DIANA DREAM off explaining. A WAITER with a telephone enters.*)

WAITER (*Carrying phone*) Phone call for Miss Esterhazy.

OZZIE Put it here.

HILDY Is he kidding? Put it over here.

(*WAITER puts the phone on the table, plugs it in.*)

Hello, hello, hello, Lucy? Where are ya? Diamond Eddie's? That's impossible. We're at Diamond Eddie's. Fifty-third Street, four blocks from the house. You're in Yonkers?

(*They all look at HILDY.*)

They got a Diamond Eddie's up there, too? All right, you made a natural mistake. Come on down here quick.

OZZIE (*Rises*) Hold on a second, Hildy. Where can we go and show Gabey a good time?

CLAIRE We need a change of atmosphere. I know, tell your friend to head for the Congacabana. And not the one in Poughkeepsie.

(*OZZIE returns to his chair.*)

"I'm Blue!"

GABEY (John Battles), OZZIE (Adolph Green), CLAIRE (Betty Comden) CHIP (Chris Alexander), HILDY (Nancy Walker), DIANA DREAM (Frances Cassard)

HILDY (*Into phone*) O.K. Lucy—look, don't come h—No, no, Don't—Come—Here—What?—Well, stop crying. Meet us at the Congacabana.—Got it?—O.K.—And stop sneezing, you'll catch cold.

(*HILDY hangs up the phone, The WAITER removes it. PITKIN enters, looking for CLAIRE.*)

CLAIRE Well, let's get the check and get out of this dive. Uh, waiter, waiter—you fat oaf—(*She turns slightly, sees someone standing near her, thinks it is the WAITER*) Oh, there you are.

(*OZZIE sees PITKIN.*)

PITKIN Hello, darling.

CLAIRE Why, Pitkin, darling.

(*She rises, as does OZZIE.*)

What are you doing here? Oh, how stupid of me. I was supposed to meet you here, wasn't I?

PITKIN (*With his arm around her*) That's quite all right, darling.
(*Singing.*) I understand—

(*Greets OZZIE warmly.*)

Oh, glad to see you again, old man.

(*PITKIN makes a slight move toward OZZIE, who backs away.*)

OZZIE I can explain everything.

PITKIN Explain what? Why, I'm indebted to you.

(*Grabs OZZIE's hand, shakes it and they pile their hands one on the other.*)

I appreciate your bringing Claire to the club.

CLAIRE (*Coming between them and separating them*) Oh, Pitkin, these are Ozzie's friends—uh, Gabey, Hildy, Chip.

(*They ad lib "hellos."*)

This is Judge Bridgework, my fiancé.

PITKIN Why don't you all have a drink with the two of us? Waiter!

CLAIRE (*Quickly*) Uh, look, Pitkin, darling, I can't explain now, but we were just leaving. Why—why don't you meet us in a few minutes over at the Conga-cabana. I'd tell you all about it, but we're in an awful hurry. Just take care of the check, will you? You understand.

PITKIN Of course, of course, I understand. The Congacabana in a few minutes, darling. Waiter, let me have the check for that table.

WAITER Yeah, yeah.

(*PITKIN and WAITER exit.*)

CLAIRE Come on, everybody, we're off to the Congacabana.

(*Blackout.*)

SCENE 1B

The Congacabana. The scene has shifted to the Congacabana. A large palm tree stands in the center of the stage. Otherwise, the setting is the same. When the lights come up, the PATRONS are indulging in a Conga line, which grows more strenuous, until by the final bars, HILDY, who is in the line, is completely knocked out and has to be assisted back to the table.

OZZIE (*When the commotion has subsided, spies a GIRL with a tray of shawls*) Hey, girlie! Come here. What have you got there?

GIRL Shawls.

OZZIE (*Takes one back to GABEY*) Oh. Shawls!

GABEY I don't want a shawl.

OZZIE Here's a nice one. Take it.

GABEY What would I do with a shawl?

OZZIE Sure, sure, make yourself a hammock, make believe you're a piano. Anything.

CLAIRE (*Calming him down again*) Calm down.

> (*CLAIRE pays for the shawl. There is a fanfare and the MASTER OF CEREMONIES dashes on, all teeth.*)

MASTER OF CEREMONIES At this time, we have the pleasure to bring to you direct from Havana, Cuba, Señorita Dolores Dolores. Give her a nice hand.

> (*To a smattering of applause, the SEÑORITA enters.*)

DOLORES DOLORES (*The same song as before, in very broken English. GABEY's head sinks down*)

> Su-fro, desilusion,
> I thought I had a date wichew,
> I guess I just don't rate wichew,
> I veesh I vass d-a-a-d—and buried!
> Su———

HILDY (*Interrupting DOLORES DOLORES*) I'm awfully sorry, but my friend's allergic to that song.

MASTER OF CEREMONIES You mustn't interrupt this show.

HILDY Oh, I've been requested to sing.

MASTER OF CEREMONIES Who requested it?

GABEY I did.

HILDY Yeah, I've had a request from a serviceman in uniform.

> (*CHIP, OZZIE and GABEY and OTHER SOLDIERS and SAILORS rise and come toward the MASTER OF CEREMONIES in threatening silence.*)

MASTER OF CEREMONIES (*Seeing the situation, hastily*) Well, in that case . . .

> (*CHIP waves "thanks" to the BOYS and they return to their seats.*)

GABEY O.K. It's just a contest. They're trying to cheer me up.

HILDY

> I'm eager to share my love and devotion,
> It's deep as the ocean.
> I've plenty to spare and since it's so ample,
> I'll throw you a sample.

I will fix you up on the spot,
So forget the things you have not.
Can't you see, kid, what a very rare treasure you got?

Ya got me, baby, ya got me!
You got my affection, baby, and my sympathy.
You got my whole muscular equipment, from A to Z,
And it's free, baby, it's all free.

CLAIRE, HILDY, CHIP, OZZIE
It's all free, it's all free, it's all free.

OZZIE
Ya got me, Gabey, ya got me!
You got my enthusiasm on the land and sea.

CLAIRE, HILDY, CHIP
Whoop! Whoop! Whoop!

OZZIE
You got my whole knack of getting ladies,
It can't be beat,
And it's free, Gabey, it's all free.

CLAIRE, HILDY, CHIP, OZZIE
It's all free, it's all free, it's all free.

CLAIRE
I'm filled to the brim with eager affection
That seeks a direction.
My vigor and vim leave no one excluded,
And you are included.

I will get you out of your lull,
You won't feel unwanted or dull,
If you'll get this through that normal, Neanderthal skull:

Ya got me, baby, ya got me.
You got my extensive knowledge of anatomy.

HILDY, CHIP, OZZIE
Of anatomy!

CLAIRE
You got my whole interest in mankind—of every breed—
And it's free, baby, it's all free.

CLAIRE, HILDY, CHIP, OZZIE
It's all free, it's all free, it's all free.

CHIP
Ya got me, Gabey, ya got me!
You got a guy who always functions systematically.

CLAIRE, HILDY, OZZIE
'Matically!

CHIP
You got my whole family in Peoria, for you to see!
And it's free, Gabey, it's all free.

CLAIRE, HILDY, CHIP, OZZIE
It's all free, it's all free, it's all free.

(They dance)

CLAIRE & HILDY
Ya got we, Gabey, ya got we!

CHIP & OZZIE
> You got a date with Lucy Schmeeler, girl of mystery.

CLAIRE & HILDY
> Mystery!

CLAIRE, HILDY, CHIP, OZZIE
> You got her whole reservoir of passion
> To fill your need,
> And it's free, Gabey,
> Without fee, Gabey.
> Can't you see, Gabey?
> It's all free!

CLAIRE & HILDY (*Pointing to OZZIE and CHIP*)
> Ya got he!

CHIP & OZZIE (*Pointing to HILDY and CLAIRE*)
> Ya got she!

CLAIRE, HILDY, CHIP, OZZIE
> Ya got we!!

> (*Encore—Ya got me!*)

CLAIRE. HILDY, CHIP, OZZIE (*As the dance ends*)
> Ya got me!!!

CLAIRE I'll tell you what, let's go on to the Slam Bang Club. The music's primitive, the atmosphere primeval—

OZZIE Swell.

> (*He grabs CLAIRE and pulls her down in a clinch.*)

You and I can go back a couple of centuries.

> (*OZZIE kisses her. PITKIN has entered and comes to the table merrily.*)

PITKIN Hello, darling!

> (*CLAIRE and OZZIE break violently. CLAIRE comes to her feet.*)

CLAIRE (*Flustered*) Oh, Pitkin darling, what are you doing here? How stupid of me! I was supposed to meet you here, wasn't I?

PITKIN Darling, I UNDERSTAND! Getting a little scatterbrained. Working too hard on the book.

CLAIRE Well, darling, we're on our way to the Slam Bang. Meet us over there, won't you? This is so important. I can't give you the details, but pay the check, won't you?

PITKIN (*A little puzzled*) Yes, of course, I understand, the Slam Bang . . .

HILDY (*A sudden horrid thought*) Hey, what about Schmeeler?

CLAIRE (*Back to PITKIN*) Oh, Pitkin, while you pay the check, wait for a girl who answers to the name of Lucy Schmeeler, will you? And bring her along.

PITKIN Schlam Bang—Schmeeler.

HILDY You can't miss her. She's wearing a sneeze.

> (*PITKIN exits.*)

CLAIRE O.K. On to the Slam Bang!

> (*Blackout.*)

Publicity photo
Betty Comden,
Leonard Bernstein,
Adolph Green

SCENE 1C

The Slam Bang Club. The club is very small. The palm tree has disappeared, the customers have almost all gone, except a few people having a last dance to a dying orchestra. GABEY sits with his head on the table. MADAME DILLY enters, sits at a table, obviously very drunk.

MADAME DILLY (*As she enters*) Waiter—waiter—

> (*The WAITER approaches and she orders a drink during the opening music. When it stops, she begins to sing drunkenly, a cappella.*)

> Do-do-re-do.
> Do-re-mi-do.
> Do-re-mi-fa-do.

GABEY (*His head comes up as he hears her. Suddenly, he recognizes her and dashes over to her*) Maud P. Dilly. Oh, Madame Dilly! (*Very excited*) Where is she?

MADAME DILLY Where's who? (*With slight difficulty, she focuses on him and a slight glimmer of recognition floats over her face*) O-o-o-h-h-h, the young tar I hurled so uncermoniously out—(*Starts singing bravura*) Out—out of my lodge at Eventi-i-i-d-d-e!!

> (*GABEY shakes her impatiently.*)

I know where she is. (*Laughs*) You'll find her hobnobbing in the social whirl . . .

GABEY (*Bursting with impatience*) Where? Where?

MADAME DILLY At the corner of Tilyou and the Boardwalk—Coney Island.

GABEY Tilyou and—what kind of place is that?

MADAME DILLY O-o-o-h—iss an exlusive resort—The playland of the rich!! Yesshir!!

GABEY Tilyou and the Boardwalk—Coney Island!

> (*There is a second's pause, then he dashes out of the club. The OTHERS have watched and listened in complete bewilderment and are now shocked to see GABEY run out. OZZIE and CHIP jump up.*)

CHIP Gabey!

OZZIE Hey, Gabe. Come back.

> (*He rises and exits after him.*)

CHIP (*Goes over to DILLY and shakes her as she has apparently fallen into a stupor.*) Hey, lady. Lady!

MADAME DILLY (*Raises her head and looks at him*) Bellbottom, how you've grown.

CHIP Lady, who were you talking about?

OZZIE (*Re-entering, coming to table*) He'll never get to the ship on time.

CHIP We might lose him.

> (*Crosses to HILDY and kneels.*)

Oh, gee, Hildy, it's been swell!!

> (*CHIP puts his arms around her and kisses her on the cheek. HILDY sighs, he rises to go, but she trips him and he falls sprawling on his back. She goes quickly over to him and hauls him up.*)

Opposite:

"That's the nicest thing anyone's ever said to me!"

LUCY (Alice Pearce), PITKIN (Robert Chisholm)

HILDY A-a-a-a-ah-h, no ya don't. I'm going along.

OZZIE (*Goes to CLAIRE*) Well, we know where he is. (*Grabs the shawl*) Come on, Claire.

> (*THREE WAITERS take table and chairs away.*)

CLAIRE Look, specimen, I've just . . . I've just got to wait for Pitkin . . .

OZZIE (*Pats her shoulder*) O.K., kid, see you in another six million years.

> (*He starts to leave.*)

CLAIRE That's such a long time.

> (*BOTH pause. LUCY enters, beaming as she sneezes.*)

HILDY Lucy! (*LUCY turns to her expectantly*) Oh, Lucy, your date's gone!

LUCY (*Crushed and still with a cold in her nose*) Do! (*"No!" with a cold*)

HILDY Don't cry. I'll explain just as soon as I get home.

> (*CLAIRE gets her coat from chair, preparing to leave.*)

He couldn't wait any longer. Goodbye, Lucy.

LUCY So long!

> (*CHIP and HILDY start off. PITKIN enters. They collide.*)

PITKIN Hello, darling!

CLAIRE O-o-h-h-h, Pitkin, what are you doing here? We're going to Coney Island.

PITKIN Are you?

CLAIRE Yes, uh, well, look, you just stay here and take care of the check.

> (*Gets LUCY and passes her to PITKIN.*)

And, uh, take care of Miss Schmeeler. You understand. G'bye.

> (*CLAIRE grabs OZZIE and rushes out. LUCY and PITKIN look after them. LUCY sneezes.*)

PITKIN Gesundheit!

LUCY That's the nicest thing anybody ever said to me. Do you understand?

PITKIN I always have.

> When I was five my brother stole my lollipop.
> My lollipop stole he!
> But I didn't mutter "Damn your hide,"
> He needed candy more than I'd,
> So instead of biting off his hand,
> I just said, "Goo! I understand!"
>
> When I was ten, my mother trounced me with a mop.
> With a mop trounc-ed she me!
> But I didn't mutter "Damn your eyes,"
> I knew she needed exercise,
> So instead of joining a gypsy band,
> I just said, "Mom, I understand."

(*LUCY sneezes. He gives her his handkerchief.*)

At thirty a man in a car ruthlessly ran me down.
He ruthlessly down ran me!
But I didn't mutter "Damn your spleen,"
For a man's a man, but a car's a machine.
So instead of stripping him of his land,
I just said, "Jack—

(*He puts out his hand and she hands him back his handkerchief.*)

I understand."

Now I'm forty-five and I've met Claire,
We're engaged to wed.
Engaged to wed are we!
But tonight I tell you, "Damn you Claire!"
You played me evil,

(*LUCY giggles, jumps up and down.*)

And that's not fair!

LUCY (*Still stuffed up*) Do!! (*Rhymes with "No!"*)

PITKIN

So instead of remaining calm and bland,
I hereby do not understand!!!

I've had enough. I'm going after them! Come along, Miss Schmeeler.

LUCY Call me Lucy.

(*The Fifth Chase Interlude begins. FIGMENT sees PITKIN, demands arrest, runs off. POLICEMAN follows. UPERMAN follows in chase, followed by a COP. LITTLE OLD LADY tears across, finally PITKIN and LUCY join in, exiting.*)

Technical and business staff of *On the Town* minus Oliver Smith, co-producer and set designer

SCENE 2

The subway train to Coney Island. GABEY is seated, his doll in his hand. TWO COUPLES are in the car. A GIRL passes through, fishing in her pocketbook. GABEY's head drops, he is asleep, and in his dreams . . .

The IMAGINARY CONEY ISLAND BALLET begins. The swaying of the PEOPLE in the car becomes rhythmic. The music picks up and the PEOPLE dance to it, in a trance-like movement, their eyes closed, their movements detached. Suddenly, IVY appears from one end of the subway, dressed as the doll now lying in GABEY's lap. She comes toward GABEY, who looks up. The dance becomes wilder, and she motions him to come into the resplendent world which is now visible through the car windows—the Dream Coney Island of GABEY's imagination. IVY leads him invitingly to the center doors of the subway car, which open. The entire car splits in two, rolls off to either side of the stage, and IVY and GABEY step into the dream world.

*Dream Coney
Island Ballet*

IVY (Sono Osato)

SCENE 3

*The Dream Coney Island. A limitless void of blue. In the distance soar the
myriad lights of Coney Island—deeper, richer, higher, more exotic than the
real place. The Dream continues with the DREAM BALLET. GABEY is conscious of motion around him—a swirl of skirts, the scuffling of passing feet.
The lights slowly come up and he realizes where he is—a wonderful, sus-
pended, fluid and dreamy, sophisticated place for rich people. Suave, well-
groomed MEN and lovely, unattainable WOMEN dance by easily and coldly,
with a great impersonal quality about them. IVY is seized by the MEN and
they carry her off over GABEY's head. There is great excitement. The real
GABEY goes off to one side to see his DREAM COUNTERPART enter. TWO GIRLS
carry on a poster, advertising "Gabey The Great Lover."*

*The stage is a swirl of excitement as his DREAM SELF enters. They all watch
as the GREAT LOVER dances for them—a jazzy, slick, ingratiating, torchy,
sexy dance. He finishes with a bang. There is a fanfare. The MASTER OF
CEREMONIES from Diamond Eddie's enters.*

MASTER OF CEREMONIES Good evening, ladies and gentlemen. Welcome to
Coney Island—Playground of the Rich. Ha! Ha! (*Stamps his feet as he did in
the real nightclub*) And now, ladies and gentlemen, for the main event of
the evening: Gabey the Great Lover versus Ivy Smith!

*(With much ceremony, a prize ring is set up, a fight light comes down,
and IVY enters the ring. The match begins. IVY starts toward the
GREAT LOVER with soft, voluptuous movements—and the attacking
feints of the GREAT LOVER become slow motion movements, until
finally they are caresses rather than punches. She lures him into
unwrapping her turban. Suddenly, in her grasp, the length of red cloth
becomes a rope with which she proceeds to ensnare the GREAT LOVER,
until he is helpless in its coils. He is overcome, and IVY is lifted to
receive the plaudits of the multitude in triumph. The real GABEY, who
has watched horrorstruck, is brushed away, and he glides rapidly backward off stage.)*

*Dream Coney
Island Ballet*

IVY (Sono Osato),
GABEY THE GREAT
LOVER (Ray
Harrison)

SCENE 4

The Coney Island Subway Express. FLOSSIE and her GIRL FRIEND are seated to one side; on the other side are CHIP, HILDY, OZZIE and CLAIRE.

FLOSSIE So I said to him, "Listen, Mr. Gadolphin, I've come to your house to deliver the brassieres, not to model them."

FRIEND So what did he say?

FLOSSIE (*Rises*) So I said, "Mr. G.—I'll thank you to keep your distance."

FRIEND So what did he say?

FLOSSIE So I said, well, suddenly, I had nothing left to say.

FRIEND Well, for heaven's sake. What are you going to do now?

FLOSSIE Oh, let's stop off and get a malted.

(*They exit.*)

OZZIE (*Pointing to the subway ad of Miss Turnstiles*) There she is! There's the cause of all Gabe's trouble.

CHIP (*Rising to look at the picture*) Do you think he really met her?

(*HILDY rises, pulls CHIP down on bench beside her.*)

OZZIE Damn it, we just missed him. Why did that door have to slam in our faces just as we got there?

CLAIRE It always does. It's the unwritten law of the subway.

OZZIE Well, how long does it take to get to Coney Island?

CHIP (*Rises, looks at map*) Let's see. From here, to Coney Island, there are two— three—

HILDY Relax. You've got one hundred and ninety-six more stops to go.

CHIP What? We'll never get to the ship on time.

OZZIE Yeah, statistics show we've got to be back in a couple of hours.

CHIP Aw, gee, Hildy, I'll hate to leave you.

HILDY Oh, John.

(*They embrace. They are aware there is so little time left.*)

CLAIRE

Twenty-four hours can go so fast,
You look around, the day has passed.
When you're in love
Time is precious stuff;
Even a lifetime isn't enough.

Where has the time all gone to?
Haven't done half the things we want to.
Oh, well, we'll catch up
Some other time.

This day was just a token,
Too many words are still unspoken.
Oh, well, we'll catch up
Some other time.

Dream Coney Island

GABEY THE GREAT LOVER (Ray Harrison), IVY (Sono Osato)

Just when the fun is starting,
Comes the time for parting,
But let's be glad for what we've had
And what's to come.

There's so much more embracing
Still to be done, but time is racing.
Oh, well, we'll catch up
Some other time.

HILDY

Didn't get half my wishes,
Never have seen you dry the dishes.
Oh, well, we'll catch up
Some other time.

Can't satisfy my craving,
Never have watched you while you're shaving.
Oh, well, we'll catch up
Some other time.

CLAIRE, HILDY, CHIP, OZZIE

Just when the fun's beginning,
Comes the final inning . . .

(They embrace.)

CONDUCTOR *(Passing through the car)* Coney Island. All out.

OZZIE *(OZZIE and CLAIRE rise)*

Haven't had time to wake up,
Seeing you there without your make-up.
Oh, well, we'll catch up
Some other time.

CLAIRE, HILDY, CHIP, OZZIE

Just when the fun is starting,
Comes the time for parting,
But let's be glad for what we've had
And what's to come.

There's so much more embracing
Still to be done, but time is racing.
Oh, well, we'll catch up
Some other time.

SCENE 5

The Real Coney Island. It is a gaudy honky-tonk sort of place. Somewhat later than 2 AM, all the revelry that is left is concentrated in this place. SOL-DIERS and SAILORS and their GIRLS are drifting around, some tired, some happy, some drunk. On one side of the stage is the entrance to the Tunnel of Love. On the other side is a platform and large sign advertising "Rajah Bimmy's Night in a Harem." CHIP, OZZIE, CLAIRE and HILDY wander through the crowd and out. GABEY wanders around in a daze, looking for IVY. RAJAH BIMMY comes onto his platform to advertise the show.

RAJAH BIMMY (*Over music*) Hurry, hurry, hurry! Folks, it's our last red-hot, sizzling show of the evening—and what I'm about to show you is the most blood-tingling exhibition of the female form weaving in action—that you and I have ever had the tantalizing privilege of witnessing! Might as well warn you—the cops have their eye on this place! We keep the girls just within the bounds of decency—but there might be a slip—who can tell? One of the girls might go too far—

> (*Corny "hootch" music as THREE GIRLS enter in cheap Turkish costumes. BIMMY keeps up a running commentary.*)

Rajah Bimmy's Harum-Scarum
Where you see the pretty girl who picks
The handkerchief up with her teeth

And the girl who picks the handkerchief up,
And the girl who picks the handkerchief up,
And the girl who picks the handkerchief up
With her teeth.

> (*The GIRLS cavort sexily.*)

Rajah Bimmy's Harum-Scarum
Where you see the pretty girl who picks
The handkerchief up with her teeth

And the girl who picks the handkerchief up,
And the girl who picks the handkerchief up,
And the girl who picks the handkerchief up
With her teeth.

> (*He introduces IVY. IVY and the GIRLS do their bumps and grinds and parades. IVY takes a handkerchief from a MAN's pocket and proceeds, with the aid of her fellow DANCERS, to pick the handkerchief up with her teeth. GABEY enters, and realizes with horror that this is IVY.*)

GABEY Ivy!

IVY Gabey!

> (*He makes a grab for her, and pulls her skirt off. There is a pause of shock, then a police whistle.*)

POLICEMAN Hey, that's indecent exposure. I'll arrest you.

> (*General movement as PEOPLE flock around the COUPLE. OZZIE, CLAIRE, CHIP and HILDY enter and see GABEY and IVY. The COP approaches HILDY. She hits him and he backs away. The six of them start to run, but encounter FIGMENT, COPS, LITTLE OLD LADY, and UPERMAN, entering, who recognize their quarry and chase the six back. HILDY grabs CHIP, who grabs CLAIRE, who grabs OZZIE. GABEY grabs IVY and takes her aside.*)

GABEY A fine thing. Miss Turnstiles—the pride of New York—too good for me.

IVY Gabey, I wanted to come to Nedick's to meet you, but I owe Madame Dilly fifty-six dollars and she made me come to work.

GABEY Is that true?

IVY Yes, Gabey. I wanted to go out with you more than anything in the world.

GABEY Ivy—Ivy—you're beautiful—you're wonderful—uh, you haven't got much clothes on.

(A GIRL rushes on with a coat for IVY.)

IVY (*As she struggles into the coat*) Oh, I know. I'm gonna be arrested for dis-nuding in public.

PITKIN (*Entering with LUCY, pushing his way through the CROWD*) All right, all right, officer. I'll take charge here.

WORKMAN Who is that guy?

GIRL Judge Bridgework.

PITKIN Come on, officer, line 'em up.

CLAIRE Oh, Pitkin, darling—what are you doing here? Oh, this is wonderful. All these people are following us. We've got into a little trouble—you'll get us out—you understand.

PITKIN Claire, I do *not* understand!

CLAIRE What?

PITKIN I do *not* understand. Officer, arrest these people.

(As the CROWD murmurs and protests.)

You three men will be turned over to the Naval Authorities.

OZZIE Well, you see, it's this way . . .

PITKIN That means you, too, specimen. And I will hold the three accused females for further questioning.

CLAIRE Pitkin, this is ridiculous. You know I'm not a criminal.

PITKIN I don't know what you are, Claire. I'll never trust a woman again. You are all under arrest.

(The CROWD murmurs as the LOVERS rush to each other.)

Silence!

IVY Gabey!

GABEY Ivy!

HILDY They can't do this to us.

CHIP Gee, Hildy.

CLAIRE Goodbye, Ozzie.

PITKIN (*Pushing*) No fond farewell, please, just go.

(POLICEMAN escorts OZZIE, CHIP and GABEY off.)

HILDY (*To PITKIN*) A fine guy you are. Won't let your fiancée go with the guy she loves.

CLAIRE Pitkin, darling, please understand and forgive. Haven't you ever committed an indiscretion?

HILDY Yes, haven't you ever, uh, uh—(*She gestures suggestively*)

PITKIN Never.

> (*There is a moment's pause, then PITKIN sneezes the sneeze of SCHMEELER.*)

LUCY Gesundheit!

> (*She giggles wickedly.*)

ALL (*Realizing*) A-ha-ah!

Publicity Photo "Ivy—Ivy, you're beautiful!"
GABEY (John Battles), IVY (Sono Osato)

SCENE 6

The Brooklyn Navy Yard. It is the same as the opening of the play. It is almost the same time of day, early morning. A STREET SWEEPER goes his round. A SAILOR is saying goodbye to his GIRL. OZZIE, CHIP and GABEY come on, escorted by a POLICEMAN. They are disconsolate.

OZZIE
New York, New York.

GABEY
The lights are out.

CHIP It's six o'clock.

(The music picks up and the BOYS hear their names called from off-stage. It's the GIRLS. They rush on.)

HILDY (*Calls offstage*) Chip!

CLAIRE Ozzie!

IVY Gabey!

CLAIRE, HILDY, IVY (*Singing in time to the music as they throw themselves into the arms of CHIP, OZZIE and GABEY*)

Pitkin understood!

(As they embrace)

He really understood!

(Suddenly, the six o'clock whistle blows and the stage is alive with WORKERS going to work, SAILORS returning and fresh SAILORS out on their day of leave. The THREE COUPLES look around, realizing that this is goodbye.)

THREE SAILORS (*Entering excitedly from the ship*)
New York, New York,
It's a helluva town!

We've got one day here and not another minute
To see the famous sights.
We'll find the romance and danger waiting in it,
Beneath the Broadway lights.

And we've hair on our chest,
So what we like the best
Are the nights.
Sights, lights, nights!

(GABEY, CHIP, and OZZIE, with IVY, HILDY, and CLAIRE look at one another, realizing what they have been through and what lies ahead, as three new SAILORS take off on the town. They are joined by the entire company.)

ENTIRE COMPANY
New York, New York,
A helluva town!
The Bronx is up, and the Battery's down.
The people ride in a hole in the groun'.
New York, New York.
It's a helluva town!

(Curtain. End of Play.)

Wonderful Town

Music by Leonard Bernstein
Book by Joseph Fields & Jerome Chodorov
Lyrics by Betty Comden & Adolph Green

BASED ON THE PLAY *MY SISTER EILEEN*
BY JOSEPH FIELDS AND JEROME CHODOROV
AND THE STORIES BY RUTH MCKENNEY
ORIGINAL DIRECTION BY GEORGE ABBOTT

Wonderful Town

A phone call from George Abbott always held promise of excitement. Late in 1952, I (Betty) got a phone call and it was George asking if we could write the lyrics for a show based on *My Sister Eileen* to star Rosalind Russell. I (Adolph) was in Paris and got a call from me (Betty) telling about it, which caused me (Adolph) to rush home at once. It seems they had a partial score they were unsure of. George asked if we could write a score in four weeks because after that they would lose Miss Russell to other commitments, and wanted to know what composer we could suggest. We thought of Leonard Bernstein, knowing he had just returned from his honeymoon with Felicia, and mentioned him dubiously to George. George said: "Go over and ask him right away!" We did, although we were very doubtful if Lenny would be interested. Among other things he had promised his mentor Serge Koussevitsky that after *On the Town* he would get down to serious business and never, never write another show. We had no sooner entered Lenny's apartment and were blurting out the facts about the show when the phone rang. It was George, never one to waste time, barking at us impatiently, "Well, is it yes or no?!!" To our surprise, with no hesitation Lenny said "Yes." He always liked deadlines, and four weeks to write a score was an irresistible challenge.

The play by Jerome Chodorov and Joseph Fields written in the 1940's had been based on stories by Ruth McKenney about two girls from Columbus, Ohio, who come to New York in the mid-30's to seek fame and fortune. We resisted all pressure to update it to the 50's, and knew we were on our way when Lenny exuberantly banged out on the piano the Eddie Duchin vamp, a characteristic musical sound of the 1930's. We were creatively on our way to Greenwich Village and adventure in the "Big City," and were able to complete the score in the prescribed four weeks.

This show celebrates New York as the magnet for young people from all fields of endeavor who, like Ruth and Eileen, still come here to fulfill their aspirations in this Wonderful Town.

"This show celebrates New York as the magnet for young people … who … still come here to fulfill their aspirations in this Wonderful Town."

Wonderful Town was presented first by Robert Fryer at the Winter Garden,
New York City, on February 25, 1953 with the following cast:

GUIDE	Warren Galjour
APPOPOLOUS	Henry Lascoe
LONIGAN	Walter Kelvin
HELEN	Michele Burke
WRECK	Jordan Bentley
VIOLET	Dody Goodman
VALENTI	Ted Beniades
EILEEN	Edie Adams
RUTH	Rosalind Russell
A STRANGE MAN	Nathaniel Frey
DRUNKS	Lee Papell, Delbert Anderson
ROBERT BAKER	George Gaynes
ASSOCIATE EDITORS	Warren Galjour, Albert Linville
MRS. WADE	Isabella Hoopes
FRANK LIPPENCOTT	Chris Alexander
CHEF	Nathaniel Frey
WAITER	Delbert Anderson
DELIVERY BOY	Alvin Beam
CHICK CLARK	Dort Clark
SHORE PATROLMAN	Lee Papell
FIRST CADET	David Lober
SECOND CADET	Ray Dorian
POLICEMEN	Lee Papell, Albert Linville, Delbert Anderson, Chris Robinson, Nathaniel Frey, Warren Galjour, Robert Kole
RUTH'S ESCORT	Chris Robinson
GREENWICH VILLAGERS	Jean Eliot, Carol Cole, Marta Becket, Maxine Berke, Helena Seroy, Geraldine Delaney, Margaret Cuddy, Dody Goodman, Ed Balin, Alvin Beam, Ray Dorian, Edward Heim, Joe Layton, David Lober, Victor Moreno, William Weslow, Pat Johnson, Evelyn Page, Libi Staiger, Patty Wilkes, Helen Rice, Delbert Anderson, Warren Galjour, Robert Kole, Ray Kirchner, Lee Papell, Chris Robinson

Production directed by George Abbott
Dances and Musical Numbers Staged by Donald Saddler
Sets and Costumes by Raoul du Bois
Musical Direction and Vocal Arrangements by Lehman Engel
Miss Russell's Clothes by Main Bocher
Lighting by Peggy Clark
Orchestrations by Don Walker

SETTING

The play takes place in Greenwich Village in the '30s.

Act One

SCENE 1: CHRISTOPHER STREET

Christopher Street   Guide and Villagers

SCENE 2: THE STUDIO APARTMENT

Ohio   Ruth and Eileen

SCENE 2A: NEW YORK CITY

Conquering New York   Ruth, Eileen and Company

SCENE 3: THE STREET OUTSIDE THE STUDIO APARTMENT

One Hundred Easy Ways   Ruth

SCENE 4: BOB BAKER'S OFFICE

What a Waste   Baker and Editors

Story Vignettes   Miss Comden and Mr. Green,
Rexford, Mr. Mallory, Danny,
Trent, and Ruth

SCENE 5: THE STREET OUTSIDE THE STUDIO APARTMENT

A Little Bit in Love   Eileen

SCENE 6: THE BACKYARD OF THE STUDIO APARTMENT

Pass The Football   Wreck and the Villagers

Conversation Piece   Miss Comden and Mr. Green,
Ruth, Eileen, Frank, Baker,
and Chick

A Quiet Girl   Baker

SCENE 7: THE BROOKLYN NAVY YARD

Conga   Ruth; Danced by The Cadets

SCENE 8: THE BACKYARD OF THE STUDIO APARTMENT

Act Two

SCENE 1: THE CHRISTOPHER STREET STATION HOUSE

My Darlin' Eileen   Eileen and Policemen

SCENE 2: THE STREET OUTSIDE THE STUDIO APARTMENT

Swing!   Ruth and the Villagers

SCENE 3: THE STUDIO APARTMENT

Ohio (Reprise)   Ruth and Eileen

SCENE 4: THE STREET OUTSIDE THE VILLAGE VORTEX

It's Love   Baker and the Villagers

SCENE 5: THE VILLAGE VORTEX

Wrong Note Rag   Ruth, Eileen and The Villagers

Act One

SCENE 1

In front of the curtain, which a semi-abstract impression of Greenwich Village, a GUIDE and a group of gaping TOURISTS enter to a musical vamp in a style highly characteristic of the 1930s.

GUIDE Come along!

> (*Singing in the brisk, off-hand manner of a barker and indicating points of interest in a lilting song.*)

> On your left,
> Washington Square,
> Right in the heart of Greenwich Village.

TOURISTS (*Looking around ecstatically*)

> My, what trees—
> Smell that air—
> Painters and pigeons in Washington Square.

GUIDE

> On your right,
> Waverly Place,
> Bit of Paree in Greenwich Village.

TOURISTS

> My, what charm,
> My, what grace!
> Poets and peasants on Waverly Place.

GUIDE (*Reeling off his customary spiel*) Ever since 1870, Greenwich Village has been the Bohemian cradle of painters, writers, actors, etc., who've gone on to fame and fortune. Today in 1935, who knows what future greats live in these twisting alleys? Come along!

> (*As the GUIDE and group cross to the side, the curtain opens, revealing Christopher Street. The scene looks like a cheery postcard of Greenwich Village, with Village characters exhibiting their paintings, grouped in a tableau under a banner which reads "Greenwich Village Art Contest, 1935."*)

GUIDE

> Here you see
> Christopher Street,
> Typical spot in Greenwich Village.

TOURISTS

> Ain't it quaint,
> Ain't it sweet,
> Pleasant and peaceful on Christopher Street?

> (*Suddenly the tableau comes to life and all hell breaks loose. An angry ARTIST smashes his painting over the head of an art-contest JUDGE who retires in confusion.*)

VILLAGER Here comes another judge.

> (*A SECOND JUDGE enters, examines the paintings, and awards First Prize to a bewildered JANITOR, whose well-filled ashcan the JUDGE mistakes for an ingenious mobile sculpture. The angry ARTIST smashes another painting over the second JUDGE's head and all freeze into another tableau.*)

GUIDE

> Here is home,
> Christopher Street,
> Right in the heart of Greenwich Village.

VILLAGERS

> Life is calm,
> Life is sweet,
> Pleasant and peaceful on Christopher Street.

(They freeze into another tableau as a cop comes in, a friend of the street, named LONIGAN. He goes up to one of the artists, a dynamic, explosive character named APPOPOLOUS.)

GUIDE

> Here's a famous Village type:
> Mr. Appopolous, modern painter,
> Better known on this beat
> As the lovable landlord of Christopher Street.

(Music is interrupted.)

APPOPOLOUS *(Breaking out of tableau. To LONIGAN—violently)* Throw that Violet woman out of my building!

LONIGAN What's the beef now, Appopolous?

APPOPOLOUS I'm very broadminded, Lonigan, but when a woman gives rumba lessons all night, she's gotta have at least a phonograph!

(Music resumes. LONIGAN enters building. WRECK exits from building, carrying bird cage with canary. He meets a cute young girl named HELEN on the street. As they kiss the stage "freezes" again.)

GUIDE

> Here's a guy known as The Wreck,
> Football professional out of season,
> Unemployed throughout the heat,
> Living on nothing on Christopher Street.

(Music is interrupted. Freeze breaks. WRECK kisses HELEN.)

HELEN Hi! Where you goin' with Dicky Bird?

WRECK Takin' him down to Benny's to see what I can get on him . . .

HELEN Oh no, Wreck! You can't hock Dicky!

WRECK Take your choice—we either hock him or have him on toast.

(Music resumes. He goes off. VIOLET comes out of building, followed by LONIGAN.)

VIOLET Let go of me, ya big phony!

(Freeze. VIOLET drops valise on the sidewalk, leans down, pointing angry finger at LONIGAN. She carries a large pink doll.)

GUIDE

> Here is yet another type.
> Everyone knows the famous Violet,
> Nicest gal you'd ever meet
> Steadily working on Christopher Street.

(Music is cut off.)

"Such interesting people live on Christopher Street."

95

VIOLET (*To* LONIGAN) Don't shove me, ya big phony!

LONIGAN On your way, Violet.

(*VIOLET is pushed off by LONIGAN.*)

VIOLET (*As she goes*) You're a public servant—I pay your salary! So just you show a little respect!

(*Music resumes.*)

"Don't shove me, ya big phony."
APPOPOLOUS (Henry Lascoe), VIOLET (Dody Goodman)

ALL

    Life is gay,
    Life is sweet,
    Interesting people on Christopher Street.

    (*Everybody dances*)

    Such interesting people live on Christopher Street!

A PHILOSOPHER (*Enters, carrying a sign—"Meeting on Union Square"*)
    Down with Wall Street! Down with Wall Street!

    (*He freezes with the others, fist in air.*)

GUIDE

    Such interesting people live on Christopher Street!

YOGI (*Enters with sign "Peace"*)
    Love thy neighbor! Love thy neighbor!

    (*Another freeze.*)

TOURISTS

    Such interesting people live on Christopher Street!

    (*Two MODERN DANCERS enter.*)

MODERN DANCERS (*Working hard*)
    And one—and two—and three—and four—
    And one—and two—and three—and four

TOURISTS

    Such interesting people live on Christopher Street!

ALL

    Look! Look!
    Poets! Actors! Dancers! Writers!
    Here we live,
    Here we love.
    This is the place for self-expression.
    Life is mad,
    Life is sweet.
    Interesting people living on Christopher Street!

    (*The VILLAGERS perform a mad dance of self-expression, which involves everything from a wild can-can to imitations of a symphony orchestra. It works its way up to a furious climax which ends with a last tableau like the opening one, the final punctuation being the smashing of yet another painting over the first JUDGE'S head.*)

GUIDE (*Leading TOURISTS off, as music fades*)
    Come along,
    Follow me.
    Now we will see MacDougal Alley,
    Patchen Place,
    Minetta Lane,
    Bank Street and
    Church Street and
    John Street
    And Jane.

VALENTI (*A strange zoot-suited character struts in*) Skeet—skat—skattle-ee-o-do—

APPOPOLOUS Hey, Mister Valenti! My most desirable studio is about to become available, and I'm going to give you first chance at it.

VALENTI Down there? (*Pointing to bars of a basement room, below street level*) When I go back to living in caves—I'll see ya, cornball.

(*There is a scream offstage and a KID runs in, carrying a typewriter. APPOPOLOUS twists him very expertly. The KID runs off, dropping the typewriter.*)

EILEEN (*Runs on*) Stop him, somebody! He grabbed it right out of my hand! Ruth!

(*RUTH enters with two valises.*)

RUTH (*To APPOPOLOUS*) Oh, you've got it! Thank goodness! Thank you, sir. Thank you very much.

APPOPOLOUS (*Pulls typewriter back*) You're welcome, young lady.

RUTH (*Holding out for the case*) Well?

APPOPOLOUS Only how do I know this property belongs to you? Can you identify yourself?

RUTH Identify myself?

APPOPOLOUS Yes, have you got a driver's license?

RUTH To operate a typewriter?

EILEEN Now you give that to my sister!

APPOPOLOUS How do I know it's hers?

RUTH The letter "W" is missing.

APPOPOLOUS Now we're getting somewhere. (*Opens the case.*)

RUTH It fell off after I wrote my thesis on Walt Whitman.

APPOPOLOUS (*Closes case*) She's right. Here's your property. The incident is closed. Case dismissed.

RUTH Who are you, Felix Franfurter?

APPOPOLOUS (*Laughs*) You can tell they're out-of-towners. They don't know me!

EILEEN We don't know anybody. We just got in from Columbus today.

RUTH Please, Eileen, they're not interested.

HELEN Columbus? That's the worst town I ever played in.

EILEEN Are you an actress?

(*HELEN nods.*)

That's what I came to New York for—to break into the theatre—

WRECK Well, you certainly got the face and build for it—

APPOPOLOUS (*Steps in, to RUTH*) And you, young lady, are you artistic like your sister?

RUTH No. I haven't the face and build for it.

EILEEN Don't listen to her. She's a very good writer—and very original.

RUTH Yes. I'm the only author who never uses a "w." (*RUTH picks up case and valise*) Come on, Eileen. It's getting late, and we've got to find a place.

"How do I know this property belongs to you?"
EILEEN (Edie Adams), RUTH (Carol Channing who followed Rosalind Russell in the part), APPOPOLOUS (Henry Lascoe's replacement in the role)

APPOPOLOUS (*Laughing*) Remarkable! You're looking for a place, and I got just the place! Step in—I'll show it to you personally!

RUTH What floor is it on?

APPOPOLOUS What floor? Let me show you the place before you start raising a lot of objections.

EILEEN Let's look at it anyway, Ruth. What can we lose?

APPOPOLOUS Of course! What can you lose?

RUTH I don't know, Eileen—

APPOPOLOUS What do you gotta know? (*He opens door*) Step in.

    (*EILEEN steps through. RUTH follows.*)

A Chinese opium den it isn't, and a white slaver I ain't!

    (*APPOPOLOUS steps in, closes door behind him.*)

VILLAGERS
> There they go
> Down the stairs.
> Now they will live
> In Greenwich Village.
>
> Life is mad,
> Life is sweet,
> Interesting people living on
> Christopher Street.

    (*They all dance off.*)

SCENE 2

The studio: a basement horror with two daybeds, an imitation fireplace and one barred window that looks out on the street above. It's a cross between a cell in solitary confinement and an iron lung.

APPOPOLOUS Isn't it just what you've been dreaming about?

RUTH It's very nice, only—

APPOPOLOUS Note the imitation fireplace—(*Steps to bed, patting it*) the big, comfortable daybeds—

> (*RUTH goes to bed, starts to pat it; APPOPOLOUS takes her hand away and points it to window.*)

Look! Life passes up and down in front of you like a regular parade!

> (*Some people pass by—only their legs are visible.*)

RUTH Well, really—

APPOPOLOUS Let me point out a few salient features. In here you have a model kitchenette, complete in every detail.

> (*RUTH goes to door—APPOPOLOUS closes it quickly. He goes to bathroom door. She follows.*)

And over here is a luxurious bathroom—

> (*RUTH starts to look. APPOPOLOUS closes door quickly.*)

RUTH They're awfully small.

APPOPOLOUS In those two rooms you won't entertain. (*He indicates a hideous painting on the wall*) You see that landscape? That's from my blue-green period.

RUTH You mean *you* painted that?

APPOPOLOUS Yes, of course. This studio is merely a hobby—a sanctuary for struggling young artists—and since you are both in the arts, I'm gonna let you have this studio for the giveaway price of sixty-five dollars a month.

RUTH Sixty-five dollars for *this?*

EILEEN (*Weakly*) Couldn't we stay here tonight, and then if we like it—

> (*RUTH shakes head "no."*)

APPOPOLOUS I'll do better than that. You can have the place for a month—on trial—at absolutely no cost to you!

RUTH Oh, we couldn't let you do that, could we, Eileen?

APPOPOLOUS And then, if you're not one hundred percent satisfied, I'll give you back your first month's rent!

EILEEN (*Pathetically*) Please, Ruth—I've got to get to bed.

> (*RUTH gives her a look, sighs and starts to count out some bills.*)

RUTH Twenty, forty, sixty-one, sixty-two . . .

> (*There is a tremendous boom from below. The girls freeze in terror as APPOPOLOUS quickly grabs the money from RUTH.*)

APPOPOLOUS That's enough.

EILEEN My God!

RUTH What—what was that?

APPOPOLOUS (*Innocently*) What was *what?*

RUTH That noise—the whole room shook!

APPOPOLOUS (*Chuckles*) That just goes to show how you'll get used to it. I didn't even notice it.

EILEEN Get used to it?

APPOPOLOUS You won't even be conscious of it. A little blasting—the new subway—(*He points to the floor.*)

RUTH You mean they're blasting right underneath us?

APPOPOLOUS What are you worrying about? Those engineers know how much dynamite to use.

EILEEN You mean it goes on all the time?

APPOPOLOUS No—no—they knock off at midnight and they don't start again until six o'clock in the morning! (*Goes to door and turns*) Good night—Sleep tight! (*He goes out.*)

RUTH Yes, Eileen—sleep tight, my darling—and you were in such a hell of a hurry to get to bed!

EILEEN Ruth, what are we going to do?

RUTH We're gonna do thirty days.

> (*EILEEN exits to bathroom with suitcase. RUTH follows, looks in, and steps back in horror*)

Thank God, we took a bath before we left Columbus!

> (*She opens her suitcase and starts to take out her things. Woman with dog passes at window, dog stops and looks through the bars.*)

Oh! You get away from there!

> (*The woman and her dog go off.*)

EILEEN (*Comes out of bathroom, combing her hair. She is in pajamas*) I wonder what Billy Honnecker thinks now?

RUTH He's probably at the country club this minute with Annie Wilkinson, drinking himself to death.

EILEEN He can have her.

RUTH Don't you suppose he knows that?

EILEEN And she can have him, too—with my compliments.

RUTH That's the advantage of not leaving any men behind—you don't have to worry what becomes of them.

EILEEN Oh, it's different with you. Boys never meant anything in your life.

RUTH (*Going to bathroom with pajamas*) Not after they got a load of you they didn't.

(She goes into bathroom. EILEEN sits on her bed and a moment later a man comes in the front door and calmly crosses to a chair and sprawls out on it.)

FLETCHER Hello. Hot, isn't it?

(He offers EILEEN a cigarette.)

EILEEN (*Rising fearfully*) I think you're making a mistake. What apartment do you want?

FLETCHER Is Violet home?

EILEEN No. No Violet lives here.

FLETCHER It's all right. Marty sent me.

EILEEN I don't know any Marty. You'll have to get out of here!

FLETCHER Aw, don't be like that. I'm a good fella.

EILEEN I don't care *what* you are! Will you please go!

FLETCHER Are you sure Violet Shelton doesn't live here?

EILEEN If you don't get out of here, I'm going to call the police!

(He laughs.)

All right—you asked for it—now you're going to get it! (*She goes to front door*)

FLETCHER Ha! They won't arrest me—I'm a fireman!

EILEEN (*In the hall*) Help—somebody—help!

(RUTH comes out of the bathroom, stops in surprise as she sees FLETCHER, and backs away.)

RUTH Oh, how do you do?

FLETCHER Hello.

EILEEN (*Comes in*) Don't "how do you do" him, Ruth! He's nobody!

(She runs behind RUTH.)

He just walked in and he won't go away. Make him go 'way, Ruth!

RUTH (*Diffidently*) Now you go 'way. And stop bothering my sister.

FLETCHER No.

(WRECK dashes in, still in his shorts.)

WRECK What's the trouble, girls?

EILEEN This man walked in and he won't go 'way!

WRECK (*To FLETCHER—who rises*) What's the idea of crashing in on these girls?

FLETCHER Now don't get yourself excited. It was just a mistake.

WRECK You bet it was a mistake! Now get movin'!

FLETCHER (*Goes calmly to door*) Okay. (*To girls*) Good evening— (*To WRECK*) You're the hairiest Madam I ever saw!

Left: WRECK (Jordan Bentley), FLETCHER (Nathaniel Frey)

Right: RUTH (Rosalind Russell), EILEEN (Edie Adams)

104

WONDERFUL TOWN

(*He runs out as* WRECK *starts after him angrily.*)

EILEEN (*Hastily*) Oh, thank you—Mr.—

WRECK (*Turns*) Loomis—but call me The Wreck.

RUTH The Wreck?

WRECK That's what they called me at Trenton Tech. I would have made All-American, only I turned professional. Well, girls, if anyone busts in on you again, just holler. "I'm a ramblin' Wreck from Trenton Tech—and a helluva engineer—"

(*He goes off singing.*)

EILEEN Ruth, I'm scared!

RUTH It's all right, darling, go to bed—

(*She leads* EILEEN *to a daybed, then goes to fireplace and bumps her hips.*)

Aw, the hell with it! Let it spread! (RUTH *switches off light. There's no perceptible difference*)

Didn't I just put out the light?

(*She pushes button again. Then, she pushes the button a third time.*)

EILEEN There's a lamp post right in front of the window. Pull down the shade.

RUTH There isn't any shade.

EILEEN No shade? We're practically sleeping on the street!

RUTH Just wait till I get that Appopolous! (*Sits on bed and winces*) Boy! What Bernarr MacFadden would give for this bed!

EILEEN Let's go to sleep.

RUTH Maybe we can forget.

EILEEN Good night—

RUTH Good night—

(*A kid runs by window, scraping a stick against the iron bars. It sounds like a volley of machine-gun fire. The girls sit up, terrified.*)

EILEEN What was that?

RUTH It sounded like a machine gun!

KID (*Runs by again, shouts*) Hey, Walyo—wait for me!

EILEEN (*Wails*) Gee, Ruth—what I got us into.

RUTH Oh, go to sleep!

(*Girls settle back wearily. Drunks are heard singing "Come to Me My Melancholy Baby." They come up to the window, their legs visible.*)

EILEEN (*Covering herself—shouts to window*) You go 'way from there, you drunken bums!

(*Drunks stoop down, leering in.*)

FIRST DRUNK Ah! A dame!

RUTH You go 'way from there or we'll call the police!

FIRST DRUNK Another dame! Look, Pete! There's two broads—one for you, too!

> (*Wiggling his fingers happily at* RUTH.)

EILEEN Ruth! Close the window!

RUTH *Me* close the window!

FIRST DRUNK No—the hell with her— (*To* EILEEN) You close it!

EILEEN Ruth, please!

SECOND DRUNK Don't you do it, Ruth!

FIRST DRUNK Leave me in! I'll close it!

> (*The cop's legs appear, nightstick swinging.*)

OFFICER LONIGAN What's goin' on here? Come on! Break it up!

> (*The drunks hurry away.* LONIGAN *stoops, looks in window*)

Oh, I get it!

RUTH I'm awfully glad you came, Officer.

OFFICER LONIGAN (*Heavily*) Yeah, I'll bet you are.

RUTH We just moved in today.

OFFICER LONIGAN (*Grimly*) Well, if you're smart, you'll move out tomorrow. I don't go for this stuff on my beat. I'm warning you.

> (*He goes off. The girls stare at each other in dismay.*)

EILEEN Oh, *Ruth!*

RUTH (*Goes to her dismally*) Now, Eileen, everything's going to be all right.

EILEEN It's awful!

RUTH Never mind, Eileen—try and sleep.

EILEEN I *can't* sleep.

RUTH Try, darling—make your mind a blank.

EILEEN I did, but I keep thinking of Ohio.

> (RUTH *puts arm around* EILEEN.)

RUTH Oh, Eileen—me, too.

> (*They sing, plaintively.*)

EILEEN AND RUTH
Why, oh why, oh why, oh—
Why did I ever leave Ohio?
Why did I wander to find what lies yonder
When life was so cozy at home?
Wond'ring while I wander,
Why did I fly,
Why did I roam,
Oh, why oh, why oh
Did I leave Ohio?
Maybe I'd better go home.
Maybe I'd better go home.

> (*Music continues.*)

RUTH (*Rises, defiantly*)
>Now listen, Eileen,
>Ohio was stifling.
>We just couldn't wait to get out of the place,
>With Mom saying—"Ruth, what no date for this evening?"

EILEEN
>And Pop with, "Eileen, do be home, dear, by ten—"

RUTH AND EILEEN
>Ugh!

RUTH
>The gossipy neighbors
>And everyone yapping who's going with whom—

EILEEN
>And dating those drips that I've known since I'm four.

RUTH
>The Kiwanis Club Dance.

EILEEN
>On the basketball floor.

RUTH
>Cousin Maude with her lectures on sin—

RUTH & EILEEN
>What a bore!

EILEEN
>Jerry Black!

RUTH
>Cousin Min!

EILEEN
>Ezra Nye!

RUTH
>Hannah Finn!

EILEEN
>Hopeless!

RUTH
>Babbity!

EILEEN
>Stuffy!

RUTH
>Provincial!

RUTH AND EILEEN
>Thank heavens we're free!

>(*By this time each is in her own bed, reveling in newfound freedom. There is a terrific blast from the subway below and they dash terrified into each other's arms and sing hysterically.*)

>Why, oh why, oh why, oh—
>Why did we ever leave Ohio?!

(*They cut off as music continues and go over to RUTH's bed, huddling together under the covers.*)

RUTH & EILEEN (*Quietly and sadly*)
Wond'ring while we wander,
Why did we fly?
Why did we roam?
Oh, why oh, why oh—
Did we leave Ohio?
Maybe we'd better go

EILEEN	**RUTH**
Home.	O—H—I—O.

RUTH & EILEEN
Maybe we'd better go home.

(*They sink back exhausted as the lights dim. There is a fanfare of a bugle reminiscent of "Reveille," followed by the sound of an alarm clock as the lights come up sharply. It is early morning.*

RUTH springs up as if shot from a cannon, turns off the alarm and shakes EILEEN. RUTH is full of determination.)

RUTH Come on, Eileen. Up and at 'em! Let's get an early start. We're going to take this town. Get up, Eileen!

(*She starts briskly toward the bathroom, suddenly winces and clutches her aching back, but limps bravely on. The lights black out.*

There is a dance pantomime depicting the girls' struggle to get ahead in the "Big City" beginning with determined optimism and ending in utter defeat. Everywhere RUTH goes with her manuscripts, publishers are either out to lunch, in conference, or just not interested. Everywhere EILEEN goes, looking for theatre work, she receives many propositions, but they are never for jobs. As the number comes to a finish, the two sisters join each other sadly, collapsing glumly on each other's shoulders as the hostile city crowds sing to them "Maybe you'd better go home!" There is a blackout.)

SCENE 3

The street, same as Scene 1.

ESKIMO PIE MAN Eskimo Pies—Eskimo Pies—Eskimo Pies—

> (*RUTH enters from house with milk bottles in a sack.*)

RUTH Hey, Eskimo Pies! Will you take five milk bottles? You can cash them in on the corner!

ESKIMO PIE MAN I got no time for milk bottles!

> (*He goes. RUTH puts bottles down.*)

EILEEN (*Enters with a large paper bag*) Be careful, Ruth—they're valuable!

RUTH (*Wearily*) Oh, hello, Eileen. What have you got in the bag?

EILEEN Food.

RUTH (*Eagerly*) Food? Let's see! Where'd you get it?

> (*They sit on the stoop.*)

EILEEN At the food show. I saw people coming out with big bags of samples. So I went in, and I met the nicest boy. He was the floor manager—

RUTH (*Nods sagely*) Oh, the floor manager.

EILEEN He loaded me up! We've got enough junk here for a week.

RUTH (*Taking out small boxes of cereal*) "Pep-O," "Rough-O," "Vita-Bran," "Nature's Broom." We're going to have breakfast all day long.

EILEEN It's good for you—it's roughage.

RUTH I'd like to vary it with a little smoothage—like a steak!

> (*Puts stuff back in bag. VALENTI enters and crosses, snapping his fingers in rhythm.*)

VALENTI Skeet—skat—skattle-o-do—

EILEEN Oh, hello, Mr. Valenti!

VALENTI
> Hi yah, gate! I got my eye on you! *Solid.*
> Skeet—skat—skattle-e-o-do—

RUTH Who was *that?*

EILEEN That's Speedy Valenti! He runs that advanced night club—the Village Vortex. He's a very interesting boy. He had a cow and he studied dairy farming at Rutgers and then got into the nightclub business.

RUTH Naturally.

EILEEN I auditioned for him this morning.

RUTH You did? How'd he like it?

EILEEN He said I should get myself a reputation and he'd give me a trial.

> (*HELEN and WRECK enter.*)

HELEN Oh, girls! Can we see you a minute?

RUTH Sure, Mrs. Loomis—what is it?

HELEN Well, this is awfully embarrassing—I don't know how to tell you—

WRECK It's like this. Helen got a wire that her old lady is coming on, which kind of straight-arms me into the alley.

RUTH Haven't you room?

WRECK You see, Helen's mother doesn't know about me.

EILEEN You mean she doesn't know that you're married?

WRECK Well, you might go a little deeper than that. She doesn't even know we're engaged.

> (*RUTH looks at EILEEN.*)

HELEN So, while Mother's in town we thought you wouldn't mind putting The Wreck up in your kitchen?

EILEEN What?

RUTH You mean *sleep* in our kitchen?

"Keep up your strength. You're eating for two now."

EILEEN (Edie Adams), RUTH (Rosalind Russell)

HELEN You'd feel a lot safer with The Wreck around. And he's awful handy. He can clean up and he irons swell.

WRECK But no washing—that's woman's work.

EILEEN Well, maybe we could do it for one night, but—

RUTH Wait a minute—

HELEN Oh, thank you, girls. You don't know how much you're helping us out! (*She goes.*)

RUTH But, look, we haven't—

WRECK (*Quickly*) Gee, that's swell! (*Follows her*) I'll get my stuff together right away!

RUTH (*Grimly*) Something tells me you weren't quite ready to leave Columbus.

EILEEN (*Smiles guiltily and goes to door*) Coming in?

"That's Speedy Valenti. He runs that advanced nightclub—the Village Vortex!"
EILEEN (Edie Adams), RUTH (Rosalind Russell), SPEEDY (Ted Benaides)

RUTH No. I'm taking these stories down to the *Manhatter*— (*Holding up envelope with manuscript*) and I'm going to camp beside the water cooler till that editor talks to me. See you later—

EILEEN I won't be here later. I've got a date.

RUTH With whom?

EILEEN Frank Lippencott.

RUTH *Who's* Frank Lippencott?

EILEEN Didn't I tell you about the boy who manages the Walgreen drugstore on 44th Street?

RUTH No.

EILEEN He hasn't let me pay a single lunch check since I've been going there. Today I had a pimento sandwich, a tomato surprise, and a giant double malt—with marble cake.

RUTH That's right, dear—keep your strength up. You're eating for two, now.

EILEEN I want you to meet him, so when you're in the neighborhood, you can have your lunches there, too.

RUTH Gee, since I've been in New York, I only met one man, and he said, "Why the hell don't you look where you're going?" (*Shrugs*) Maybe it's just as well. Every time I meet one I gum it up. I'm the world's leading expert on discouraging men. I ought to write a book about it. "Girls, are you constantly bothered by the cloying attentions of the male sex? Well, here's the solution for you. Get Ruth Sherwood's new best-seller: 'One Hundred Easy Ways to Lose a Man.' "

> (*EILEEN laughs and goes into house as RUTH sings in a spirit of rueful self-mockery.*)

Chapter One.
Now the first way to lose a man—

(*Sings with exaggerated romanticism.*)

You've met a charming fellow and you're out for a spin.
The motor fails and he just wears a helpless grin,
Don't bat your eyes and say, "What a romantic spot we're in."

(*Spoken flatly:*)

Just get out, crawl under the car, tell him it's the gasket and fix it in two seconds flat with a bobby pin.

That's a good way to lose a man—

(*Sung:*)

He takes you to a baseball game,
You sit knee to knee—
He says, "The next man up at bat will bunt, you'll see."
Don't say, "Oooh, what's a bunt? This game's too hard for little me."

(*Spoken*)

Just say, "Bunt? Are you nuts?!! With no outs and two men on base, and a left-handed batter coming up, you'll walk right into a triple play just like it happened in the fifth game of the World Series in 1923."

(*Sung*)

That's a sure way to lose a man.

A sure sure sure sure way to lose a man,
A splendid way to lose a man.
Just throw your knowledge in his face,
He'll never try for second base.
Ninety-eight ways to go.

The third way to lose a man—
The life-guard at the beach that all the girlies adore
Swims bravely out to save you through the ocean's roar.
Don't say, "Oh, thanks, I would have drowned in just one second
more"—

(*Spoken*)

Just push his head under water and yell, "Last one in is a rotten egg" and
race him back to shore!

(*Sung*)

That's a swell way to lose a man.
You've found your perfect mate and it's been love from the start.
He whispers, "You're the one to who I give my heart."
Don't say, "I love you too, my dear, let's never never part."

(*Spoken*)

Just say, "I'm afraid you've made a grammatical error—it's not 'To who I give
my heart,' it's 'To whom I give my heart'—You see, with the use of the prepo-
sition 'to,' 'who' becomes the indirect object, making the use of 'whom'
imperative which I can easily show you by drawing a simple chart"—

(*Waving goodbye toward an imaginary retreating figure*)

That's a fine way to lose a man.

A fine fine fine fine way to lose a man,
A dandy way to lose a man.
Just be more well-informed than he,
You'll never hear "O, Promise Me."

Just show him where his grammar errs,
Then mark your towels "hers" and "hers"—
Yes, girls, you too can lose your man,
If you will use Ruth Sherwood's plan:
One hundred easy ways to lose a man!

(*She goes off as the lights dim.*)

SCENE 4

BAKER's office at the "Manhatter." At rise: BAKER is seated behind desk.
RUTH is seated in a chair opposite, talking fast.

RUTH —So you see, Mr. Baker, I worked on the Columbus *Globe* a couple of years—society page, sports, everything—and did a lot of writing on the side—but I'm afraid my stuff was a little too sophisticated for Columbus— so I took the big plunge and came to New York—

BAKER (*Breaks in*) Yes, I know—I did it myself but this is a mighty tough town. Maybe you should have come here gradually—by way of Cleveland first.

RUTH Yes. They're awfully short of writers in Cleveland—

BAKER Well, at least a few people in Ohio know you—

RUTH That's why I left—

BAKER (*Laughs*) Look, Miss Sherwood, I'd like to help you, but I'm so swamped now—If you just leave your stories here, somebody will read them.

RUTH (*Puts envelope down*) Are you sure? I get them back so fast that unless I take the subway, they beat me home!

BAKER We read them, all right— (*He takes eyeglasses from breast pocket*) I had 20-20 vision when I left Duluth.

Act One
SCENE 4

BOB: "At least a few people in Ohio know you." *RUTH:* "That's why I left."

RUTH (ROSALIND RUSSELL), BAKER (GEORGE GAYNES)

RUTH Duluth? Maybe *you* should've come here gradually—and stopped at St. Paul.

BAKER (*Grimly*) Huh?

RUTH —95 ways to go—

BAKER What?

RUTH Oh, dear—Mr. Baker, please—would you mind if I went out that door and came back in and started all over again?

BAKER Forget it!

RUTH And I was so anxious to make a good impression!

BAKER Well, you made a strong one.

> (*ASSOCIATE EDITORS enter with a pile of manuscripts. They put them on BAKER's desk.*)

FIRST EDITOR Light summer reading, Bob!

BAKER Oh no, not any more! (*To RUTH*) See what I mean? Every one of those authors is convinced he's an undiscovered genius!

RUTH (*Looks at pile of manuscripts, then up to BOB*) Well, what do you advise me to do?

BAKER (*From behind his desk*)
> Go home!
> Go west!
> Go back where you came from!
> Oh, why did you ever leave Ohio?

RUTH (*Rises*)
> Because I think I have talent!

BAKER
> A million kids just like you
> Come to town every day
> With stars in their eyes.
> They're going to conquer the city,
> They're going to grab off the Pulitzer Prize,
> But it's a terrible pity,
> Because they're in for a bitter surprise.
> And their stories all follow one line,

(*Pointing with his arm to FIRST EDITOR*)

> Like his,

(*Pointing to SECOND EDITOR*)

> Like his,

(*To himself with both hands*)

> Like mine.

(*To RUTH*)

> Born in Duluth,
> Natural writer,
> Published at seven—genius type—

Wrote the school play,
Wrote the school paper,
Summa cum laude—all of that tripe—
Came to New York,
Got on the staff here—
This was my chance to be heard.
Well, since then I haven't written a word.

BAKER & EDITORS (*Strumming imaginary guitars*)
What a waste,
What a waste,
What a waste of money and time!

(*RUTH turns and goes angrily as BAKER looks after her sympathetically.*)

FIRST EDITOR
Man from Detroit,
Wonderful artist,
Went to Picasso—Pablo said "Wow!"
Settled in France,
Bought him a beret,
Lived in Montmartre,
Really learned how.
Came to New York—had an exhibit,
Art critics made a big fuss.
Now, he paints those toothpaste ads on the bus!

EDITORS AND BAKER
What a waste,
What a waste,
What a waste of money and time!

SECOND EDITOR
Girl from Mobile,
Versatile actress,
Tragic or comic,
Any old play,
Suffered and starved,
Met Stanislavsky.
He said the world would
Cheer her some day.
Came to New York,
Repertoire ready,
Chekhov's and Shakespeare's and Wilde's.
Now, they watch her flipping flapjacks at Childs'.

EDITORS AND BAKER
What a waste,
What a waste,
What a waste of money and time!

BAKER
Kid from Cape Cod,
Fisherman's family,
Marvelous singer—big baritone—
Rented his boat,
Paid for his lessons,
Starved for his studies,
Down to the bone—
Came to New York,

Aimed at the opera—
Sing "Rigoletto" his wish.
At the fulton market now he yells "Fish!"

EDITORS
What a waste,
What a waste,
What a waste of money and time!

BAKER (*Looking off after RUTH*)
Go home! Go west!
Go back where you came from!

(*EDITORS go.*)

Go home!

(*BAKER goes to his desk, his mind still on RUTH, and picks up the envelope containing her manuscripts. he takes them out and starts to read one.*)

BAKER (*Reading*) "For Whom the Lion Roars"—by Ruth Sherwood.

"It was a fine day for a lion hunt. Yes, it was a good clean day for an African lion hunt—a good clean day for a fine clean kill."

(*The lights go up on stage left as BAKER continues reading. In the ensuing STORY VIGNETTES, played stage left and musically underscored, RUTH portrays all the heroines. These are RUTH's ideas of sophisticated writing, and are acted in exaggerated satiric style.*)

BAKER (*Reading*) "Sandra Mallory stalked into the clearing with the elephant gun."

(*SANDRA MALLORY [RUTH] enters dazzlingly attired in a glamorous version of an African hunting outfit, a huge gun tucked casually under her arm.*)

BAKER (*Reading*) "Just behind Sandra was Harry Mallory, her husband, and Randolph Rexford, the guide."

(*They enter. REXFORD is an open-shirted, tight-lipped Gary Cooper type and HARRY is a small, ineffectual-looking man in an obvious state of terror, his gun shaking in his hands.*)

BAKER (*Reading*) "Nearby, they could hear the fine clean roar of the lion."

(*There is a loud, ominous lion roar.*)

REXFORD (*Pointing out front*) There he is, right in front of you, Mr. Mallory!

(*MALLORY points his gun toward the oncoming roars, which become louder and louder as REXFORD continues.*)

No, not yet—Wait until you see his eyes. That will be the fine clean way to bag the Simba. No—not yet—Not yet, Mr. Mallory.

(*MALLORY dashes off, screaming.*)

SANDRA (*Flatly*) My cigarette has gone out. (*She holds her cigarette up to her mouth. Contemptuously*) He ran—Harry, the brave hunter!

(*Her hand is trembling exaggeratedly.*)

REXFORD (*Tensely*) Your hand is trembling, Mrs. Mallory—

(*He grabs her hand, helping her light the cigarette.*)

SANDRA (*Conscious of his grip*) It is nothing.

BAKER (*Reading*) "He gripped her hard. It was a clean fine grip. She remembered Harry's grip. Like clean, fine oatmeal. Suddenly Sandra Mallory felt the beat, beat, beat of Africa—"

(*Drums are heard nearby.*)

SANDRA (*Sexily to REXFORD as she undulates to the rhythm*) Rexford—why do you hate me?

REXFORD (*Tight-lipped*) I have my job—Mrs. Mallory—and Mr. Mallory is your husband.

(*There is a roar and terrified scream from offstage.*)

SANDRA (*Calmly*) He *was* my husband.

(*She drops her gun and cigarette and walks toward him passionately.*)

Rexford—

REXFORD (*Moving toward her with equal passion*) Mrs. Mallory—

SANDRA (*Stepping nearer*) Rexford—

REXFORD (*Nearer—and now seething*) Sandra—

SANDRA (*Throwing her arms around him*) Randolph!

(*He bends her backward in a movie kiss.*)

BAKER (*Incredulous*) No!

(*There is a blackout on the African scene, as BAKER picks up the next manuscript a little more cautiously.*)

BAKER (*Reading*) "Twentieth-Century Blues." "It was squalid in that one room flat in Williamsburg without the windows, with the gray peeling plaster and the sound of rats scurrying inside the walls and the scratching phonograph across the hall screaming gee I'd like to see you lookin' swell baby diamond—" (*BAKER finally has to take a deep breath and plunge on*) "—bracelets Woolworth doesn't sell baby and Danny coming in gray and drawn like the gray plaster coming in clutching his guts with the gray rats inside his walls too yeah the gray rat pains of hunger yeah the twentieth-century hunger yeah—"

(*DANNY enters, a ragged proletarian figure in his undershirt, in the depths of despair and hunger. He is followed by ESSIE [RUTH], ludicrously ragged and obviously somewhat with child. They speak in the singsong Brooklynese used in the social-problem dramas of the '30s.*)

ESSIE (*Dully*) Danny—when we gonna get married?

DANNY When—when—when—always naggin'—

ESSIE They're talkin'—the neighbors are talkin'. Mama looks at me funny like.

DANNY It takes money, dream boat, to get married. The green stuff with the pictures of Lincoln.

ESSIE Lincoln should see me now. Remember how swell life was gonna be? We was gonna have everything—a four-star trip to the moon—diamonds—yachts—shoes!

DANNY Baby—

ESSIE What's left, Danny—what's left?

(*They approach each other lumberingly with the same growing passion as in the first vignette.*)

DANNY (*Stepping closer, arms open*) Baby—

ESSIE Danny—

DANNY Baby—

ESSIE (*Clutching him in an embrace*) Danny!

BAKER No!

(*There is a blackout on the vignette as he hurls the script down and very warily picks up the third.*)

"Exit Laughing"—"Everyone agreed that Tracy Farraday was marvelous. Everyone agreed that this was her greatest acting triumph. Everyone agreed that her breathtaking performance in 'Kiss Me, Herman' was the climax of a great career."

(*The lights go up on an elegantly dressed party. Guests are discovered in a tableau.*)

"Everyone agreed that the plush opening night party at the Astor Hotel was a memorable occasion."

(*Everyone is indulging in upper class merriment, with laughter and hysterical chitchat. TRENT FARRADAY, a stuffy society type, is kissing a girl as he holds her in a deep embrace.*)

WOMAN GUEST (*Looking off*) Here comes Tracy now!

ALL GUESTS Tracy!

(*TRACY enters in superb evening clothes—the perfect picture of the glamorous actress. She takes a glamorous pose.*)

BAKER (*Reading*) "Everyone agreed that perhaps Tracy drank a bit too much."

(*TRACY suddenly staggers in cross-eyed, exaggerated drunkenness.*)

TRACY (*Tallulah-ish*) Has anyone seen that silly old husband of mine?

(*TRACY staggers to TRENT—taps him on the shoulder. He is still deep in the embrace.*)

Oh, Trent—

(*TRENT looks up from the kiss*) —

Have you got a match?

TRENT Tracy—I'm leaving—I have found someone who needs me—appreciates me—

TRACY You cahn't!

TRENT (*Exiting with girl*) You are not a woman, Tracy. You are a billboard.

TRACY (*After him*) No, no, Trent—I'll be different—I will—Don't go!

BAKER (*Reading*) "Everyone agreed that Tracy was a hypochondriac. Otherwise, why did she always carry a bottle of iodine?"

> (*TRACY, throughout speech, is rummaging through her purse, pulls out a red bottle of iodine and downs the contents.*)

TRACY (*With bitter abandon, giving her greatest performance*) Everybody! On with the party! (*She executes a wild fandango—then, suddenly clutching her midriff in a paroxysm of agony, she crashes to the floor*)

MALE GUEST Tracy!

WOMAN GUEST Ah—she's just passing out!

TRACY (*Pulling herself up on one elbow with difficulty—gallant to the end*) Yes! Everyone agrees—I'm just passing out—exit laughing! Ha—Ha—Ha—Ha! (*She laughs wildly and falls back dead, after a last, convulsive twitch*)

GUESTS (*Raising glasses in a toast to a noble lady, singing in solemn chorale fashion*)
What a waste,
What a waste,
What a waste of money and time!

> (*BAKER joins in the chorus—hurling his script down on the desk. Blackout.*)

SCENE 5

The street. At rise: MRS. WADE and HELEN come on.

MRS. WADE Whatever possessed you to move into a dreadful neighborhood like this, Helen? How do you ever expect to meet a nice young man down here?

HELEN Oh, Mother, please! Let me live my own life!

MRS. WADE (*Climbing steps—turning from top before going into house*) Life! You're just a child! You don't know what life is!

> (*MRS. WADE exits into the house—HELEN following. VALENTI enters, followed by two BOP GIRLS. FRANK LIPPENCOTT enters. He carries a box of candy.*)

VALENTI Skeet—skat—skattle-e-o-do—

> (*To GIRLS:*)

Don't bother me, kids! Wait until you grow up!

> (*He's off, followed by the KIDS. EILEEN comes on and sees FRANK peering in their window.*)

EILEEN Oh, hello, Frank!

FRANK Hello, Eileen! I just came down during my lunch hour. I've been thinking about you all morning.

EILEEN You have?

FRANK I brought you some chocoloate-covered cherries we're running. We're featuring them all this week during our annual one-cent sale.

EILEEN (*Taking candy from him*) You're sweet.

FRANK Well, I've got to get back to the drugstore. It's pandemonium down there.

EILEEN Don't forget—we expect you for dinner tonight. I want you to meet my sister—she's in your neighborhood a lot.

FRANK Oh—I'll be here all right.

EILEEN Thanks for the chocolate-covered cherries.

FRANK 'Bye, Eileen—

EILEEN 'Bye, Frank! (*She watches him go off and, all starry-eyed, starts to sing*)
> Mm—Mmm—
> I'm a little bit in love,
> Never felt this way before.
> Mm—Mmm—
> Just a little bit in love,
> Or perhaps a little bit more.
>
> When he
> Looks at me,
> Everything's hazy and all out of focus.
> When he
> Touches me,
> I'm in the spell of a strange hocus-pocus.
> It's so—
> I don't know.
> I'm so—

I don't know.
I don't know—but I know,
If it's love,
Then it's lovely!

Mm—Mmm—
It's so nice to be alive
When you meet someone who bewitches you.
Will he be my all,
Or did I just fall
A little bit,
A little bit in love?

(*BOB BAKER enters, goes to the grill window and looks in. EILEEN pulls the ribbon off candy box, goes to steps. She sees BAKER and stares coldly.*)

EILEEN *Well?*

BAKER (*Looking up from window*) I was just looking for the young lady who lives in there—my name's Baker—Robert Baker.

EILEEN Did *Marty* send you?

BAKER I beg your pardon?

EILEEN I hate to ruin your afternoon, Mr. Baker, but Violet doesn't live here any more.

BAKER Violet?

EILEEN You might tell Marty and all the boys. It'll save them a trip.

BAKER I'm afraid you've got me confused with somebody else.

EILEEN I have?

BAKER Yes. I'm looking for Ruth Sherwood. She lives here, doesn't she?

EILEEN Who—are you, Mr. Baker?

BAKER I'm an associate editor of the *Manhatter.*

EILEEN Oh, oh, I'm terribly sorry! Ruth'll be furious—I'm her sister, Eileen.

BAKER How do you do, Miss Sherwood?

EILEEN Ruth isn't in right now—but I'm sure she'll be right back. Won't you come in and wait?

BAKER No, thanks. I'll drop by later.

EILEEN You're sure, now?

BAKER Oh, yes—

EILEEN Because I know Ruth must be terribly anxious to see you—

BAKER Well?

EILEEN How about a nice, cool drink?

BAKER Not now—thanks, Miss Sherwood—

EILEEN Oh—*Eileen!*

BAKER Eileen.

EILEEN Mr. Baker—I mean, Robert—I have a wonderful idea! Why don't you come back and take pot luck with us?

BAKER Well, I don't know—

EILEEN Oh, please! I'm making a special dish tonight!

BAKER Okay—what time?

EILEEN Any time after seven!

BAKER Swell, Eileen—see you later.

EILEEN 'Bye, Bob!

> (*She watches him go with the same starry-eyed look as before.*)

> Mm—Mmm—
> I'm a little bit in love,
> Never felt this way before.
> Mm—Mmm— (*music continues*)

> (*LONIGAN enters slowly.*)

Oh, hello, Officer!

LONIGAN (*Suspiciously*) Yeah.

> (*THE WRECK enters and goes to house. He is carrying a rolled-up Army mattress.*)

WRECK I borrowed a mattress, Eileen. That floor in your place is awful hard!

> (*WRECK disappears into the house. LONIGAN looks warily to EILEEN, who turns, startled, and puts a hand to her mouth. Blackout.*)

SCENE 6

The back yard. This is the "garden" that APPOPOLOUS boasts about. It's a dismal place, sunk deep among the tenements that surround it. There are a moldy tree, a couple of chairs, and a bench. Across from the girls' kitchen we see the back entrance of Nino's, an Italian restaurant. At rise: WRECK is at an ironing board, pressing some of the girls' things.

WRECK

"I'm a ramblin' Wreck—
From Trenton Tech—
And a helluva engineer—"

(*WAITER comes out of Nino's and is joined by Italian CHEF.*)

CHEF E arrivato il padrone—e meglio cominciare a lavorare.

WAITER Peccato. Si sta così bene qui fuore.

CHEF Be. Così è la vita.

(*RUTH comes in from kitchen.*)

RUTH Any mail?

WRECK Yeah, one of your stories came back.

RUTH From the *Manhatter?*

WRECK No, *Collier's.*

(*RUTH picks up manuscript in envelope at window sill, changing address with a pencil*)

Hot, ain't it?

RUTH Yah. I feel as if I'm living in my own little world, mailing these to myself.

WRECK Hey, which way do you want these pleats turned?

RUTH (*Glances at him wearily*) Toward Mecca.

(*The phone rings. WRECK goes to window sill and answers it.*)

WRECK The Sherwood residence—who do you want? Eleanor? You mean Eileen. She's not in. (*Annoyed*) This is the butler—Who the hell are *you?*

RUTH (*Grabbing phone*) Wreck! Hello? . . . Who is this, please? . . . Chick Clark? Oh, yes, Mr. Clark. This is her sister—Ruth . . . No, she's not in right now . . . any minute . . . I'll tell her . . . 'Bye. (*Hangs up. Makes note on pad at window sill.*)

WRECK That Eileen does all right for herself. And the funny part of it is, she's a good girl.

RUTH (*Eyeing him*) When did you find *that* out?

WRECK No, you sense those things. I never made a pass at you, but I could swear *you're* all right.

RUTH That's the story of my life.

(*She goes off with manuscript as HELEN enters.*)

WRECK Hy'ah, Sugar Foot!

HELEN Hi.

WONDERFUL TOWN

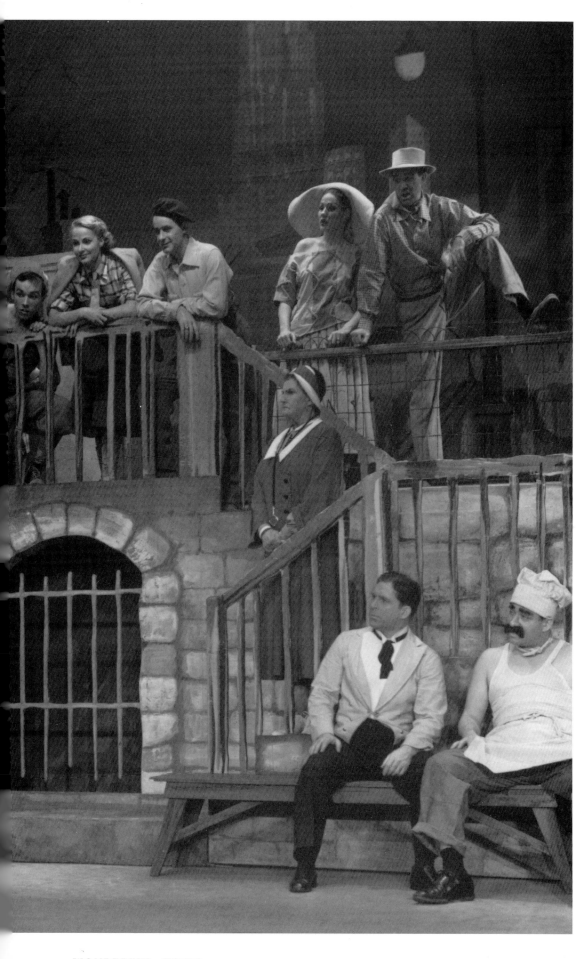

WONDERFUL TOWN

WRECK Do you miss me, honey?

HELEN Of course I miss you. Now I have to do all the housework. (*Looking at laundry*) Huh! You never ironed that good for me!

WRECK Now look, honey—!

> (*MRS. WADE appears in the street above them. HELEN ducks behind the ironing board, her rear facing the audience.*)

MRS. WADE (*Staring at WRECK*) Well, I never!

WRECK What are *you* lookin' at, you old bat?

MRS. WADE How dare you!? (*She goes off indignantly.*)

WRECK (*Shouting after her*) Didn't you ever see a man in shorts before?

HELEN (*Wails*) Wreck! That was Mom!

WRECK You mean that old wagon was your mother?

HELEN You've got to get out of here!

WRECK Where am I gonna sleep?

HELEN If we could scrape up a few dollars you could stay at the "Y" till Mother leaves.

WRECK We're tryin' to dig up a coupla bucks and your mother's got a mattressful!

HELEN If only we had somethin' left to hock.

WRECK Hey—wait a minute! (*Goes to kitchen*) If anyone comes, whistle "Dixie."

> (*There is a blast from the subway, making HELEN jump. WRECK returns from the kitchen with APPOPOLOUS' "blue-green" canvas.*)

HELEN That's one of Appopolous'. They won't lend you a dime on it!

WRECK This fancy frame might be good for a coupla bucks. Take it over to Benny's and see what you can get on it!

> (*HELEN exits, lugging the heavy picture. DELIVERY KID enters from the street with a basket of vegetables.*)

DELIVERY KID (*Adoringly*) Hey, Wreck—getting ready for the football season?

WRECK Oh, I keep in shape!

DELIVERY KID (*Centering the "ball"—a head of cabbage*) Hey—signals?

WRECK 45—26—7—hip!

> (*WRECK catches the cabbage.*)

CHEF (*Enters in front of Nino's—to KID*) E tu che diavalo fai con quel cavallo?

DELIVERY KID (*To WRECK*) Pass!

> (*WRECK passes to KID—who passes to the WAITER, who catches the cabbage in his stomach.*)

CHEF Che pazzerela!

> (*Waving an angry hand at KID, who passes him basket with vegetables. CHEF exits.*)

KID Well, you certainly look in good shape for the football season.

WRECK Yeah—for all the good it does me!

(*Goes wearily back to ironing and sings*)

Look at me now,
Four years of college,
Famous professors
Tutoring me;
Scholarship kid,
Everything paid for,
Food and vacations,
All of it free.
Day that I left,
Everyone gathered,
Their cheering still rings in my ears—

(*Carried away by memories, he executes some old cheers with great vigor.*)

Ray Wreck rah
Rah Wreck ray
Rah Wreck
Wreck rah
Rah Wreck Wreck
W-E-C, R-E-K, R-E-Q,
Wreck, we love you!

(*Singing bravura*)

'Cause I could pass that football
Like nothin' you have ever seen!

(*A CROWD has gathered on the street, watching him. They cheer.*)

Couldn't spell a lick,
Couldn't do arithmetic;
One and one made three,
Thought that dog was c-a-t,
But I could pass that football
Like nothin' you have ever seen.

Couldn't write my name,
Couldn't translate "je vous aime,"
Never learned to read
Mother Goose or André Gide,
But I could pass that football
Like nothin' you have ever seen.

Couldn't figure riddles,
Puzzles made me pout:
Where the hell was Moses when the lights went out?
I couldn't even tell red from green,
Get those verbs through my bean,
But I was buddies with the Dean
Like nothin' you have ever seen.

Passed without a fuss
English Lit and Calculus.
Never had to cram,
Even passed the bar exam,
Because I passed that football
Like nothin' you have ever seen.

Then there was the week
Albert Einstein came to speak:
Relativity!
Guess who introduced him? Me!
'Cause I could pass that football
Like nothin' you have ever seen.

Had no table manners,
Used ta dunk my roll,
Always drunk the water from the fingerbowl.
Though I would not get up for any she,
The Prexy's mom—age ninety-three—
Got up and gave her seat to me,
Like nothin' you did ever see.

In our Hall of Fame,
There's a statue with my name.
There we stand, by heck,
Lincoln, Washington and Wreck.
'Cause I could pass that football
Like nothin' you have ever seen!

(*WRECK and CROWD of assorted VILLAGERS do a "football" dance, with WRECK ending up with a pile of players, hopelessly outclassed. He sticks his head out from under, weakly.*)

'Cause I could pass that football!
Like nothin' you have ever—ever seen!

(*CROWD pulls away. WRECK staggers and collapses in their arms. At the end of the number, the CROWD goes off. HELEN enters with a pawn ticket.*)

HELEN Two bucks—here's the ticket.

EILEEN (*Enters from studio*) Gee, Wreck—the laundry looks swell.

HELEN (*Coldly*) Too bad he's leaving, isn't it?

EILEEN Oh, is he?

HELEN Yes, and it's about time, too.

(*RUTH enters from the alley.*)

WRECK Stop racin' your motor! I told her there was nothing to it!

RUTH Nothing to *what?*

EILEEN Ruth, do you know what she had the nerve to insinuate?

RUTH Was it something with sex in it?

WRECK Why, if I thought about Eileen in that way—May God strike me dead on this spot!

(*He raises his hand solemnly and there's a tremendous BOOM! from below. He shrinks guiltily.*)

RUTH (*Looking up*) He's everywhere, all right.

HELEN Come on, Wreck!

(*They go off. VIOLET enters from house.*)

VIOLET (*Cheerfully*) Hello, girls.

RUTH (*Stares*) Hello.

VIOLET I'm Violet. I used to live in this fleabag before you girls got it.

EILEEN Oh, so *you're* Violet.

VIOLET Say, have I had any callers the last coupla weeks—since you kids moved in?

RUTH (*Grimly*) One or two.

VIOLET I thought so. A lot of my friends don't know I moved yet. In case they come around would you mind giving out my new cards?

> (*She takes a thick pack of calling cards from her purse and hands them to EILEEN*)

Thanks loads. So long. (*She goes*)

RUTH The spiritual type.

> (*EILEEN carries the cards to window sill.*)

EILEEN (*Looking at note pad*) Oh, did Chick Clark call?

RUTH Yes. Who's he?

EILEEN He's a newspaperman. I met him in an elevator. We got to talking and I told him about you. He seemed very interested in you.

RUTH So interested in me, I'll bet he can't wait to get you alone.

EILEEN What've we got for dinner, Ruth?

RUTH What do you think? Spaghetti and meat balls.

EILEEN Haven't we polished that off yet? We've had it all week!

RUTH (*Flatly*) It closes tonight.

EILEEN Well, we simply can't give that to Bob.

RUTH Bob? I can't keep up with you. Who's *Bob*?

EILEEN You know, Bob Baker, from the *Manhatter*. Don't play dumb!

RUTH Mr. Baker! No!

> (*Turns EILEEN around.*)

Where did you meet him?

EILEEN He dropped by to see you, and naturally I asked him to dinner.

RUTH Naturally!

> (*Grabs EILEEN, kisses her.*)

Oh, darling! You are terrific! I'd never have the nerve!

EILEEN Well, for goodness sake, why not? He's just a *boy*—

RUTH (*Looks around helplessly*) How can we fix this dump up a little? (*Closing kitchen door*) Eileen, promise me you won't take him in there!

EILEEN Of course not. We'll eat in the garden—al fresco.

RUTH Ah—

EILEEN Oh, dear—I just remembered. I asked Frank over tonight.

RUTH Who?

EILEEN You know—Walgreen's—

RUTH Oh, no! How can you mix a soda jerk with an editor?

EILEEN He's *not* a jerk! He's the manager!

RUTH Okay—okay—Gee, if a man like Mr. Baker comes to see me personally, he must really be interested!

EILEEN Of course he's interested.

RUTH And we can't even offer him a cocktail.

EILEEN We could tell him it's too hot to drink.

RUTH (*Nods*) But cold enough for spaghetti.

EILEEN Hmmm—smell that chicken cacciatore at Nino's. Maybe I ought to have a little talk with Mr. Nino.

RUTH Do you know him too?

EILEEN No, but I will—he's our neighbor, isn't he?

> (*She goes into Nino's. CHICK CLARK enters from street above.*)

CHICK Hello. (*Coming down stairs, consulting matchbook*) I'm lookin' for a party named Sherwood—Eleanor Sherwood.

RUTH You mean Eileen. You must be Mr. Clark?

CHICK Yeah. Who are you?

RUTH I'm her sister.

CHICK (*Doubtfully*) Her sister? She's a blonde, *good-looking* kid, ain't she?

RUTH (*Grimly*) Yes, she's a blonde, good-looking kid.

CHICK (*Loosening his collar*) Wow, it's absolute murder down here, ain't it? (*Staring overhead*) What is this—an abandoned mine shaft?

RUTH Are you planning to be with us long, Mr. Clark?

CHICK Eileen asked me to take pot luck with her.

FRANK (*Offstage*) Hello? Anyone home? (*FRANK appears at window in studio*) Oh, hello, the front door was open. Is Eileen home?

RUTH You're Mr. Lippencott, aren't you? Come in.

> (*She motions to steps. The door opens, LIPPENCOTT appears, carrying a bottle of red wine. Trips down stairs. Recovers himself. Pulls out comb and combs hair.*)

FRANK Gee, I'm sorry. I didn't know there was any—

> (*Shakes hands with RUTH.*)

RUTH Oh, that's all right. Everybody does that.

FRANK I guess you're Eileen's sister. I can see a family resemblance, all right.

RUTH Why, I'm very flattered.

FRANK Of course, you're a different type.

RUTH Yes, I see what you mean. Eileen'll be back in a minute— (*Glancing to café.*) She's just fixing dinner. (*Looking at CHICK*) Oh, I want you to meet Mr. Clark—

> (*FRANK goes to CHICK, to shake hands. CHICK ignores his hand.*)

CHICK There ain't too much oxygen down here as it is.

RUTH Mr. Lippencott is with Walgreen's.

CHICK Yeah? I buy all my clothes there.

FRANK No, it's a drugstore.

CHICK (*Groans and looks at bottle with interest*) What's in the bottle?

FRANK (*To CHICK coldly*) A very fine California Burgundy-type wine.

> (*To RUTH:*)

I thought it would go good with the spaghetti.

> (*Hands her wine.*)

It's a special we're running this week.

RUTH (*Looking at the bottle sadly*) So's our spaghetti.

FRANK Huh?

RUTH Has this heat affected your business?

FRANK Why, we pray for heat waves.

CHICK Oh, you *do,* eh?

FRANK Our fountain turnover is double. I'm lucky to get away at all.

RUTH Oh, *we're* the lucky ones.

EILEEN (*Entering, to FRANK*) Oh, Frank, I'm terribly sorry I wasn't here to greet you.

> (*To RUTH:*)

Ruth, what do you think?

RUTH What?

EILEEN Mr. Nino's in Italy. He won't be back till Labor Day.

> (*To CHICK, in dismay:*)

Oh, hello, Mr. Clark!

CHICK Hy'ah, gorgeous!

EILEEN Oh, Ruth, this is that newspaper gentleman I was telling you about who was so interested in you.

CHICK That's right. I gave the city editor a big pitch already— (*Lasciviously*) You won't believe this, baby, but I've been turnin' you over in my mind all afternoon.

> (*EILEEN laughs uneasily as RUTH nods.*)

FRANK Gee, this is great. I always wanted to live in the Village in a place like this.

RUTH What stopped you?

FRANK Well, in my position in the drugstore you've got to keep up appearances.

RUTH I see. Where the Liggetts speak only to the Walgreens and the Walgreens speak only to God.

(*CHICK grabs EILEEN's hand. She pulls away.*)

EILEEN I'd better set the table. (*Goes to kitchen*) Where shall we dine—inside or outside?

CHICK Which is this?

(*BOB BAKER appears from street, waving envelope with manuscript.*)

BAKER Hello!

EILEEN Oh, hello, Bob!

RUTH Hello, Mr. Baker! Sorry I wasn't in when you called.

BAKER That's all right—

RUTH I'd like you to meet Mr. Clark, Mr. Lippencott. This is Mr. Baker.

FRANK Pleased to meet you.

(*Holds out his hand, which BAKER shakes.*)

CHICK What the hell is this, a block party?

RUTH You're quite a card, aren't you, Mr. Clark? (*Puts wine on window sill*) Mr. Lippencott brought you some wine, dear.

EILEEN Oh, how sweet! Shall we sit down?

(*She motions the others to join her and there is a general embarassed shuffling about for chairs. She pulls BOB down beside her on her chair. CHICK brings a chair forward and RUTH, assuming it is for her, goes toward it, but CHICK sits on it himself. She gets her own and the five wind up in a tight uncomfortable group facing one another with nothing to say. EILEEN after a pause:*)

Well—here we are—all together—

(*There is a dry, discordant vamp in the orchestra expressing the atmosphere of embarrassed silence, which is repeated during every pause in the following song and conversation. It seems to grow more mocking and desperate at each repetition. After another pause, they all start speaking at once very animatedly and then dwindle off. Pause again. EILEEN giggles nervously. Pause.*)

FRANK (*Starting bravely*) At the bottom of the vanilla—

(*He has a terrific coughing fit. BAKER slaps his back, and he sits down—and combs his hair*)

It's nothing!

(*Vamp.*)

EILEEN (*Singing, over-brightly, after a pause*)
Mm—mmm—it's so nice to sit around—
And chat.

Nice people, nice talk
A balmy summer night,
A bottle of wine—
Nice talk—nice people,
Nice feeling—nice talk—
The combination's right
And everything's fine—

Nice talk—nice people,
It's friendly—it's gay
To sit around this way.
What more do you need?
Just talk—and people,
For that can suffice,
When both the talk and people are so nice—

(*She finishes lamely as the dreaded vamp is played again. Pause.*)

FRANK (*Settling back in chair with a hollow, unconvincing laugh*) Ha ha—Funny thing happened at the counter today—Man comes in—Sort of tall like—Nice looking refined type—Red bow tie—and all. Well, sir, he orders a banana split—That's our jumbo special—twenty-eight cents—Three scoops—chocolate, strawberry, vanilla—choice of cherry or caramel sauce—chopped nuts—whipped cream. Well, sir, he eats the whole thing—I look at his plate and I'll be hornswoggled if he doesn't leave the whole banana—doesn't touch it—not a bite— Don't you see? If he doesn't like bananas, what does he order a banana split for? He coulda had a sundae—nineteen cents—Three scoops—Chocolate—Strawberry—Vanilla—(*He dwindles off as vamp is played again.*)

RUTH (*Making a noble attempt to save the day*) I was re-reading *Moby Dick* the other day and—Oh, I haven't read it since—I'm sure none of us has—It's worth picking up again—It's about this whale—

(*Her futile attempt hangs heavy on the air. Vamp again.*)

CHICK (*Even he is driven by desperation to attempt sociability*) Boy, it's hot! Reminds me of that time in Panama—I was down there on a story—I was in this, well, dive—And there was this broad there—What was her name?—Marquita?—Maroota? (*Warming to his subject*) Ahh, what's the difference what her name was—That dame was built like a brick—

(*A sharp drum crash cuts him off and the vamp is played with hysterical speed and violence. The four others spring to their feet horrified and, as CHICK stands by puzzled, they cover up with a sudden outburst of animated talk and laughter expressed by a rapid rendition of "Nice People, Nice Talk" with EILEEN singing an insane coloratura obbligato as the music builds to a thunderous close.*)

ALL

Nice people, nice talk,
A balmy summer night,
A bottle of wine—
Nice talk, nice people,
Nice feeling—nice talk,
The combination's right
And everything's fine.

Nice talk, nice people—
It's friendly, it's gay
To sit around this way.

What more do you need?
Just talk and people,
For that can suffice,
When both the talk and people are so nice
It's nice!

(*A closing orchestra chord.*)

RUTH (*Gets bottle*) Let's have a drink, shall we?

EILEEN (*To FRANK*) Do we need ice?

FRANK No, this wine should be served at the temperature of the room.

CHICK Then you'd better cook it a coupla hours.

APPOPOLOUS (*Entering from stairs*) Congratulate me, young ladies! Today is the big day! I'm entering my painting in the WPA Art Contest!

(*He goes into studio.*)

BAKER Ruth, who's that?

RUTH Our landlord—Rasputin.

APPOPOLOUS (*Comes back, heavily*) What kind of a funny game is going on here? Where is it? Who took it?

RUTH What?

APPOPOLOUS You know everybody who goes into your apartment.

RUTH We don't know *half* of them.

APPOPOLOUS Please, I know you girls are hard up. Tell me what you did with it and there'll be no questions asked.

EILEEN You don't think we stole it?

APPOPOLOUS If you didn't—who did?

RUTH Maybe it was the same gang that swiped the Mona Lisa.

APPOPOLOUS (*Goes angrily*) You won't be so humorous when I come back with a cop!

RUTH (*To BAKER anxiously*) I hope you don't take any of that seriously, Mr. Baker.

BAKER Of course not.

FRANK (*Scared*) Do you think he's really going to call the police?

EILEEN The police won't pay any attention to him—he's always calling them!

CHICK (*Breaking between FRANK and EILEEN*) Well, let's crack that bottle before the wagon gets here!

EILEEN I'll open it and get some glasses. Do you want to help me, Frank?

CHICK (*Stepping in*) I'll help ya, Eleanor—(*Turning to FRANK*) You stay out here and hand them a few laughs.

(*EILEEN starts into house. CHICK follows.*)

FRANK Oh, is that so?

(*Trips up steps into house.*)

RUTH (*To* BAKER, *sadly*) If you'd like to make your getaway now, Mr. Baker, I'll understand.

BAKER No, I'm enjoying it.

RUTH Did you get a chance to read those stories?

BAKER I certainly did!

(*WRECK and HELEN appear in the street.*)

RUTH Well, what did you think?

WRECK (*Coming down stairs*) Oh, I'm sorry, Ruth—didn't know you had company.

HELEN (*With him*) Can we come in?

RUTH (*Groans*) Yes, please do. (*To kitchen*) Two more glasses, Eileen!

WRECK I talked it over with Helen, and she wants to apologize.

RUTH (*Quickly*) That's not necessary—Mr. Baker—This is Mr. Loomis—and his intended.

(*They shake hands.* BAKER *eyes his shorts anxiously.*)

Mr. Loomis is in training.

BAKER Oh.

(*FRANK enters from studio with tray and glasses of wine.*)

FRANK (*From top of steps*) This wine was—(*Stepping carefully down*) made by a Frenchman in California.

(*EILEEN comes through studio door, carrying two more glasses.*)

EILEEN Oh, hello there—

(*She hands glass to* RUTH. CHICK *follows through studio door, carrying his own glass.* FRANK *passes tray to* WRECK *and* HELEN *and moves upstage with tray.*)

What a magnificent bouquet!

RUTH Drink up, everyone—it's later than you think! Here's to us and Burgundy, California!

(*They all have raised glasses in toast. There's a BOOM! from below.* FRANK *jumps and spills his wine all over his new white suit.*)

FRANK Gee, what was that?

EILEEN (*Stares at the wine stain miserably*) Oh, Frank, I'm terribly sorry!

FRANK (*Looking down at his suit pathetically*) What—what happened?

RUTH The new subway—

(*Wipes off wine.*)

FRANK (*Wails*) Does red wine stain?

EILEEN Not if you rub salt on it.

(*Wipes off wine.*)

CHICK You better get a bagful!

FRANK I just got this suit. It's brand new!

CHICK Ah, you can't even notice it!

(*He starts to laugh. They all join in, hysterically. FRANK stands in the center, stricken. HELEN sinks to the floor in her laughter.*)

FRANK (*Backing to stairs, he starts up*) Well, if you think it's so funny, I'll go!

EILEEN (*Starts to follow*) Frank—don't go! Wait!

(*Turning to the others.*)

Oh, dear—he's really angry.

MRS. WADE (*Offstage*) Helen, are you in there?

"Does red wine stain?"

EILEEN (Edie Adams), FRANK (Chris Alexander), RUTH (Rosalind Russell)

WONDERFUL TOWN

HELEN Yes, Mother.

RUTH Won't you come in, Mrs. Wade?

MRS. WADE (*Entering*) Most certainly not. Helen, I want you to come out of there immediately!

HELEN But, Mother—

MRS. WADE I will not have you associating with those depraved women and their consort!

RUTH & EILEEN *What?!*

WRECK *Who's* a consort?

HELEN Please, Mother—

MRS. WADE Not another word. You come right along with me. Don't you dare talk to my Helen again. You're not fit to associate with decent people!

> (*She pushes* HELEN *out.*)

WRECK I'm gonna wait till Mother's Day— (*Making fist*) and sock her! (*He goes.*)

EILEEN Bob, I don't know what you must think of us, but really, it isn't so.

BAKER (*Grins*) I'm sure it isn't.

RUTH Well, you must admit—for a place with a bad location and no neon sign, we're doing a hell of a business.

EILEEN (*Brightly*) Dinner, anyone?

BAKER Fine!

EILEEN (*Going to kitchen*) I'd better heat the entrée.

CHICK (*Following close behind*) We'll warm it up together, Eleanor!

> (*They go off.*)

RUTH Funny, I'm not a bit hungry.

BAKER I'm starving. And I smell something delicious!

RUTH (*Looks at Nino's*) Trade Winds.

EILEEN'S VOICE Mr. Clark, please! Not while I'm trying to cook!

BAKER While we have a minute, before anything else happens, I'd like to talk to you about your stories—

RUTH Oh, do, please! You mean you actually read them yourself?

BAKER I certainly did—You have a lot of talent, Miss Sherwood—

RUTH Do you really think so?

BAKER Yes, I do—

> (RUTH *turns away, tearfully*)

What's the matter?

RUTH Nothing—

BAKER You're crying—

RUTH (*Turning back to him*) It's just an allergy I have to good news—

BAKER You really should have more faith in yourself—

RUTH Thanks, I'm beginning to—

BAKER And once you get on the right track, you're going to do some good work.

RUTH Right track?

BAKER Look, Ruth. Have you ever gone on a safari in the African veldt?

RUTH No.

BAKER And have you ever lived in a cold-water tenement?

RUTH No.

BAKER Then why do you write that stuff? Write about something you know— something you've actually experienced.

RUTH I write the things I feel! I put myself in every one of those characters!

BAKER Then you must be hopelessly repressed.

RUTH That's a terrible thing to say! I'm the most normal person you'll ever meet!

BAKER That's a sure sign. All inhibited people think they're normal.

RUTH Oh! So now I'm inhibited!

BAKER (*Turns to her*) I'm afraid so—if you claim you're really those frustrated heroines.

RUTH Repressed! Inhibited! Frustrated! What *else* am I?

BAKER Don't take it personally—

RUTH How else can I take it?

BAKER I'm just trying to help you—

RUTH What are you, an editor or a psychoanalyst?

BAKER I should've known better—You can't take it—You'll never get anywhere till you learn humility—

RUTH When did you learn yours?

(*Runs into studio quickly. BAKER watches her.*)

BAKER (*With weary anger*)
All right! Goodbye!
You've taught me my lesson!
Get mixed up with a genius from Ohio!
It happens over and over;
I pick the sharp intellectual kind.
Why couldn't this time be different?
Why couldn't she—only be
Another kind—a different kind of girl?

(*With sudden longing and reflection*)
I love a quiet girl,
I love a gentle girl,
Warm as sunlight,
Soft, soft as snow.

Her smile, a tender smile,
Her voice, a velvet voice,
Sweet as music,
Soft, soft as snow.

When she is near me
The world's in repose.
We need no words;
She sees—she knows.

But where is my quiet girl?
Where is my gentle girl?
Where is the special girl,
Who is soft, soft as snow?

Somewhere—
Somewhere—
My quiet girl.

(*As he walks slowly off, RUTH enters from the kitchen and watches him go, with the hopeless feeling of having lost him.*)

RUTH (*Sings*)
I know a quiet girl,
Hoping—waiting—
But he'll never know.

(*The music continues. There is a crash of dishes from the kitchen. RUTH turns suddenly—looks toward kitchen—her reverie broken.*)

EILEEN (*Offstage*) Now look what you made me do!

(*Entering from studio, CHICK follows.*)

The spaghetti—it's all over the kitchen floor! Really, Mr. Clark!

CHICK You're so darn jumpy! (*Goes to stairs*) Okay, I'll run down to the corner and get some sandwiches and beer! Be right back! (*He's off.*)

EILEEN Where's Bob?

RUTH Gone.

EILEEN Isn't he coming back?

RUTH If he does, he's crazy after the way I treated him.

EILEEN Gee, Ruth, what happened?

RUTH I'd rather not discuss it—I'm too frustrated.

(*There's a BOOM! from below. She looks down wearily.*)

Go on! Blow us up and get it over with!

EILEEN Gee, Ruth, if you start to feel that way, who's going to hold me up?

RUTH Oh, I'm not worried about you—not while there's a man alive.

EILEEN After all, men are only an escape.

(*The phone rings. EILEEN hurries to it.*)

RUTH Comes another escape—

EILEEN (*On phone*) Sherwood residence—Miss *Ruth* Sherwood?

RUTH For *me?*

EILEEN Who's calling please?—What? Wait a minute—Just a second!

> (*To RUTH:*)

Ruth, it's Chick Clark's paper. Mr. Bains of the city room wants to talk to you—

> (*EILEEN hands the phone to RUTH.*)

RUTH Hello?—Yes—yes, Mr. Bains. This is she—her—she. Thank you, Mr. Bains. That's wonderful! Yes, yes, of course.

> (*To EILEEN:*)

Paper and pencil, quick. Take this down!

> (*EILEEN reaches over for pad and pencil from window.*)

EILEEN What is it? What happened?

RUTH Yes, Mr. Bains, I'm ready!—Sands—Street—Brooklyn—I understand— Yes, right away, Mr. Bains! Thank you—thank you very much. (*She hangs up, looks up excitedly*) I can't believe it!

EILEEN What did he say? What did he want?

RUTH He's giving me a chance to show what I can do—an assignment over in Brooklyn!

EILEEN Brooklyn? What happened there?

RUTH A Brazilian training ship just came in—like Annapolis—only these fellows are all young coffee millionaires. I'm going aboard to get a human interest story.

EILEEN Coffee millionaires! Well, you're not going over there with a run in your stocking! Take it off!

> (*They sit on bench. Both remove stockings, exchange them. Conversation continues throughout.*)

RUTH What a break! Isn't it wonderful? I'll show him!

EILEEN Who?

RUTH Never mind! Inhibited, huh?

EILEEN What?

RUTH I'll get a job on my own! Who does he think he is? (*Finished with stockings, she jumps up*) Have you got any money?

EILEEN Who—*me?*

RUTH How am I going to get over there?

EILEEN The milk bottles!

> (*RUTH picks up bottles near door, grabs her hat and rushes to stairs.*)

RUTH (*Climbing stairs*) Wish me luck!

> (*EILEEN follows.*)

EILEEN Good luck!

(*RUTH exits noisily, milk bottles clanging. EILEEN turns back, picks up tray with wine glasses, exits into studio. WAITER enters from Nino's with gallon glass jug of cheap wine. CHEF enters with two Chianti bottles in straw and funnel.*)

CHEF Il vino?

WAITER Porta qui le bottiglie. Ecco!

(*Pulls two straw bottles from behind back. WAITER pours from cheap bottle into straw one. When first bottle is full, CHEF takes funnel and puts it into second bottle.*)

CHICK (*Entering from street carrying package from grocery store. EILEEN comes out of studio*) Dinner for two—comin' right up!

EILEEN (*Taking sandwiches*) Oh, how nice!

CHICK Let's go in the kitchen—it's stiflin' out here!

(*CHEF and WAITER go off with bottles.*)

EILEEN (*Going to bench*) Oh, this is much pleasanter!

"You're not going with a run in your stocking— Take it off!"

EILEEN (Edie Adams), RUTH (Carol Channing— followed Rosalind Russell)

(CHICK sits next to her and makes a pass at her shoulder, which she shrugs off. She puts the bag with food between them)

It was awfully sweet of you to get Ruth a chance.

(Opening wrapper, pulling out sandwich.)

CHICK A pleasure!

(He pats her hand and puts arm around her. She hands him sandwich in hand which has been groping around her back. He puts sandwich on bench, his arms around her again)

—And the next thing, we're gonna get your career straightened out.

EILEEN *(Struggling, rises)* Please! You'll have to excuse me, Mr. Clark!

CHICK Excuse ya! After all the trouble I went to get rid of that eagle-eyed sister of yours.

EILEEN *(Staring)* What? That call Ruth got was from the editor, wasn't it?

CHICK What are you worrying about? I'm handling it—

EILEEN It was *you!* You sent Ruth on a wild goose chase!

CHICK *(Shrugs)* I'll give her a coupla bucks for her trouble.

EILEEN She was so excited. How am I ever going to tell her? You get out of here!

CHICK Now that's a lousy attitude to take!

(Phone rings.)

Let it ring!

EILEEN *(Answering phone)* Hello? Oh, Mr. Baker—hello, Bob!

CHICK *(Into phone)* Call back later!

EILEEN *(To CHICK)* How dare you! *(Into phone)* Oh, just somebody who's leaving.

(To CHICK:)

Now stop this nonsense! *(Into phone)*—Ruth? No, she's gone to Brooklyn.

(To CHICK—hand over the phone:)

Skunk! *(Into phone, elegantly)* Oh, you don't have to apologize, we never got to dinner anyway—Me?—I guess I'll wait for Ruth, I always feel silly eating alone—

CHICK Alone! How about me and them baloney sandwiches!?

EILEEN *(Into phone)* Why, Bob, how nice! I'd love to have dinner with you.

(Glaring at CHICK:)

Yes, I'll be waiting. *(Hangs up. Picks sandwich from window sill.)*

CHICK That's the worst double-cross I ever got! A fine little sneak you turned out to be!

(EILEEN starts to eat sandwich. CHICK grabs it from her hand as she is taking a bite. CHICK goes to the bench, picks up the empty bag, and stuffs EILEEN's sandwich into it)

I ain't fattenin' you up for someone else!

(Blackout.)

SCENE 7

The Navy Yard. At rise: SHORE PATROLMAN doing sentry duty. RUTH enters, passing SHORE PATROLMAN.

SHORE PATROLMAN Just a minute, Miss! Where's your pass?

RUTH Oh, it's all right—Press—I'm a reporter.

SHORE PATROLMAN You gotta have a pass.

RUTH I just want to interview those Brazilian cadets.

SHORE PATROLMAN Look, I'm tryin' to tell you—a pass—

RUTH Well, where can I get one?

SHORE PATROLMAN You can't—Commandant's office is closed. Tomorrow.

RUTH Oh, please—my job depends on it!

SHORE PATROLMAN So does mine.

(*BRAZILIAN CADET enters.*)

FIRST CADET (*Eyeing RUTH with some interest. After all, she's a woman*) Hello.

RUTH (To SHORE PATROLMAN) Is that one of them?

(*SHORE PATROLMAN nods. She steps to CADET.*)

Excuse me, Admiral. I'm from the press, and I'd like to ask you a few questions—

(*CADET shrugs his shoulders, blankly.*)

SHORE PATROLMAN That means he don't understand.

RUTH Thanks. I know that much Portuguese myself.

(*Seven more CADETS enter, enveloping RUTH in their midst, and talking loudly*)

Ah! Any of you Admirals speak English?

SECOND CADET Si! English!

RUTH What do you think of America?

SECOND CADET American dance—Conga!

RUTH No, no! Conga's a Brazilian dance!

FIRST CADET No—Cubano!

SECOND CADET Conga *American* dance! You show Conga!

RUTH Then will you tell me?

ALL Si! Si!

RUTH It's like this. One, two, three, kick. One, two, three, kick.

(*She shuffles from side to side in Conga step. They follow clumsily. She ad-libs: That's fine! You've got it! That's right! But they don't quite stop. Music:*)

What do you think of the USA—NRA—TVA?
What do you think of our Mother's Day?
What do you think of the—

ADMIRALS

Conga!

(*They dance. She attempts to get her interview, but each time the CADETS cut in with shrieks of "Conga!" As the number becomes more violent and RUTH is hurled about from one CADET to the other, she remains grimly resolved to disregard them and get her story.*)

RUTH

What do you think of our native squaws,
Charles G. Dawes,
Warden Lawes—
What's your opinion of Santa Claus?
What do you think of the—

ADMIRALS

Conga!

(*They dance.*)

RUTH

Good neighbors—Good neighbors,
Remember our policy—
Good neighbors—I'll help you,
If you'll just help me—

ADMIRALS

Conga!

(*They dance. RUTH gets more and more involved.*)

RUTH

What's your opinion of Harold Teen,
Mitzi Green,
Dizzy Dean?
Who do you love on the silver screen?
What do you think of the—

ADMIRALS

Conga!

(*More dancing, with RUTH struggling to get out of it.*)

RUTH

What do you think of our rhythm bands,
Monkey glands,
Hot dog stands?
What do you think of Stokowski's hands?
What do you think of the—

ADMIRALS

Conga!

(*Dance.*)

RUTH

Good neighbors—Good neighbors,
Remember our policy—
Good neighbors—I'll help you,
If you'll just help me—

ADMIRALS

Conga!

(*By now the dancing is abandoned and wild.*)

RUTH

What's your opinion of women's clothes,
Major Bowes,
Steinbeck's prose?
How do you feel about Broadway Rose?
What do you think of the—

ADMIRALS

Conga!

RUTH

What do you think of our rocks and rills,
Mother Sills' sea-sick pills?
How do you feel about Helen Wills?
What do you think of the—

ADMIRALS

Conga!

RUTH

Good neighbors—Good neighbors,
Remember our policy—
Good neighbors—I'll help you,
If you'll just help me—

(*ADMIRALS sing a serenade, strumming on imaginary guitars, while RUTH stands listening, totally exhausted. They yell "Conga!" again, and lift her on their backs. Careening about, RUTH still tries to get her interview.*)

RUTH

Stop!
What do you think of our double malts,
Family vaults,
Epsom Salts?
Wouldn't you guys like to learn to waltz?
I know—you just want to—Conga!

(*She is whirled about piggy-back in Conga rhythm, her hat over her eyes—and finally lifted aloft and carried offstage—as the music builds to a frenetic finish.*)

Following page:

RUTH (Rosalind Russell)

SCENE 8

The back yard. RUTH enters, immediately after rise, followed by ADMIRALS.

RUTH Good night! Au revoir! Auf wiedersehn! Goodbye! (*To EILEEN, who enters from studio*) Eileen. Eileen!

EILEEN What's going on?

RUTH The Fleet's in!

EILEEN (*To ADMIRALS*) How do you do?

RUTH Listen, Emily Post—How do you say, "Get the hell out of here" in Portuguese?

EILEEN Why? What's the matter?

RUTH Suppose *you* take 'em outside and walk 'em around! I'm sick of having kids whistle at me.

EILEEN You mean they don't understand any English at all?

RUTH Yes—three words: American dance—Conga!

A CADET Conga! Da-da-da-da-da-da!

(*He starts to dance. The others restrain him hastily.*)

RUTH Listen boys—Go! Leave! Goodbye!

(*She waves. ADMIRALS return wave, then mutter happily "Goo-bye." RUTH turns back to EILEEN, shrugs and steps to her.*)

EILEEN What did you bring them here for?

RUTH Bring them?! They've been on my tail ever since I left the Brooklyn Navy Yard.

EILEEN What do they want, anyway?

RUTH What do you *think* they want?

EILEEN Oh, my God! We've got to get them out of here! Make them go, Ruth!

RUTH Suppose you take a crack at it.

EILEEN (*Sweetly*) Look, boys. Go back to your boat. Boat!

(*She salutes. ADMIRALS snap to attention, salute in return.*)

RUTH Admiral Sherwood, I presume.

(*They drop salute.*)

EILEEN Boys—go 'way—please!

(*Supplicating—her arms extended—they take it wrongly—howl and step forward after her. EILEEN shrieks, runs back to RUTH.*)

RUTH That's fine.

EILEEN Gee, they can't be *that* dumb.

RUTH They're *not* that dumb.

EILEEN What are we going to do?

RUTH I've tried everything. I guess, Eileen, we'll just have to stand here grinning at each other.

(*She turns to ADMIRALS and grins broadly. ADMIRALS all grin back. She motions helplessly, steps back to EILEEN.*)

EILEEN Look—boys—sick! Very sick! (*Sits on bench and leans all the way back—on "bed"*) Bed! Bed!

(*The ADMIRALS rush in at her. EILEEN jumps up, shrieks, makes a dash for RUTH, swings behind her for protection.*)

RUTH For God's sake, don't let 'em get any wrong ideas!

EILEEN You brought them here! The least you can do is help me get rid of them!

   (*The ADMIRALS start to toss coins.*)

   What are they tossing for?

RUTH I don't know, but I've got a hunch it's not me!

   (*An ADMIRAL approaches them gravely.*)

FIRST CADET (*Bowing*) Senorita, eu tive é grande prazer de a ganhar está noite.

RUTH Isn't it a romantic language?

EILEEN No understando—no spikee Portuguese—

FIRST CADET American dance—Conga!

> (*He turns EILEEN, takes her by the wrist and other ADMIRALS join in. RUTH dances backwards in front of EILEEN.*)

RUTH Eileen, we've got get them out of here.

> (*There is a blast from below. The ADMIRALS stop and cross themselves in fear.*)

EILEEN Run—Earthquake!

> (*EILEEN runs to doorway, hides against it, to see if ADMIRALS disperse. ADMIRALS make for the stairway. WAITERS and the CHEF enter from Nino's. Passers-by on the street stop to stare down. The ADMIRALS stop on the steps, look at one another and laugh.*)

RUTH What a performance! Helen Hayes couldn't have done better. Listen, I've got an idea. Lead 'em out through the alley and lose them on the street!

EILEEN Okay, but tell Bob I'll be right back.

RUTH Bob?

EILEEN Yes, I'm having dinner with him.

> (*To ADMIRALS.*)

Come on, boys—Conga!

> (*Boys make a line. EILEEN exits into the alley, ADMIRALS Conga-ing after her. RUTH stares off unhappily. The WAITERS from Nino's start to Conga gaily. BAKER enters from the street and stares strangely at CHEF and two WAITERS in Conga line. He goes to RUTH.*)

BAKER Ruth, what's going on?

RUTH (*Looks at him and starts to Conga by herself*) Oh, a few friends dropped in. We're losing our inhibitions!

> (*She grabs a piece of celery from WAITER, puts it between her teeth and starts to Conga wildly. She starts her own line, with the CHEF, and WAITERS following. As they go off, they are met by EILEEN coming back, still followed by the ADMIRALS and a huge snake line of mixed VILLAGERS. RUTH backs away in dismay.*)

EILEEN I couldn't lose them!

> (*MRS. WADE comes on with LONIGAN and another cop. Whistles are blown by LONIGAN. Meanwhile, RUTH has been hoisted up in the air by the ADMIRALS. COP makes a grab for EILEEN, picks her up. She turns in the air, kicks LONIGAN in the stomach. He drags her off. MRS. WADE has made for the stairs and stands on the first landing, motioning wildly. RUTH gets down from her perch and desperately starts to run across after EILEEN. She is grabbed by one of the ADMIRALS, carried, slid back and overhead by the ADMIRALS. BAKER runs after EILEEN as RUTH is Conga-ed aloft amidst a swirl of VILLAGERS, all caught up in the frenzy of the Conga rhythm.*)

> *Curtain.*

Act
Two

Act Two

SCENE 1

SCENE 1

The Christopher Street station house. A couple of COPS are talking as WRECK and HELEN enter. WRECK is carrying a dress of EILEEN's.

COP Hey, what are you doing in here?

HELEN Good morning.

WRECK Can we see Miss Sherwood, please?

FIRST COP What do you think this is, the Barbizon Plaza? Miss Who?

HELEN Eileen Sherwood.

COP Eileen? Why didn't you say so? (*Calls offstage*) Oh, Eileen!

EILEEN (*Offstage*) Yes? What is it, Dennis?

> (*Enters. Sees WRECK and HELEN. She is carrying a malted milk.*)

Oh, hello, Wreck—Helen—

WRECK Hi, Eileen!

HELEN The Wreck ironed this dress especially. He thought you'd want to look fresh in court.

EILEEN (*Taking dress*) Oh, thanks, Wreck. That's awfully sweet of you.

> (*To COP:*)

Dennis—

SECOND COP Yeah, Eileen?

EILEEN (*Hands dress to him*) Dennis, would you mind hanging this up in my cell?

SECOND COP Sure, Eileen.

> (*He goes off, holding dress carefully over arm. SECOND COP enters.*)

SECOND COP Oh, Eileen.

EILEEN Yes, Dan—

SECOND COP There's a man on the phone—wants to talk to you—says it's important.

EILEEN Who is it, Dan?

SECOND COP Chick Clark. Says he knows you.

EILEEN (*Angrily*) You tell Mr. Clark I'm not in to him and hang up on him if he ever calls again!

SECOND COP Leave it me, Eileen.

> (*He pats her shoulder and goes.*)

HELEN (*To WRECK*) And we were worried about her?

EILEEN Oh, I'm fine. How are you two getting along?

WRECK Pretty good. If everything works out all right, we'll be leavin' on our honeymoon next week.

EILEEN Congratulations! Are you getting married?

HELEN We decided not to wait for the football season.

WRECK Yeah. Ya see, Helen went to the doctor—

HELEN (*Turns to him*) Wreck!

WRECK Anyway, the decision was taken out of our hands.

HELEN Yes, we've got a plan and Appopolous is puttin' up all the dough.

EILEEN Appopolous!

HELEN Yes, as soon as I collect my dowry, he'll get his back rent.

EILEEN Good luck. I hope you'll be very happy.

WRECK Well, we've been happy so far—I don't see why marriage should change it.

(*They go off.*)

EILEEN (*To COP*) And to think I was always afraid of being arrested!

FIRST COP Ah, that Lonigan's a bum sport—just because you kicked him!

THIRD COP (*Enters*) Eileen, there's a girl outside—claims she's your sister.

EILEEN Ruth? Send her in please!

(*COP waves RUTH on.*)

RUTH (*Embracing EILEEN tearfully*) Eileen! Oh, you poor kid!

EILEEN (*Startled*) What happened?

RUTH What do you mean, what happened? This!

EILEEN Oh—Oh, yes—this!

RUTH I've been all over New York, trying to raise your bail—Maybe I'd better send a wire to Dad.

EILEEN Gee, don't do that! He'll ask a lot of foolish questions—

RUTH Well, we've got to do something.

EILEEN I'm all right! Everybody's very sweet to me here!

FIRST COP (*Enters*) Phone, Eileen.

EILEEN Who is it, Dennis?

SECOND COP A Mr. Lippencott. He'd like to know when he can call on you.

EILEEN (*Thoughtfully*) Tell him—any time before five.

RUTH (*Stares*) Tell me, Eileen, how many do you keep in help here?

EILEEN Huh?

RUTH I just love the way you've done this place. Well, I've got to get to work!

EILEEN Where?

RUTH The Village Vortex. Your old pal Speedy Valenti gave me a job.

EILEEN Doing what?

RUTH (*Hesitates*) Well, it pays—

FOURTH COP (*Enters*) Eileen, there's a gentleman to see you.

(*Hands* EILEEN *a business card.*)

EILEEN (*Reading*) Robert Baker! Why, it's *Bob!* Send him in, please.

RUTH (*Turning unhappily*) I'd better go.

BAKER (*Enters*) How are you, Eileen?

(*Turns to* RUTH.)

Oh, hello, Ruth.

RUTH (*Flatly*) Hello.

BAKER What happened to you, Ruth? I looked for you after the patrol wagon left.

RUTH I went for a walk—had a lot of things to think over—

BAKER You do look a little tired.

RUTH I am. I didn't sleep all night—

(*To* EILEEN:)

—worrying about *you*—So I sat at that typewriter and wrote the story about the Brazilian Admirals. It's a darn good story—I know it is! I took your advice—a slice of my own life—and I sent it to Chick's city editor— Mr. Bains. (*Sadly*) But they didn't print it, so I guess it wasn't so good after all.

BAKER Want *me* to read it?

RUTH If you feel up to it—

(*To* EILEEN:)

Sorry to eat and run, darling—but I've got to get to work!

(*Kisses her.*)

BAKER (*To* RUTH) Did you get a job? What are you doing?

RUTH Oh, it's in the advertising game. (*Looks at wrist watch*) Cocktail time, already? Well, I've got to fly! 'Bye dear—lovely party—such fun! *Do* ask me again! (*She hurries off.*)

EILEEN Poor Ruth! I didn't have the heart to tell her. There isn't any Mr. Bains—

BAKER What?

EILEEN It was all a big lie! That Chick Clark's an utter snake! Oh, if I could only get out of here, I'd—

BAKER Look, I'm working on this. I'm going to get you out. I just tried to pay your fine, but they haven't set it yet.

EILEEN Why not?

BAKER I don't know. Washington wants them to hold you here.

EILEEN (*Gasps*) Washington—D. C.?

BAKER Something about Pan-American relations.

EILEEN Oh, my God!

BAKER But don't worry—I'm working on this.

FOURTH COP (*Entering, making a butler's announcement*) Frank Lippencott.

EILEEN Send him in, Pat.

BAKER I'm going over to see the Brazilian Consul right now.

> (*He starts out. FRANK enters. They collide. FRANK carries a small box.*)

FRANK Oops! Sorry.

> (*BAKER exits irritatedly. FRANK combs his hair quickly.*)

Gee, this is the first time I was ever in a police station.

EILEEN It's *my* first time, too.

FRANK I brought you an electric fan we're running. I though it would cool off your cell.

> (*Holds out box to her.*)

EILEEN Isn't that thoughtful!

FRANK It's given away free with every purchase over five dollars.

EILEEN Thanks.

FRANK (*Opening box*) Somebody forgot it.

EILEEN You're sweet.

FRANK (*Removing small rubber fan from box*) You'd be surprised at the breeze that little thing gives off.

> (*He spins blade, hods it up to EILEEN's face.*)

Everybody in the store's got a cold.

> (*He hands her fan. FOURTH COP enters.*)

EILEEN (*To COP*) Pat, would you mind putting these things in my cell?

> (*She gets suitcase, hands it to ANDERSON.*)

FOURTH COP Yes, sure.

EILEEN Thank you.

> (*FOURTH COP exits.*)

FRANK Eileen, I want to ask you something. It's the most important decision I ever made in my life.

EILEEN Frank, you're a very sweet boy, and I'm fond of you, but I'm really not thinking of getting married.

FRANK No, neither am I.

EILEEN You're not?

FRANK No.

EILEEN Then what are you thinking of?

FRANK Listen, Eileen, I suddenly realize I've been wasting my life—

EILEEN What are you talking about?

FRANK You know—*Life*—the way you girls live it—free to follow your natural bent whatever it is—

EILEEN What's all that got to do with me?

FRANK Don't you see? We'd have our freedom and we'd have each other. I thought we could have a sort of ideal relationship, like Helen and the Wreck—

EILEEN (*Aghast*) Timothy!

FRANK Gee, Eileen, it was only an idea!

"You came from Killarney. You're Irish, Eileen!"

EILEEN (Edie Adams)

EILEEN Show this gentleman out—and don't ever let him in here again!

(*FRANK goes quickly. As he passes COP, COP stamps his foot menacingly. FRANK quickens speed, exits.*)

FIFTH COP (*Enters excitedly*) Eileen! Did you see the paper?

EILEEN No.

FIFTH COP Look! You're in it!

SECOND COP (*Enters*) Eileen's in the papers!

FIFTH COP A big story! Your picture and everything!

EILEEN Oh, for goodness sakes!

FOURTH COP (*Comes in with others*) Hey! That's me! Not bad, huh?

FIRST COP That jerk Lonigan has his back to the camera! He'll fry!

THIRD COP Look, Lonigan!

>   (*LONIGAN enters.*)

FOURTH COP You're famous, Eileen!

EILEEN Do you think so? I wonder if Mr. Valenti saw it?

>   (*To LONIGAN:*)

Oh, John, it's on your beat. Would you do me a great favor? Would you take this over to the Village Vortex and show it to Speedy Valenti personally?

FIRST COP He'd better!

LONIGAN Sure, Eileen. I'll serve it on him!

FIRST COP Atta boy, John!

>   (*To EILEEN as music begins:*)

Oh, Eileen, you brought a breath of the old country into the station house.

LONIGAN (*In greatly exaggerated Irish brogue*)
Sure and I been feelin' twice as Irish since you came into our lives.

>   (*Singing à al John McCormack*)

Take it from me,
In Dublin's fair city
There's none half so pretty
As pretty Eileen.
Take it from me,
The Mayor of Shannon
Would shoot off a cannon
And crown ye the queen.

ALL

Darlin' Eileen,
Darlin' Eileen,
Fairest colleen that iver I've seen.
And it's oh, I wish I were back
In the land of the green
With my darlin' Eileen.

FIRST COP

I've seem them all:
There's Bridget and Sheila,

SECOND COP

There's Kate and Deli—lah

And Moll and Maureen.

THIRD COP

    I've seen them all,
    Not one can compete with

FIRST COP

    Or share the same street with
    My Darlin' Eileen.

ALL

    Darlin' Eileen,
    Darlin' Eileen,
    Fairest colleen that iver I've seen.
    And it's oh, I wish I were back
    In the land of the green
    With my darlin' Eileen.

(They dance a lusty jig of the Old Country, lumbering but full of life, all vying for her attention.)

EILEEN *(Somewhat apprehensive, cutting them off)*
    Listen, my lads,
    I've something to tell you
    I hope won't compel you
    To cry and to keen.
    Mother's a Swede and Father's a Scot,
    And so Irish I'm not—And I never have been.

ALL COPS *(They will not hear of this)*
    Hush you, Eileen! Hush you, Eileen!
    Fairest colleen that iver I've seen.
    Don't you hand us none of that blarney,
    You come from Killarney,
    You're Irish, Eileen!

(The dance resumes and ends in a "hats off" salute to the girl of their dreams, EILEEN.)

Blackout.

SCENE 2

The street. At rise: MRS. WADE is sitting on a camp stool, posing; APPOPOLOUS is painting her picture.

MRS. WADE May I look?

APPOPOLOUS No, it's still an embryo. Let it kick and breathe first. As a model you will be immortalized like Van Gogh's herring!

(The WRECK and HELEN enter. HELEN pushes him in. He wears a navy-blue suit, carries a hat. She motions to his head. He puts hat on, starts to step in. HELEN grabs him, motions to glasses. He puts bone glasses on. HELEN goes off as WRECK crosses to APPOPOLOUS and looks over his shoulder at canvas.)

WRECK Bravo! Magnificent! You've captured the inner soul of this lovely lady!

APPOPOLOUS Thank you, Mr. Loomis.

(MRS. WADE looks at WRECK.)

That's indeed a compliment coming from a great collector like you!

WRECK Not at all!

APPOPOLOUS May I present you? Mr. Loomis—Mrs. Wade—

MRS. WADE Pleased to meet you.

WRECK (*Removing his hat*) I'm delighted. Maestro, I'd like to add this to my collection. Is it for sale?

APPOPOLOUS Sorry! I'm presenting this to Mrs. Wade!

HELEN (*Enters*) Hello, Mother.

MRS. WADE Oh, Helen. Come here a moment! I want you to meet someone! This is my daughter, Helen—Mr. Loomis.

WRECK Daughter? You're spoofing! You look more like sisters!

HELEN I'm very pleased to meet you, Mr. Loomis.

WRECK Likewise, I'm sure! Well, this is delightful! May I invite you all to tea at the Purple Cow?

MRS. WADE Oh.

APPOPOLOUS Fine! You young people go along, and we'll join you in a minute.

(WRECK smiles, offers his arm to HELEN. She takes it.)

HELEN Do you get down to the Village very often, Mr. Loomis?

(They go off.)

MRS. WADE Who *is* he?

APPOPOLOUS He comes from a very aristocratic family from Trenton Tech.

(APPOPOLOUS and MRS. WADE go off. RUTH enters with MAN with sign. As passers-by come on, they turn on electric signs reading "VORTEX" across their chests.)

RUTH (*To MAN*) I feel like a damn fool!

MAN (*Shrugs*) It's a living.

Act Two
SCENE 2

(Another couple passes by. RUTH and MAN turn on signs.)

VILLAGER You ever been there?

SECOND VILLAGER Yeah, last night.

(They go off.)

RUTH (*To MAN*) I'm really a writer, you know.

MAN I'm really an architect, but they haven't built anything since the Empire State Building.

RUTH (*Spotting someone offstage*) Oh, this is awful!

MAN What's the matter?

RUTH Here comes someone I know! Please, don't light up!

MAN Sure! Don't worry about it.

(RUTH turns, faces MAN, simulates fixing his tie. BAKER enters. After he has passed RUTH, she and MAN turn and stroll off. BAKER recognizes RUTH, turns.)

BAKER *Ruth!*

RUTH (*Turns, brightly*) Oh, hello there!

(Hastily, she folds her arms across the electric sign.)

BAKER Well, this is a surprise! Going out?

RUTH Yes, we are—to the opera. Mr. Stevens, I'd like you to meet Mr. Baker. Mr. Stevens is in Washington with the Reconstruction Finance Corporation.

(They shake.)

BAKER (*To RUTH*) I read your piece about the Brazilian Navy. Now that's the idea! It's fine!

RUTH Really? No repressions? No inhibitions?

BAKER No, just good clean fun. I gave it to the boss to read. I'm sure he'll go for it.

RUTH Oh, thank you, Bob. That's wonderful of you.

(VALENTI enters.)

MAN (*To RUTH*) Hey, Ruth, we're going to be late for the opera!

RUTH Just a minute, please. This is important!

MAN So is this! More important!

(Points to VALENTI.)

VALENTI What's going on here? Get on the ball!

(MAN snaps light on. BAKER stares in wonder. RUTH looks at him unhappily.)

Well? What's with you sister—run out of juice?

RUTH (*Lights up sign and smiles feebly at BAKER*) Well, it's a healthy job. Keeps me out in the air!

BAKER (*Pats her arm reassuringly*) Good girl.

(*He smiles at her and goes off.*)

VALENTI No socializing on my time. (*Goes to MAN*) Here's a pitch. You take Sheridan Square.

(*Hands flyer to MAN, who exits. Hands RUTH a flyer*)

Here's your spiel—come on, get a mob around you. Make with the pitch. Get hep.

(*VALENTI exits.*)

RUTH (*Tentatively*) Yes, sir—hep. (*Reading from flyer—very tentatively to passers-by*) Step up—step up—(*Embarrassed*) Get hep—get hep—(*Suddenly, loudly*) Step up!

(*Rhythm starts in orchestra. RUTH still reading from flyer, giving very "square" rendition.*)

Step up! Step up!
Get hep! Get hep!

(*While she reads, a crowd of '30's hepcats gathers around her.*)

Come on down to the Village Vortex,
Home of the new jazz rage—Swing!
Rock and roll to the beat beat beat
Of Speedy Valenti and his krazy kats!

(*Sings falteringly.*)

Swing! Dig the rhythm!
Swing! Dig the message!
The jive is jumpin' and the music goes around and around—
Whoa-ho—!
Goes around and around—
Cat, make it solid!
Cat, make it groovy!
You gotta get your seafood, Mama, your favorite dish is fish,
It's your favorite dish.
Don't be square,
Rock right out of that rockin' chair;
Truck on down and let down your hair;
Breathe that barrel-house air!
The Village Vortex!
Swing! Dig the rhythm!
Swing! Dig the message!
The jive is jumpin' and the music goes around and around—
Get full of foory-a-ka-sa-ke,
Get full of the sound of swing,
The solid, jivy, groovy sound of swing!

HEPCATS (*Singing and showing RUTH how to get hep*)
Swing! Dig the rhythm!
Swing! Dig the message!
The jive is jumpin' and the music goes around and around—
Whoa-ho—!

RUTH (*Getting the idea*)
Oh!

SPEEDY (Ted Beniades), RUTH (Carol Channing)

WONDERFUL TOWN

VILLAGERS
Cat, make it solid!
Cat, make it groovy!
You gotta get your seafood, Mama;
Your favorite dish is fish—

RUTH (*Catching on still more and beginning to enjoy it*)
Oh!

VILLAGERS
Don't be square,
Rock right out of that rockin' chair;
Truck on down and let down your hair;
Breathe that barrel-house air!
You gotta get with the whoa-ho-de-ho!

RUTH (*Answering Cab Calloway fashion*)
Whoa-ho-de-ho.

VILLAGERS
The gut-gut bucket.

RUTH
The gut-gut bucket.

VILLAGERS
Skid-dle-ee-oh-day!

RUTH
Skid-dle-ee-oh-day!

VILLAGERS
Heedle heedle heedle.

RUTH
Heedle heedle heedle.

VILLAGERS
Well, all right then, cats!

RUTH
Well, all right then, cats!

VILLAGERS
Yes, yes, baby I know!

RUTH (*By this time* RUTH *is in a glaze-eyed hypnotic trance, having got the message and, as the* HEPCATS *gather around her, she delivers patter in a husky dreamlike monotone*)
Well, yes, yes, baby, I know!
That old man Mose
Kicked the bucket,
The old oaken bucket that hung in the well—
Well, well, well, baby, I know—
No no; was it red?
No no no! Was it green green—
Green is the color of my true love's hair—
Hair-breadth Harry with the floy floy doy
Floy doy, floy doy, floy doy, hoy!
Hoy dre(h)eamt hoy dwe(h)elt in ma(h)arble halls—
Well that ends well, well, well—
Baby I know—No, no,
Was it green?
No no no.

Was it red sails in the sunset callin' me mc mc
You good for nothin'
Mi-mi mi-mi
Me Tarzan, you Jane,
Swingin' in the trees,
Swingin' in the trees,
Swingin' in the trees—

(This develops into an abandoned dance in which RUTH not only joins, but finally leads the HEPCATS to a "sent" finish.)

VILLAGERS

Swing—swing—swing—swing—swing—swing
Swing—Chu-chu-chu tch-chu-chu tch-chu-chu-chu
Swing—Chu-chu-chu tch-chu-chu tch-chu-chu-chu
Swing—Chu-chu-chu tch-chu-chu tch-chu-chu-chu

RUTH

Floy-doy floy-doy floy-doy hoy!

VILLAGERS

Sh-sh-sh.

RUTH

Gesundheit.

VILLAGERS

Thanks.

RUTH

You're welcome.

VILLAGERS

Whoa!

(Motioning to RUTH.)

Come on, Jackson, you're getting hep.
Come on, Jackson, you're getting hep.
Come on, Jackson, you're getting hep.

RUTH

I want my favorite dish.

VILLAGERS

Fish.

RUTH

Gesundheit.

VILLAGERS

Thanks.

RUTH

It's nothing!

VILLAGERS

Solid, groovy, jivy sound of swing—

FIRST MAN

Ah—do it.

SECOND MAN

Solid, Jackson.

FIRST WOMAN
    Seafood, Mama.

SECOND WOMAN (*A long banshee wail*)

VILLAGERS
    Go go go—yah—
    Swing—oh swing it,
    Swing—oh swing it.

    (The dance continues as the VILLAGERS back out, followed by RUTH in a trance.)

RUTH (*In a hoarse, hypnotic whisper*)
    Swing—Swing
    Green, no—red, no
    Me Tarzan—no, no, no
    That old man Mose
    He kicked that bucket
    Down in the well—well, well, well
    My favorite dish
    Ahhh—fish!

VILLAGERS
    Gesundheit.

RUTH
    Thank you.

VILLAGERS
    You're welcome.

RUTH (*Her hands before her, mesmerized, walks off in a trance.*)
    Swing—swing—swing—swing—swing—

    (She disappears.)

    Blackout.

SCENE 3

The studio. At rise: Stage empty. Through window, VIOLET's legs pass by, then man's legs. VIOLET stops, half turns. Man comes back and joins her. They stand, then go off together.

During this scene, APPOPOLOUS enters carrying blue-green painting. He steps on bed, looks about for something to stand on, picks up manuscripts off typewriter next to bed, and slips one under each foot. He hangs painting, jumps down, takes valise from under RUTH's bed, puts it on top of bed, takes typewriter from chair next to bed, puts it on bed, gets books and candlesticks off and puts them on bed. RUTH enters from bathroom in her slip. She screams.)

RUTH Ah! What are you doing with my things?

> *(She takes robe from bathroom and slips it on.)*

APPOPOLOUS You're being dispossessed! I only hope your sister has sense enough to give the wrong address!

RUTH Yes, imagine what bad publicity could do to this dump!

APPOPOLOUS (*Pointing to painting*) I found my masterpiece in Benny's. For the frame, two dollars—for my painting, nothing! At six o'clock your current occupancy terminates!

> *(Knock on door.)*

Remember! If you're not out by the stroke of six, you'll find your belongings in the street!

> *(He goes out through kitchen. There is another knock on the door.)*

RUTH Come in.

> *(BAKER enters.)*

Oh, Bob—

BAKER (*Sadly*) Oh, hello, Ruth.

RUTH What's the matter?

BAKER (*Angrily*) All I can say is, he wouldn't know a good story if he read one!

RUTH Who?

BAKER His Highness—king of the editors—pompous ass.

> *(APPOPOLOUS sticks head in from kitchen door.)*

APPOPOLOUS Fifteen minutes!

> *(Disappears again)*

BAKER What was *that?*

RUTH Bulova Watch Time.

BAKER I'm sorry, Ruth. He just didn't like it.

RUTH (*Shrugs*) Well, maybe it wasn't any good.

BAKER It's just one man's opinion.

RUTH That's enough.

BAKER I still think it's a hell of a good story and I'm going to tell him so!

RUTH Please, Bob, don't get into any trouble on my account.

BAKER This has nothing to do with you. It's a matter of principle. Either I know my business or I don't!

RUTH (*Nods slowly*) I see.

(*EILEEN enters from street with LONIGAN, who is carrying her suitcase.*)

EILEEN Ruth!

RUTH (*Embracing her*) Eileen! Darling, you're out! How did it happen?

EILEEN Bob fixed everything. Thanks, Bob.

(*CHICK CLARK appears at window.*)

WONDERFUL TOWN

CHICK Hello, kids.

EILEEN Chick Clark! You get away from there, you big snake!

CHICK Now wait a minute, Eileen! Gimme a chance.

EILEEN You had enough chances!

RUTH What are you talking about?

EILEEN Ruth, when I tell you what he did—

CHICK Wait! The city editor's read your Brazilian story and he thinks it's the absolute nuts!

RUTH (*Going to window, hopefully*) He does?

EILEEN Don't believe him, Ruth! He's the biggest liar!

CHICK Go ahead—call him up! Mr. Wilson! You know the number!

RUTH Wilson? I thought his name was Bains?

EILEEN You see, Ruth, he's lying again!

> (*To LONIGAN.*)

John, will you do me a great favor and chase him away from there?

LONIGAN Glad to!

> (*He runs out.*)

CHICK Now wait a minute, Eileen. You're gonna louse it up! Tell her to call Mr. Wilson—the city editor—I keep tellin' her all the time!

> (*CHICK runs off as LONIGAN stops at window.*)

LONIGAN (*Kneels down, offers EILEEN his whistle*) Oh, Eileen, if anything else happens, here's a police whistle.

EILEEN (*Taking whistle*) Thanks, John.

> (*LONIGAN goes.*)

RUTH Next week you'll have your own hook and ladder.

APPOPOLOUS (*Sticking head through kitchen door*) Five minutes!

EILEEN What's that about?

RUTH We're being dispossessed.

BAKER Where are you going?

RUTH (*Hands EILEEN a suitcase*) I don't know—home, I guess.

EILEEN We can't. What would people say?

RUTH "Did you hear the dirt about those Sherwood girls? On account of them, we almost lost the Naval Base in Brazil."

BAKER It's ridiculous. You can't go home now.

RUTH But, Bob—

BAKER I haven't time to argue about it. (*Looks at his watch*) I've got to get up to the office before His Highness leaves. He wants to see me—and I want to see him a damn sight more! (*Goes to door*) Now I want you to promise me you'll wait right here till I get back.

RUTH You'd better hurry, or you may find us out in the street.

BAKER Half an hour. Top.

(*He's off.*)

EILEEN Isn't he nice?

RUTH (*Sits on bed wearily*) Um—You like him a lot, don't you, Eileen?

EILEEN You know, Ruth, he's the first boy I've ever met who really seemed to care what happened to me—how I got along and everything.

RUTH Yes, I know. (*Shrugs*) I guess it doesn't make any difference now anyway—

EILEEN What?

RUTH (*Close to tears*) I said we're going home—so it doesn't matter about Bob.

EILEEN (*Goes slowly to RUTH, putting an arm around her*) Gee, Ruth, I never dreamed. You mean you like him too?

RUTH Strange as it may seem—

EILEEN Well, why didn't you say anything?

RUTH What was there to say?

EILEEN After all—you're my sister.

RUTH (*Smiles at her through her tears*) That's the side of you that makes everything else seem worthwhile.

EILEEN Gee, Ruth—I'm sorry we ever came here.

(*Puts her head on RUTH's shoulder.*)

RUTH & EILEEN
Why, oh why, oh why—oh
Why did we ever leave Ohio?
Why did we wander to find what lies yonder
When life was so cozy at home?

Wond'ring while we wander,
Why did we fly?
Why did we roam?
Oh, why oh why oh
Did we leave Ohio?
Maybe we'd better go home.

(*APPOPOLOUS enters.*)

APPOPOLOUS Time's up! Your occupancy is officially terminated.

RUTH We're not ready yet.

(*VALENTI enters.*)

VALENTI Skeet—skat—skattle-ee-o-do! (*He carries newspaper*) Where is she? I know it! I meant it! You hit me in my weak spot—(*Slaps newspaper*) Right on the front page!

EILEEN Oh, Mr. Valenti! How did you like it?

RUTH (*Takes newspaper, reading headline*) Like what? "Beautiful Blonde Bomb-shell Sinks Brazilian Navy." Oh, my—now we *can't* go home!

VALENTI (*To EILEEN*) You're in the groove, babe! I'm gonna put you in my saloon for an audition tonight. If you make good, I'll sign you!

EILEEN Oh, Mr. Valenti! Speedy! That's wonderful!

(*To RUTH:*)

Ruth, it's a job! My first break in the theatre.

(*They embrace.*)

APPOPOLOUS Girls, I'm gonna extend your time until six o'clock tomorrow morning. Make good and you can be with me for life! (*He goes.*)

VALENTI (*To EILEEN*) Get over there right away!

EILEEN Yes, yes.

(*To RUTH:*)

Only what about Bob?

RUTH We'll leave a note on the door.

EILEEN What'll I wear, Mr. Valenti?

VALENTI I'll lend you a dress. I'll lend your sister one too—

(*RUTH looks up.*)

—and without the lights. Now get over there. (*Goes to door*) What are you gonna sing, Babe?

EILEEN Ruth, remember the song we always used to do at the Kiwanis Club? The Wrong Note Rag?

RUTH Oh, yes—do that one.

VALENTI It's an oldie, but you'll never know it when I back you up with the licorice stick.

RUTH The what?

VALENTI My clarinet. Then, for an encore—tell me, kid, did you ever take 'em off?

EILEEN What?

VALENTI You know, *strip?*

RUTH My sister doesn't strip.

VALENTI Too bad. We're always looking for new faces!

(*Blackout.*)

SCENE 4

The street in front of the Vortex. At rise: HELEN and WRECK enter, followed by MRS. WADE and APPOPOLOUS.

HELEN That was a lovely dinner, Mr. Loomis!

APPOPOLOUS (*Grimly*) Yes, he's certainly a fine host—everything out of season.

WRECK Why not? You only live once!

APPOPOLOUS Only the champagne I didn't expect!

MRS. WADE It's good, though! Hit the spot!

WRECK There! You see, Maestro?

HELEN Come on! Let's get a good table!

WRECK Yeah.

> *(They go off. APPOPOLOUS takes MRS. WADE's arm.)*

APPOPOLOUS One moment, Ella. They make a lovely couple, don't they?

MRS. WADE Yes! Do you think his intentions are serious?

APPOPOLOUS I'll vouch for it.

MRS. WADE Did you notice he was holding Helen's hand under the table? My, I'd love to see my Helen settled down!

APPOPOLOUS (*Offers his arm*) Don't worry, Ella, she'll be settled down and you'll be a grandmother before you expect it!

> *(They go off. RUTH and EILEEN hurry on.)*

EILEEN Oh, dear, I'm so frightened!

RUTH Now look, Eileen, you're not afraid of anything. I know you better than that!

EILEEN You do?

> *(CHICK CLARK runs on.)*

CHICK Hey, kids! I gotta talk to you!

EILEEN Chick Clark, for the last time, stop annoying us!

CHICK I tell ya! I got it all fixed!

EILEEN All right! You asked for it—now you're going to get it!

> *(She puts whistle, attached to her arm, to her lips and blows several times.)*

CHICK What are you doin'? Ya crazy?!

> *(LONIGAN dashes on, CHICK runs off. EILEEN points in CHICK's direction. LONIGAN follows him off.)*

RUTH Eileen, are you sure you're doing the right thing?

EILEEN Some day I'll tell you the truth about Mr. Chick Clark! (*Clutches her stomach*) Oh, gee—I'm all upset again! I feel nauseous!

RUTH You do? Well, look—walk up and down in the air—and breathe deeply. That's right. I'll take your case and get you some black coffee. (*She goes off.*)

EILEEN Oh, thanks, Ruth.

(BAKER enters with piece of paper.)

BAKER Eileen—I found your note. This is wonderful news!

(Takes her hands.)

EILEEN Thanks, Bob.

BAKER Now, no more of that nonsense about going home.

EILEEN Oh, no. No.

BAKER And I'll get something for Ruth—just as soon as I land a job myself.

EILEEN Job! What happened?

BAKER Well, I left the *Manhatter*—uh—a difference of opinion.

EILEEN Oh, Bob, I'm awfully sorry. But I think it's wonderful that you feel that way about Ruth!

BAKER Well, I'm very fond of her—

EILEEN Fond? It must be more than that if you got fired on her account.

BAKER I left on a matter of principle!

EILEEN Principle! Don't play dumb!

BAKER Dumb?

EILEEN Well, you must be if you don't know what's going on in your own mind!

BAKER Will you please tell me what's going on in my own mind?

EILEEN I suppose you don't know why you fought with your editor about Ruth's story—or why you're picking a fight with me right now! Poor Bob—you're in love with Ruth and you don't even know it!

(Sings:)

It's love! It's love!

BAKER (*Sings*)
Come on now—Let's drop it.

EILEEN
It's love! It's love!
And nothing can stop it.

BAKER
You're a silly girl—It's a sign of youth.

EILEEN (*Shakes head*)
You're a silly boy—You're in love with Ruth.
It's love! It's love!
Come on now—Just try it.

BAKER (*Tentatively*)
It's love! It's love!

EILEEN
Don't try to deny it.
I know the signs,
I know it when I see it—

So just face it,
Just say it.

BAKER

It's love,
It's love,

(BAKER sings—BIG.)

It's love!!

(EILEEN watches him a moment—then exits.)

Maybe—It's love! It's love!

(As the realization grows)

Well, who would have thought it?
If this is love,
Then why have I fought it?
What a way to feel—
I could touch the sky.
What a way to feel—
I'm a different guy!

It's love, at last,
I've someone to cheer for—
It's love, at last,
I've learned what we're here for—
I've heard it said,
"You'll know it when you see it."
Well, I see it—I know it—
It's Love!

(He exits happily.)

SCENE 5

The Village Vortex, a surrealistic night club, hung with paintings from every artist who couldn't pay his tab, and dominated by a huge revolving mobile, hung from the ceiling. VALENTI leads the band with his clarinet as the crowd dances a slow, writhing jitterbug, packed tightly together like anchovies.

VALENTI (*As dance ends and a bedlam of sound from the crowd bubbles up*) Settle down! Settle down!

> (*WRECK has opened a bottle of champagne. Rises with bottle and glass.*)

WRECK Folks, here's a toast to my future mother-in-law. Long may she wave!

PATRON (*From balcony*) Sit down, you bum!

> (*WRECK starts to remove his coat and glasses, shakes an angry fist at patron.*)

HELEN (*To WRECK*) Please, Mr. Loomis—

> (*WRECK subsides.*)

VALENTI Cats and Gates! You've read about her, you've talked about her! Now here she is in person, fresh from a cellar in Christopher Street—Miss Eileen Sherwood!

> (*RUTH and EILEEN enter. RUTH is pushing EILEEN, fixing her hair at the last minute.*)

Give the little girl a great big hand!

> (*He leads applause. EILEEN climbs steps—RUTH sits on bottom step.*)

CHICK (*Enters*) Hey, Ruth, I gotta square myself with you.

RUTH Go away—my sister's going to sing!

EILEEN You get out of here, Chick Clark!

FRANK (*Stepping in*) Is he annoying you, Miss Sherwood?

CHICK (*Pushing FRANK*) Go on back to your drugstore! No! Look, Ruth! I got your press card, signed by the city editor! You start Monday!

RUTH Is it true?

CHICK It's official—I tell ya!

LONIGAN (*To CHICK*) All right you—come on!

> (*He takes CHICK's arm.*)

CHICK Ruth, tell this clown I'm okay!

RUTH No, no, Officer—he's all right!

EILEEN Yes, John—you can let him go now.

LONIGAN (*Disgustedly*) Ah!

RUTH (*Going up to EILEEN on the platform*) Oh, thanks, Chick! Eileen, I can't believe it! Look, it's a press card! I've got a job—I can go to work!

> (*They embrace.*)

EILEEN Ruth, that's wonderful!

VALENTI What is this—a nightclub or an employment agency?

VOICES Come on! Sing it! Let's hear her sing!

VALENTI Come on, what are you cryin' for?

EILEEN I'm happy!

RUTH We're both happy!

VALENTI Well, I ain't! And the customers ain't! Sing or blow!

RUTH She'll sing! Go on, Eileen—

EILEEN I can't—I can't just stop crying and start singing!

RUTH Of course, you can!

EILEEN Do it with me, Ruth, please!

RUTH In front of all those people?!

VALENTI Come on! Come on!

EILEEN Ruth!

RUTH Should I, Mr. Valenti?

VALENTI Sure! Do something—do anything!

RUTH All right! Play the band—the "Wrong Note Rag"!

> *(RUTH and EILEEN stand up. RUTH explains the routine. RUTH and EILEEN hurriedly whisper directions to each other during the announcement.)*

VALENTI Folks, something new has been added. Another glorious voice joins us. The Wrong Note Rag—Hit it, boys!

> *(There is an old-fashioned blaring introduction and RUTH and EILEEN march forward and perform the number they have known since their early childhood. They work in a dead-pan sister-act style circa 1913.)*

RUTH AND EILEEN
> Oh, there's a new sensation that is goin' aroun'—
> Goin' aroun'—Goin' aroun'—Goin' aroun'—
> A simple little ditty that is sweepin' the town,
> Sweepin' the town—swee—eepin' the town.
> Doo—Doo—Doo
> Doo—Doo—Doo—Doo—Doo—Doo
> They call it the wrong note rag!
>
> It's got a little twist that really drives you insane,
> Drives ya insane, drives ya insane, drives ya insane,
> Because you'll find you never get it out of your brain,
> Out of your brain—Ou-out of your brain!
> Doo—Doo—Doo—
> They call it the Wrong Note Rag!
>
> *(The music and the girls' spirit and energy become infectious and the crowd joins in.)*

WONDERFUL TOWN

ALL
> Bunny Hug!
> Turkey Trot!
> Gimme the Wrong Note Rag!

RUTH & EILEEN
> Please play that lovely wrong note,
> Because that wrong note
> Just makes me
> Doo—Doo Da—Doo, Doo-Doo—Da—Doo, Doodoo!
>
> That note is such a strong note,
> It makes me

EILEEN
> Rick-ricky-tick, rick-ricky-tick tacky.

RUTH
> Wick-wicky-wick, wick-wicky-wick wacky.

RUTH & EILEEN
> Don't play that right polite note,
> Because that right note
> Just makes me
> Blah-blah-bla-blah, blah-blah-bla-blah blah blah!
> Give me that new and blue note
> And sister
> Watch my dust!
> Watch my smoke!
> Doin' the Wrong Note Rag!

(They break out into a corny ragtime dance, and the couples at the Vortex, loving it, pick up the steps and join them, building the number to a high-spirited finish. There is wild enthusiasm from the Vortex patrons as RUTH and EILEEN hug each other happily.)

VALENTI Well, that's what drove 'em out of Ohio. What are you gonna do for an encore?

EILEEN Encore? Did I get one?

RUTH Of course you did! You were terrific! Go on!

VALENTI What's it gonna be?

(EILEEN whispers, "It's Love!" She goes upstage and all face her. RUTH sits on a step downstage)

For an encore our little premier donna is gonna get nice and mellow—
Keep it low, folks.

(The music to "It's Love" starts and EILEEN sings—all eyes on her. She is in a spotlight—and so is RUTH, watching her.)

EILEEN *(As she sings)*
> It's love! It's love!
> Well, who would have thought it?

(BAKER enters, looks about, sees RUTH, goes to her and touches her shoulder. She turns, shushes him and turns back to watch EILEEN.)

> If this is love,
> Then why have I fought it?

(RUTH does a take as she realizes it is BAKER, but she shushes him again. This time he takes her in his arms and kisses her. Still dazed, she pushes him away, again shushing him. Then, suddenly realizing what is happening, she turns back to him and rushes into his arms.)

What a way to feel,
I could touch the sky.
What a way to feel,
I have found my guy.

BAKER *(Holding RUTH, as all turn to watch them, EILEEN beaming happily at them across the club)*
It's love, at last,
I've someone to cheer for.

RUTH
It's love, at last,
I've learned what we're here for.

ALL
I've heard it said,
"You'll know it when you see it."

(RUTH and BAKER hold hands, oblivious to everything but each other.)

Well, I see it—I know it—
It's love!

(The curtain falls.)

Technical and business staffs. Sixth from left is Hal Prince, Assistant Stage Manager.

Bells Are Ringing

Book and Lyrics
by Betty Comden and Adolph Green
Music by Jule Styne

ENTIRE ORIGINAL DIRECTION BY **JEROME ROBBINS**

DANCES AND MUSICAL NUMBERS BY
JEROME ROBBINS & BOB FOSSE

Bells Are Ringing

We wanted to write a show for the great Judy Holliday, our close friend and partner from our old nightclub days. While searching desperately for an idea, our eyes happened to light on the back of the telephone book, where an ad for an answering service showed rows of girls wearing earphones, seated at banks of switchboards, wires growing out of their heads, seemingly plugged into the entire city. A possible idea. We decided to visit my (Adolph's) answering service, located a block away from my apartment, and instead of what we expected, walked into the cellar of a dilapidated brownstone. The one room contained an old sofa with springs and stuffings bursting out, several empty coffee containers, a small puppy relieving himself in a corner, and in the center, one lone switchboard at which sat a very large young woman plugging in and saying, "Gloria Vanderbilt's residence." A very possible idea.

We called composer Jule Styne, and he, with customary restraint, yelled, "They have got to fall down!!!," meaning that critics and audiences alike would be so entranced with it they would simply collapse on the floor in adoration. Jerome Robbins directed and co-choreographed with Bob Fosse, and the Theater Guild were our producers.

Judy, who was by this time a big movie star and had won the Academy Award for *Born Yesterday*, liked our idea but did not commit until we had written a goodly hunk of the book and read it to her. Happily she loved it.

Somewhere in this seemingly cold and indifferent town there lurk unexpected pockets of warmth and love. In *Bells are Ringing*, Judy played an answering service operator who felt that people should care about one another every day, the same way they seem to only in times of crisis. She puts her philosophy into practice by trying to help her unseen subscribers. Her need to help others may make her atypical as a New Yorker, but there *are* such people and that is why the "Big City" works.

"We called composer Jule Styne, and he, with customary restraint, yelled, 'They have got to fall down!!!'"

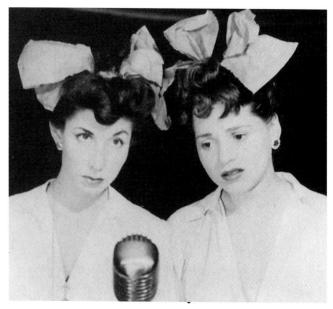

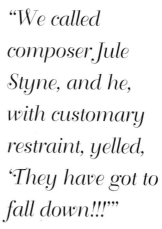

Bells Are Ringing was first presented by The Theatre Guild at the
Sam S. Shubert Theatre, New York City, on November 29, 1956, with the following cast:

SUE SUMMERS	Jean Stapleton
GWYNNE SMITH	Pat Wilkes
ELLA PETERSON	Judy Holliday
CARL	Peter Gennaro
INSPECTOR BARNES	Dort Clark
FRANCIS	Jack Weston
SANDOR	Eddie Lawrence
JEFF MOSS	Sydney Chaplin
LARRY HASTINGS	George S. Irving
TELEPHONE MAN	Eddie Heim
LUDWIG SMILEY	Frank Milton
CHARLES BESSEMER	Frank Green
DR. KITCHELL	Bernie West
BLAKE BARTON	Frank Aletter
ANOTHER ACTOR	Frank Green
CLERK	Tom O'Steen
OLGA	Norma Doggett
HENCHMAN FROM CORVELLO MOB	John Perkins
OTHER HENCHMAN	Kasimir Kokich
CAROL	Ellen Ray
PAUL ARNOLD	Steve Roland
MICHELLE	Michelle Reiner
MASTER OF CEREMONIES	Eddie Heim
SINGER AT NIGHTCLUB	Frank Green
WAITER	Ed Thompson
MAITRE D'HOTEL	David McDaniel
POLICE OFFICER	Gordon Woodburn
MADAME GRIMALDI	Donna Sanders
MRS. MALLET	Jeannine Masterson
GIRL DANCERS	Norma Doggett, Phyllis Dorne, Patti Karr, Barbara Newman, Nancy Perkins, Marsha Rivers, Beryl Towbin, Anne Wallace
BOY DANCERS	Doria Avila, Frank Derbas, Don Emmons, Eddie Heim, Kasimir Kokich, Tom O'Steen, Willy Summer, Ben Vargas, Billy Wilson
GIRL SINGERS	Pam Abbott, Joanne Birks, Urylee Leonardos, Jeannine Masterson, Michelle Reiner, Donna Sanders
BOY SINGERS	Frank Green, Marc Leon, David McDaniel, Paul Michael, Julian Patrick, Steve Roland, Ed Thompson, Gordon Woodburn

Act One

OPENING SUSANSWERPHONE ADVERTISEMENT

Opening   Bells are Ringing   Girls

SCENE 1: OFFICE OF SUSANSWERPHONE. LATE AFTERNOON.

1. It's a Perfect Relationship   Ella

SCENE 2: JEFF MOSS' LIVING ROOM

2. On My Own   Jeff and Ensemble

You've Got To Do It   Jeff

SCENE 3: AN ALLEY AT NIGHT

3   It's A Simple Little System   Sandor and Ensemble

SCENE 4: THE OFFICE. EARLY MORNING

SCENE 5: A STREET IN FRONT OF THE OFFICE

5   Is It A Crime?   Ella

Better Than a Dream   Ella and Jeff

SCENE 6: JEFF MOSS' LIVING ROOM

SCENE 7: A STREET

SCENE 8: A SUBWAY CAR

8   Hello, Hello There!   Ella, Jeff and Ensemble

SCENE 9: A STREET

9   I Met A Girl   Jeff and Ensemble

SCENE 10: DR. KITCHELL'S OFFICE

SCENE 11: A STREET

SCENE 12: DRUG STORE

SCENE 13: A STREET

SCENE 14: THE OFFICE. A WEEK LATER

SCENE 15: JEFF MOSS' LIVING ROOM

15 Long Before I Knew You   Ella and Jeff

Scenes & Musical Numbers

Act Two

SCENE 1: THE OFFICE. THE NEXT NIGHT

1   Mu-Cha-Cha   Ella and Carl

     Dance   Carol, Carl and Dancing Ensemble

SCENE 2: THE PARK

2   Just In Time   Jeff, Ella and Ensemble

SCENE 3: LARRY HASTINGS' PENTHOUSE

3   Drop That Name   Ella and Ensemble

     The Party's Over   Ell

SCENE 4: THE CRYING GYPSY CAFE

4   Salzburg   Sue and Sandor

SCENE 5: THE PYRAMID CLUB

5   The Midas Touch   Singer, Boys and Girls

SCENE 6: BAY RIDGE SUBWAY PLATFORM

6   Reprise: Long Before I Knew You   Jeff

SCENE 7: THE OFFICE

7   I'm Goin' Back   Ella

     Finale   The Company

Entire production directed by Jerome Robbins
Sets and costumes designed by Raoul Pene du Bois
Dances and musical numbers staged by Jerome Robbins [and Bob Fosse]
Musical direction by Milton Rosenstock
Orchestrations by Robert Russell Bennett
Vocal arrangements and direction by Herbert Greene and Buster Davis
Dance arrangements and incidental scoring by John Morris
Lighting by Peggy Clark

Act One

OPENING

Susanswerphone Advertisement: At rise, eight GIRLS, looking lonely and disconsolate, are seen on stage.

OFF-STAGE ANNOUNCER (*With unctuous concern*) Ladies and gentlemen, has this ever happened to you? These girls missed an important telephone call.

GIRLS (*Sigh, then they sing*)
> All around there's the sound of the midsummer night;
> Bells in the air are ringing everywhere.
> I can hear footsteps that pass on the street
> And lovers rushing to meet.
> Here alone I can only imagine the sight—
> Me on the town in some bewitching gown—
> But I just wait at the end of the line
> As bells are ringing; the bells keep ringing—
> Oh why, oh why can't the next call be mine?

OFF-STAGE ANNOUNCER A sad story, girls—

> (*They nod sadly*)

But it need not have happened.

> (*They look up hopefully*)

Perhaps—during the time you were out—he called,

> (*"Ohhhh" from the GIRLS*)

but no one was there to answer your telephone.

> (*GIRLS slump despondently, sighing "Ohhhh!"*)

Don't let the same thing happen tomorrow night!

GIRLS But what can we do?

OFF-STAGE ANNOUNCER Subscribe to an answering service. Use Susanswerphone!

GIRLS Susanswerphone?

OFF-STAGE ANNOUNCER Yes. It gives and takes your messages as it does for business executives, doctors, and theatre celebrities on New York's smart East Side. Now, this is what can happen when you subscribe to Susanswerphone.

> (*Sound of phone ringing.*)

GIRLS (*Pick up imaginary phones*) Hello?

OPERATOR'S VOICE This is your answering service.

GIRLS Yes?

OPERATOR'S VOICE While you were out the agency called. You got the job!

GIRLS (*Thrilled*) Oh!

OPERATOR'S VOICE And your lawyer called. Your uncle left you all his money in his will!

GIRLS (*More thrilled*) Oh!!!

OPERATOR'S VOICE And *he* called and I gave him your message, so he's waiting for you right now!!

GIRLS (*Most thrilled*) Oh!!!!

> (*They sing.*)

Thank you Susanswerphone!

> (*They dash off joyously. One can only feel that a full, happy life is spreading before them.*)

OFF-STAGE ANNOUNCER Ring us up at our sumptuous, luxurious offices where our vast personnel of well-trained girls are ready even now to serve you! Susanswerphone!!

> (*While he is still speaking, against a musical background of celestial harps, the lights fade.*)

Dressing room make-up

JUDY HOLLIDAY, BETTY COMDEN (IN BACK-GROUND), SYDNEY CHAPLIN

SCENE 1

The Susanswerphone office. A hot New York summer day, late afternoon. A small squalid room down a few steps from street level with barely any light coming in one dirty window which looks out on a hall. An old chair on one side, with springs caved in and stuffings coming out. The place is littered with old coffee containers, filled ashtrays, empty coke bottles, movie magazines, and bedroom slippers. A door, stage left, leads to the bathroom, which girls use to change clothes.

In the center of the crowded, cluttered room is a telephone switchboard. The desk in front of the board is covered with message pads, a file, phone books, etc.

Seated at the switchboard, wearing a smock, is SUE SUMMERS, *plain and fortyish, owner of Susanswerphone. Her manner on the phone is always cool and impersonal. In the chair sits* GWYNNE SMITH, *one of her two answering service girls, reading a magazine.* GWYNNE *is plump, sedentary.*

SUE (*On phone*) Yes, Mr. Townsend. Your broker called. That is all. (*She disconnects, tears up the message briskly, and drops it in the wastebasket. The phone rings. She picks up.*) La Petite Bergère French Restaurant. (*She says this in a terrible American accent: La Pateet Burjer.*)

WOMAN'S VOICE I'd like to—

SUE We're closed for all of August. (*She disconnects. Ring*) Susanswerphone.

GIRL'S VOICE (*Gushing with happiness*) This is Miss Stevens—

SUE Yes, Miss Stevens. No messages.

GIRL'S VOICE Oh—you must be the other one. Where is—?

SUE (*Annoyed*) She'll be on later, Miss Stevens.

GIRL'S VOICE I just wanted to tell you ... Mr. Humboldt and I are getting married—(*Giggles*) So from now on we'll have *one* account with you together—instead of two.

SUE Oh. Well—congratulations. (*She unplugs, looks stricken*) Oh!

GWYNNE (*Barely looking up from her reading*) What happened, Sue?

SUE We just lost an account. I'll bet Ella had something to do with this. Ella!

ELLA (*Off stage*) I'm just cleaning the canary's cage. Be right in!

SUE (*Calling to her*) Ella! Miss No. 63 and Mr. No. 78 are getting married—!

ELLA (*Running in excitedly with the bird cage. She is blond, pretty—with a quick mind and vivid imagination that help her improvise in any situation. Warm and sympathetic, she loves her job and regards her subscribers as personal friends though, of course, she has never met them*) Ohhh, good! When did it happen?!!

SUE (*Suspiciously*) Ella, did you—?

ELLA (*Suddenly defensive, then with great innocence*) I had nothing to do with it. I just happened to know that Miss No. 63 wanted to mate her female Siamese cat and I also knew that Mr. No. 78 had a male Siamese cat—so I told her and she called him—and they *all* got together.

SUE (*Shaking her head*) My cuckoo cousin! (*Getting up*) Take over the board, please—but remember—an answering service is not the Department of Welfare!

(*She starts putting things on as* ELLA *sits at board.*)

I've told you a thousand times—you're too darn friendly with the subscribers.

> (*ELLA starts nodding her head in rhythm with this oft-heard speech and mouthing the words with her*)

> *Just give and take messages—that's all. I'll be back later.* (*She starts out, sticks head back through the window*) *I'm warning you, Ella—watch it!*

> (*She is gone. The phone rings*)

ELLA (*Her phone manner is always warm and personal. More than that, she actually assumes a different character for each subscriber, and throws herself into these continually, with an effortless abandon. At this moment she answers the phone with a flawless French accent*) La Petite Bergère Restaurant Français. *Bonjour!*

MAN'S VOICE I should like to make a reservation for—

ELLA I am sorree, we are closed for all of Auguste.

MAN'S VOICE Thank you.

ELLA De rien! (*Unplugs. Ring*) Susanswerphone.

MRS. MALLETT'S VOICE Hello. This is Mrs. Mallett. Is this Santa Claus?

ELLA Yes, Mrs. Mallett. Put Jimmy on.

JIMMY (*Child's voice*) Hello, Santa Claus.

ELLA (*Assumes booming Santa voice*) Ho, ho, ho! Jimmy! I hear you won't eat your spinach again. That makes Santa very sad. Ho! Ho! Ho!

JIMMY Ohhh—all right, Santa Claus. I will. Goodbye.

ELLA Goodbye. (*Unplugs. Ring*) Susanswerphone.

MADAME GRIMALDI'S VOICE (*Rich and operatic*) Hello! This is Rosina Grimaldi!

ELLA Oh, how's your laryngitis?

MADAME GRIMALDI'S VOICE (*Executes a coloratura trill. ELLA looks delighted and holds headpiece away from her so GWYNNE can hear*) And I owe it all to you and your wonderful mustard plaster!

ELLA Oh, I'm so glad! And listen, that mustard plaster is so pure, if there's any left over, you can put in on a hot dog.

MADAME GRIMALDI'S VOICE I'm very grateful! I'm sending you beautiful ball gown made for *Traviata!*

ELLA Oh, you mustn't! (*Click. ELLA unplugs, excitedly*) Hey, Madame Grimaldi's sending me a ball gown made for *Traviata.* (*Pause—suddenly disconsolate*) When will I ever wear it?

GWYNNE You could put it on every time Jeffrey Moss calls.

ELLA (*Innocently*) Jeffrey Moss?

GWYNNE Oh, come on. You melt every time you hear his voice.

ELLA I don't know what you're talking about. I wonder what he looks like?

> (*Ring. ELLA sits on a stool at the side of the switchboard, plugs in*)

GWYNNE Well let's see—about 80 years old, long furry tail—

ELLA Jeffrey Moss residence.

OLGA'S VOICE (*A whining screech*) Can I talk to Jeffrey, please?

ELLA (*With a weary, resigned look at* GWYNNE, *indicating "it's that one again"*) Who's calling?

OLGA'S VOICE You know who's calling! It's Olga! I've called four times already. I've been waiting since eleven for him to take me to the *races*. I can't wait around all day for him to take me to the *races*—for heavens *sake*!

    (*Click.* ELLA *disconnects.*)

ELLA (*Rising—mimicking* OLGA'S VOICE) The *races!* That's all he needs— to be taken to the *races!* As if he hasn't got enough trouble as it is.

GWYNNE Why don't you stop worrying about that playboy!

ELLA He's not a playboy! He's a very talented playwright.

GWYNNE Yeah—but all he does is play. He never writes.

ELLA He's only been doing that since his partner left him—He's afraid to write alone. You don't know him the way I do—He's sensitive—he's intelligent—he's—I wonder what he looks like—

GWYNNE (*Removing her smock*) Look—the Sleeping Prince is number 37 on the board—He's just Plaza O-double four double three.

ELLA Oh, Gwynne, he doesn't mean any more to me than any other subscriber—(*Alarm clock sounds. She rushes to turn it off*) Six thirty! I've got to wake him again. He checked in at seven this morning as usual and I've been calling him since two.

    (*She sits at the board and applies fresh lipstick.*)

GWYNNE (*Watching all this*) Yeah.

CARL (*The delivery boy from the drugstore enters with an order as* ELLA *dials*) Hi, girls. Mind if I take the short cut?

ELLA Sure, Carl—go ahead.

    (CARL *crosses in front of the switchboard, and exits.* GWYNNE *pours coffee for* ELLA *and places it on switchboard.*)

JEFF'S VOICE (*A hoarse, gravelly groan that seems to issue from some Stygian cave forlorn*) Uhhhhh.

ELLA (*Using little old lady's voice*) Hello, Mr. Moss.

JEFF'S VOICE (*Feebly conscious*) Oh, is that you, Mom?

ELLA It's six thirty—time to get up. Your producer, Mr. Hastings, called and I have another message for you. Just a minute—(*She looks through messages*)

GWYNNE Aren't you ever going to give up that old lady's voice you use with him?

ELLA (*Flatly*) He needs a mother.

    (GWYNNE *shakes her head, picks up her purse and exits with farewell gesture*)

Mr. Moss? You asked me to repeat this message to you: "Get up, you gin-soaked idiot, and write your play, *The Midas Touch.*"

JEFF'S VOICE Beautiful prose. Tell you what, Mom—call me back in a coupla hours.

ELLA Oh, no, Mr. Moss...

(*She sings a few notes of "Reveille" in a coy, sunny little soprano. JEFF'S VOICE counters with a weary rendition of "Taps" that fades away in sleep as he hangs up. She resets the alarm with a sad smile, then sings:*)

It's crazy—it's ridiculous—it doesn't make sense,
That's true—
But what can I do?

I'm in love
With a man—
Plaza O-double four, double three,
It's a perfect relationship—
I can't see him—He can't see me.
I'm in love
With a voice—
Plaza O-double four, double three.
What a perfect relationship—
I talk to him and he just talks to me.

And yet I can't help wond'ring
What does he look like?
I wish I knew!
What does he look like?
Is he six-foot-seven or three-foot-two?
Has he eyes of brown or baby blue?
Big and mighty or underfed?
Trim black moustache or beard of red?
Can he dance like Fred Astaire?
Is he dark or is he fair?
Pompadour or not a hair?
Well, I don't care!

I'm in love
With a man—
Plaza O- double four, double three.
What a perfect relationship—
And that's how things should always be.
Our love can never lose its mystery,
'Cause I'll never meet him and he'll never meet me.
No, he'll never meet me.

What does he look like?
My sleeping prince?
What does he look like?
He could be the fat and balding type,
Or rugged tweeds and a briar pipe,
Dark-rimmed glasses—super-mind,
Or the sweet, poetic kind.
It doesn't matter what he'd be—
How he'd love me.

(*A ring interrupts and brings ELLA back to reality.*)

Susanswerphone.

JEFF'S VOICE Hello. Mom? If Olga calls again, stall her for me, will you?

ELLA Yes, Mr. Moss.

JEFF'S VOICE That's good old Mom.

ELLA (*Very let-down*) Yes, Mr. Moss.

> (*He hangs up. She unplugs, shaken out of her dream, then sings*)
>
> He's still just a voice—
> Plaza O-double four, double three—
> What a perfect relationship—
> I can't see him—He can't see me.
> He calls me Mom; he thinks I'm sixty-three—
> And I'll never meet him and he'll never meet me.
> No, he'll never meet me.
>
> (*She flops down resignedly into the armchair. Two men,* BARNES *and* FRANCIS, *enter. They "case" the room quickly.* ELLA *turns to them*)

Hello.

BARNES (*Elaborately polite*) Uh—how do you do! My name is Barnes.

ELLA Yes, Mr. Barnes?

BARNES We're doing some—uh—research on answering services—for—uh—

> (*He seems to have forgotten his lines and turns to* FRANCIS, *who mouths* Fortune.)

Fortune Magazine. We'd like to ask you a couple of questions?

ELLA (*Excited and flattered*) Oh, of course! Please make yourselves at home! I'm having coffee—I'll wash out some more cups.

BARNES (*Watches her exit into bathroom*) Thanks. Thank you very much.

> (*As soon as she is out, his manner changes abruptly. He is an aggressive, not overly bright detective.* FRANCIS *is his timid, sensible assistant.*)

Francis, the minute she gets on the phone, turn on that tape recorder.

FRANCIS Are you sure about this, Inspector Barnes?

BARNES *Mr.* Barnes, you meathead! I'm going to get a promotion for closing this joint.

FRANCIS But just because the law arrests all those girls at "All-Alone—A-Phone" doesn't mean every answering service is a front for a—"lonely hearts club." She seems like such a nice girl—

> (BARNES *silences him as* ELLA *enters with cups.*)

ELLA Well—now what can I tell you?

BARNES (*With a coarse grin as he looks her up and down*) Well, let's see—Tell me—how do you like your work?

ELLA (*Open and chatty as she pours and serves the coffee*) Oh, I love it here! I used to be just a plain switchboard operator—in a lingerie house—Pretty dull except for a little modeling on the side.

BARNES (*Leering*) Modeling on the side, huh?

ELLA But here it's all so personal. I talk to so many different kinds of people—and can give each one the particular kind of help he needs. My cousin Sue thinks I spend too much time on each one. She says, "Get it over fast and on to the next!"

202

BARNES (*Exchanging look with* FRANCIS) Yes, of course.

>   (*Ring.*)

ELLA Oh, excuse me. (*She goes behind the board and plugs in.* FRANCIS *places a small tape recorder on top of the switchboard*) Madame Grimaldi's.

BARITONE VOICE Ees Madame at home?

ELLA No, the Madame is out.

>   (*They are listening intently.*)

BARITONE Are you her answering service girl?

ELLA There are several of us. Which girl do you want?

BARITONE The mustard plaster one.

ELLA (*Pleased*) Oh, that's me.

BARITONE Madame Grimaldi raved so—could you give me the formula—and how much do you charge?

ELLA Charge? Oh, for a friend of Madame Grimaldi's, it's free!

BARNES (*Grabbing her*) Okay, sister! Hang up!

ELLA Oh, excuse me. I'm sorry, sir. Good-bye. (*Hangs up and turns to* BARNES, *who has pulled her out of her chair*) What *is* this?

BARNES Get your toothbrush and come along.

ELLA My toothbrush?

GWYNNE (*Coming in*) What's going on here?

BARNES What do *you* do?

GWYNNE I work here.

BARNES (*Grabbing her*) Maybe you better come along, too.

SUE (*Entering*) Why girls, what are these men doing here?

BARNES Who's *she?*

SUE (*Angrily*) I happen to own this place—that's "who's she." What do *you* want?

BARNES (*Revealing badge with satisfaction*) We're closing up this joint. You're all coming along. Women's Detention Home—Inspector Barnes, Vice Squad!

SUE (*Gasping, almost fainting, to* ELLA) I knew it! I knew you'd get us in trouble! I warned you!

ELLA (*Completely baffled*) But, Inspector! What did we do wrong?

BARNES (*Terribly pleased with himself*) I'll just let you speak for yourself. (*Turns on tape recorder and and they all listen*)

ELLA'S VOICE "Madame Grimaldi's. No, The Madame is out. Which girl do you want? There are several of us. Oh, that's me! Charge? Oh, for any friend of Madame Grimaldi's, it's free!"

>   (ELLA *reacts with that look of surprised and approving enjoyment at hearing one's own voice played back.*)

BARNES (*Moving in for the kill*) Now, which one of you is the Madam?

ELLA (*Starting to explain reasonably*) That's Madame Rosina Grimaldi, the opera star, and I happened to recommend a mustard plaster to her for a cold, and this friend of hers—Ohhhh! (*With sudden realization*) Have *you* got a *dirty* mind! (*Very strongly, angry now*) Okay, Inspector, you take me down to the Women's Detention Home! Before I get through with you, I'll have you demoted to a chicken inspector!

SUE (*Witheringly*) And here's our list of subscribers, Inspector!

> (*She hands him the list.*)

BARNES (*Looking at it—dejected*) All right! I made a mistake—

ELLA Ha! (*She goes to sit at the board*)

BARNES *Maybe.*

FRANCIS (*Shaking his head*) Always in such a hurry to uncover a crime. I keep telling him—get the evidence like all the others do.

BARNES (*Furious*) Shut up!

> (*A face appears at the window.*)

SANDOR (*Through the window*) Liebchen!

SUE (*Flustered and excited*) Sandor!

"Ohh! Have you got a dirty mind!

SUE (Jean Stapleton), ELLA (Judy Hollday), INSPECTOR BARNES (Dort Clark)

SANDOR (*Entering. He is seedy, but suavely Middle-European. He speaks with a Continental accent, and has the silky charm of the professional con man*) Ah! My dear Sue! I—

BARNES Who's that?

SUE (*Showing him off proudly*) This is my new partner! Sandor, this is Inspector Barnes.

ELLA (*Astonished*) Partner!

SUE And this is the staff—Gwynne Smith and my cousin, Ella Peterson.

SANDOR (*Smoothly, as SUE watches him adoringly*) Charmed! Allow me to present myself—J. Sandor Prantz, President of the Titanic Record Company—purveyors of classical music—Titanic Records, the highest fi of them all! This lovely lady has persuaded me to move my recording enterprises here and join forces with Susanswerphone to expedite a wide expansion program on an over-all top urban saturation basis.

BARNES (*Taken in by him*) Uh-huh! Uh-huh! Well, Professor, she'll tell you what's been going on here.

> (*To ELLA:*)

I'll be around—and I'll be listening in.

ELLA Monitoring the phones?

BARNES Any personal or friendly talk or direct contact, little lady, and I close this joint—but quick! Come on Francis!

> (*He exits.*)

FRANCIS (*Sympathetically*) Please take care, miss. You know, it's illegal to pass on information you receive to subscribers—even for a mustard plaster—

BARNES (*Off stage*) FRANCIE!

> (*FRANCIS exits, exchanging an understanding wave of the fingers with ELLA.*)

SUE Oh, Sandor, when I came in the Inspector was about to take us all to the Women's Detention Home.

> (*Ring. ELLA plugs in.*)

ELLA Kramer Music.

VOICE Message for Kramer. This is Morty Hopper of the Pyramid Club. We need some songs fast, so Friday, 10 A.M., we're gonna have a lotta song writers in to peddle their fish. Got that?

ELLA (*Writing*) Ten a.m. Friday, Pyramid Club—song writers' auditions. Thank you. (*Disconnects, then starts dialing happily*) Hey, what an opportunity for Dr. Kitchell! He can take his songs there—and—

ALL ELLA!

ELLA (*Unplugging—very much upset*) But if he could only sell one song it might change his whole life.

SUE All right! What business is that of yours? Dr. Kitchell is a dentist and he'd rather be a song writer.

SANDOR Now, Sue, don't upset yourself. Sandor is here. He will look after things. Well—*Aufweidersehen.*

(*He starts to leave.*)

SUE Oh, Sandor—aren't you taking me to dinner?

SANDOR My dear Sue—I am desolate, but I must go to an important board of directors meeting of Titanic Records—and tell them of our new million dollar expansion program for Susanswerphone. Oh, by the way, I seem to have nothing but twenties and fifties with me. Do you have a couple of singles to spare? You know these cab drivers.

SUE (*Takes some money from her purse and hands it to him*) Here you are, Sandor.

SANDOR (*Kissing her hand*) Thank you, *Liebchen!* Good night, girls! *Aufwiedersehen!*

(*He exits. Ring.*)

ELLA Susanswerphone—

HASTINGS' VOICE (*Angry and disturbed*) This is Larry Hastings calling. Any messages? Jeff Moss call?

ELLA No, but Blake Barton, the actor, called. Wanted to know if there's a part for him in your new production, *The Midas Touch.*

HASTINGS' VOICE Blake Barton! That imitation Marlon Brando! Listen, I'm only hiring actors who show up in a suit and without a mouthful of marbles!

ELLA Oh, thanks! I mean—good-bye.

(*Disconnects and starts dialing eagerly, with a delighted chuckle.*)

SUE Ella! What are you doing?

ELLA I'm just calling Blake Barton—

SUE Ella!

BARTON'S VOICE Hello. Blake Barton here.

ELLA (*Looks up at* SUE, *shocked and hurt—then speaks in a cold, impersonal voice*) Susanswerphone.

BARTON'S VOICE (*With the slurred, faltering diction typical of the legion of would-be Brandos*) Oh, hiya, girl. Thanks a lot for that tip the other day, but No-Lucksville, Montana. They were lookin' for a Rex Harrison type—English—so I says, "Whatsa matter wi' me? I speak English."

ELLA (*Frustrated*) No messages.

BARTON'S VOICE Crazy, girl.

ELLA Crazy. (*Disconnects*) You mean I can't even tell him about wearing a suit and about his marbles?

SUE That's none of your business!

ELLA Well, if that's what it's going to be like around here, I might as well be back at the Bonjour Tristesse Brassière Company!

(*Pause.*)

SUE (*Concerned*) Ella, I'm sorry, but I worry about you. I mean, all these people on the switchboard you think of as your friends—you don't really know them. They don't care about you—

GWYNNE And that includes the Sleeping Prince, Ella.

SUE Yes—Jeffrey Moss—Remember he's just another telephone number, too.

ELLA (*Sighing, resignedly*) You're right, all right.

> (*SUE works at the table.* GWYNNE *is buried in magazine.* ELLA *sings, wistfully, to herself*)
>
> It's crazy, ridiculous; it doesn't make sense—
> But what does he look like?
> I wish I knew.
> What does he look like?
>
> (*Music builds to a rhythmic climax and blends into sound of a loud phonograph record as the set revolves to* JEFF MOSS' *apartment.*)

"That's none of your business!"

ELLA (Judy Holliday), SANDOR (Eddie lawrence), SUE (Jean Stapleton), GWYNNE (Pat Wilkes)

Act One
SCENE 2

SCENE 2

The rather nondescript living room of an expensive East Side bachelor apartment. Stage left are JEFF's desk and typewriter. Stage right, a few steps lead up to the front door and house phone. Stage center is a large couch. The telephone is on top of a console phonograph to the left of the couch. There is a small but noisy party in progress. About seven couples are dancing, drinking, and talking animatedly. One of the guests, FRANK, hears the phone ringing above the din and picks it up.

FRANK (*Yelling above the racket*) Hello! Hello! Hey—quiet! (*He switches off the phonograph*) Quiet everybody! I can't hear. (*Back to phone*) Who? Just a minute. (*He starts walking around the room, looking for the person in question, the long telephone wire trailing behind him*) Jeff! Hey—Jeff! Jeff! Hey—it's for you!

> (*A prostrate figure on the couch sits up and takes the phone. It is JEFF, who has been hidden by several ladies clustered about him. JEFF is an unusually good-looking young man, with a face that reveals both high intelligence and the easy self-indulgence of one who knows he can muddle through life on sheer charm. He dresses carelessly but well. At the moment, he is obviously pleasantly loaded.*)

JEFF Hello! (*He looks unpleasantly surprised, but continues confidently*) Oh, Olga!—Yeh—Oh—the races! I'm sorry honey, but I'm having a conference on my play.

> (*He turns toward his guests and mutters several weird syllables of gibberish reminiscent of crowd noises on a bad radio program. He motions to them to pick it up, and for a few seconds the air is filled with these heated earnest sounds from all—as JEFF holds up the phone for good, clear reception. He motions for quiet, much in the manner of a radio director, and resumes his conversation on the phone.*)

Yeah, I've been working. Call you tomorrow morning, honey. Good-bye. (*He hangs up.*)

GIRL Working? Is this the way *all* writers work?

JEFF Honey, it's not what's on paper that counts. It's what's up here—(*He taps his head significantly*) My play is all ready. One of these days I just crank my ear and it comes out in book form.

ANOTHER GIRL And wins the Pulitzer Prize, of course—

JEFF Of course! I have my speech all prepared.

> (*He puts his arms around two of the girls and speaks in humble but portentous tones.*)

Gentlemen—today you are honoring me for my maiden solo effort, *The Midas Touch.*—

> (*Loud applause and cries of "Hear! Hear!"*)

But I must decline.

> (*Murmurs of disappointment . . .*)

It is prize enough to know here—(*He indicates the area of his heart*) that I could accomplish this Herculean task without my ex-writing partner, George Livingston, and that I've learned the great lesson of independence.

> (*He leaps up on a chair and, waving a glass of whiskey aloft, sings the following oration:*)

You've got to do it!
You've got to do it!
Got to do it all alone.
Just listen to me—
That's the way to be.

Independent, self-sufficient.
Got nobody to rely on.
Independent. Self-reliant.
Crave no shoulder I can cry on.
Now I'm livin'—I'm on my own.
Goin' it alone.

I don't need anyone and no one needs me.
No need for anyone to help me
Mix martinis, roast the weinies, bake the blinis
Now that I'm free.

Self-sufficient, self-supporting,
Travelin' light and flyin' solo—
Every day is Independence Day—
Hooray!

Free and easy, blithe and breezy—
Going it alone.
I'm independent and on my own

(*The guests cheer him wildly as he downs the toast to himself. At this moment, the house phone rings and JEFF dashes to answer.*)

Hello! What? Oh Larry Hastings?! Tell him I'm not here. Tell him I'm dying. Tell him I went away for the weekend. Tell him—

(*As he is talking the front door opens and LARRY HASTINGS enters in time to hear most of the conversation. LARRY is a well-dressed, formidable-looking man of about forty.*)

LARRY Hello Jeff.

JEFF (*Pleasantly, revealing not the slightest trace of being taken aback*) Hi, Larry! (*Back to phone*) Tell him—never mind, I'll tell him myself.

(*With one sweeping gesture, he hangs up, puts his arm around LARRY and propels him into room.*)

Now, Larry, I wanted to tell you about the second act—

LARRY (*Affably*) I'm sorry to barge in when you're having a party—

JEFF (*Elaborately casual as he mixes LARRY a drink*) A party? Couple of friends drop in while I'm taking a five-minute siesta from my work, and he calls it a party! Folks, you all know Larry Hastings—he's my producer! Now, Larry, don't look like ulcers on parade. I've been working. In a couple of days you just back the ol' Mack Truck up to the door and we load the script on!

(*He hands LARRY the drink.*)

LARRY (*Grins, and sits heavily on sofa as though planning to stay for several weeks. Then outdoing JEFF in elaborate casualness*) Well, I'm relieved to hear it. Guess I've been just a finicky old fussbudget—getting so edgy just because I haven't seen a line on paper since that rough first act—six months ago!

JEFF (*Expansively*) Why, Lar—I wouldn't let you down. Who's the guy who told me I could write without my partner? And who got Paul Arnold to sign up to star in my play—sight unseen? Larry boy!

LARRY (*Chuckling*) Oh, incidentally, Paul Arnold's in town—just got in today—and he can't wait to hear the last two acts, Jeff. I tried to stall him, but I'm afraid you'll have to come to my office—sometime tomorrow—and give him at least an outline. Twelve o'clock all right?

> (*Having dropped his bomb, he rises and walks up the steps to the door.*)

JEFF (*Seemingly unruffled*) Twelve? (*With a very British accent*) Wizard, old boy! Twelve on the dot!

LARRY (*With a very grim smile*) And, Jeff—if you don't show, Paul's going to walk. And you know what else? So am I. I mean it, Jeffie boy. I've had it. It's your last chance. Well, good night, Jeff.

JEFF G'night, Larry.

LARRY (*As he goes*) Good night, everyone!

JEFF (*After a somewhat ghastly pause*) He's a million laughs, once you get to know him. (*Resuming his party manner*) Well—drink, anyone?

> (*The guests—until now frozen—are suddenly galvanized into activity of quick departure. They retreat, hastily muttering ad-lib good nights.*)

GUEST (*Leaving*) I guess we'd better be going, Jeff—

ANOTHER GUEST (*Sympathetically*) Jeff—will you be all right?

JEFF Sure—sure—A deadline's the best thing for a writer—gives him *incentive!* Something to aim at! Builds a fire under him—

> (*They are gone. He surveys the empty room littered with half-empty glasses and cigarette stubs.*)

Nothing like a nice cozy fire creeping up your trouser leg! Well—gotta get to work.

> (*The phone rings.*)

Oh shut up! (*He answers*) Hullo?

ELLA (*Mom's voice*) Mr. Moss, Mr. Hastings called and—

JEFF Yeah, I know, Mom. He was here. I've got to work tonight—all night. I don't know what time I'll get to sleep, but you've got to wake me at seven o'clock.

ELLA (*Mom's voice*) Seven A.M.?

JEFF Seven A.M.

ELLA (*Mom's voice*) Don't worry, Mr. Moss—I'll wake you. Good night!

> (*He hangs up. He looks lost—then dials quickly.*)

ELLA'S VOICE Susanswerphone.

JEFF Mom?

ELLA'S VOICE (*Changes to Mom's voice, uses it throughout the following telephone conversation*) Oh, yes—Mr. Moss.

JEFF Uh—have you got any time to talk to me tonight?

ELLA'S VOICE Well, I—uh—

JEFF You know—I thought maybe we could chew the fat for a few minutes—shoot the breeze a bit—I—uh—Mom—I'm afraid.

ELLA'S VOICE You mustn't be.

JEFF I know—You've told me that a thousand times—but it's my last chance.

ELLA'S VOICE Mr. Moss, you can write alone—I know you can—

JEFF (*With sudden determination*) Mom, you're right! And I will!

> (*He hangs up. With a look of high resolve, he sings to himself in pep-talk fashion, rather gradiosely reminiscent of Nelson Eddy exhorting his stout-hearted men.*)

> You've got to do it!
> You've got to do it!
> Got to do it all alone!
> No one else'll do it for you—
> Buddy boy! You're on your own.

> (*He hurls himself into his chair in front of the typewriter and is broken out of his manful spell as he takes several thoughtful swigs of his Scotch and soda.*)

Now let's see—the important thing is to get the first line of dialogue down on the paper. Harry says—Harry says—(*He pauses as he picks up his glass again*) I'd better set the scene first. Griswold's living room—a stuffy Victorian Mansion—Harry is seated in the armchair, stage right—Lovely touch. Enter Jenny Brewster. She looks at him; he looks at her. Then she says— she says—(*He thoughtfully strokes his upper lip with one finger as he leans forward to typewriter, his face seemingly set in creative concentration*) Wonder how I'd look with a mustache—? (*He rises*) Or maybe a beard. No, it would hurt my tennis game. Boy, I used to hit 'em pretty good. (*He executes several masterful tennis strokes*) Forehand! Zoom! Backhand! Whop! Little drinko! (*He drinks*) Whamo! Up to the net! The winner! (*He leaps imaginary net, and shakes hands with his imaginary opponent*) Thank you very much. Actually you play quite well for a loser. Really, you play very—THE PLAY! (*He rushes back to the typewriter, sings:*)

> You've got to do it!
> You've got to do it!
> Got to do it, all alone!
> No one else'll do it for you—
> Buddy boy! You're on your own.

All right—start some place else. Act Three, Scene Two—the public square. (*Pause. He rises*) Harry mounts the platform. He looks at the crowd; he clears his throat, and then he says—(*Rushes back to sit at typewriter with fingers poised over keys like a concert pianist*) Harry says—(*He looks down at his fingers*) Wouldn't it be terrible if I froze in this position? (*He rises*) It's the old writer's cramp. That's the trouble with us writers—never get any exercise— maybe a couple of push-ups—(*He stretches out with feet on the steps and hands on the floor. He does a brisk push-up and crumples instantly. He pulls himself together painfully and staggers to his feet*) You mustn't overdo it the first day. Oh well, I can get in shape when the play's on—THE PLAY!

> (*He rushes back to the typewriter, sings*)

> You've got to do it!
> You've got to do it!
> Got to do it all alone!
> No one else'll do it for you—
> Buddy boy!

> (*Suddenly all the Nelson Eddy in him is gone as he gazes dejectedly at the sheets of empty paper before him.*)

Aah, what's the use? I'll never make it alone! (*He disgustedly sweeps the papers off table. As he slumps in his chair, he reaches for the glass.*)

> *Curtain.*

SCENE 3

A disreputable-looking alley at night. Wash hangs on lines; ash cans and general refuse are visible. A nondescript crowd, including some gangster types—a barber, a bootblack, a doorman, a waitress, a pretzel woman, tarts, etc.—are waiting around with a conspiratorial air. SANDOR enters briskly, carrying his portfolio, and bangs on an ash can with his cane.

SANDOR Gentlemen! Gentlemen! (*The crowd comes to attention*) The first meeting of the sales force of Titanic Records Corporation is hereby called to order. In other words—(*He steps up on box*) Good evening, fellow bookies!

GIRL What's Titanic Records?

SANDOR That's us. The new headquarters of our little bookie ring will be located at Susanswerphone—where they are convinced that the Titanic Records Company is a record company. Now, the number one rule is we do not take bets on horses—(*Reaction from crowd*) we take "orders" for records.

GIRL I don't get it.

SANDOR (*Passing out charts as he steps down from the box*) Look these over, gentlemen. Peruse them carefully. Now, Louie, ask me about placing a typical bet—

LOUIE I'll bet five hundred bucks on the nose on Number 6 in the third race at Belmont.

SANDOR Splendid! Now consult your charts, gentlemen. As one of the agents for Titanic Records, you would call me up and say, "I would like to place an order (that's bet) for five hundred albums (that's bucks) long playing (that's on the nose) of Beethoven's (that's Belmont) Sixth Symphony (that's horse Number 6) Opus 3 (third race). I would like to place an order for 500 albums, long playing of Beethoven's Sixth Symphony, Opus 3!

> (*He chuckles and twirls his cane, highly satisfied with himself, and proceeds to teach them his simple little system. The crowd answers his questions, carefully referring to the charts each time. SANDOR sings*)

It's a simple little system any child can understand;
The composers' names, we list 'em with the racetracks of the land.
With this simple little system we'll be close by fortune's door—
And to think that no one ever, ever thought of it before!

Gentlemen, look at your charts!

What is Beethoven?

MAN

Belmont Park!

SANDOR

Where's Puccini?

MAN

Pimlico!

SANDOR

Who is Humperdinck?

MAN

Hollywood!

SANDOR

    What is Beethoven?

ALL

    Beethoven is Belmont Park

SANDOR

    Where is Puccini?

ALL

    Puccini is Pimlico.

SANDOR

    Who is Humperdinck?

ALL

    Humperdinck is Hollywood.

SANDOR

    That is correct! Turn the page.

    What's Tchaikovsky?

MAN

    Churchill Downs!

SANDOR

    Who's Moussorgsky?

MAN

    Monmouth Park!

SANDOR

    What's Rachmaninoff?

MAN

    Rockingham!

SANDOR

    What's Tchaikovsky?

ALL

    Tchaikovsky is Churchill Downs.

SANDOR

    Who's Moussorgsky?

ALL

    Moussorgsky is Monmouth Park.

SANDOR

    Who's Rachmaninoff?

ALL

    Rachmaninoff is Rockingham.

SANDOR

    That is correct! Turn the page.

ALL

    It's a simple little system—we're impatient to begin.
    It's a simple little system when the law is list'ning in.

SANDOR

    We will take those record orders in a very cultured tone,
    While we'really booking horses over at Susanswerphone!

ALL

    We'll be rich! We'll be rich! We'll be rich!
    Debussy is Del Mar; Humperdinck is Hollywood.

Cesar Franck is Fairgrounds; Sibelius is Sportsman's Park.
Berlioz is Bainbridge; Hindemith is Hawthorne.
Offenbach is Omaha—

SANDOR

Everybody! All together now!

ALL

Who is Beethoven?
Belmont Park!
Who's Puccini?
Pimlico!
Who's Tchaikovsky?
Churchill Downs
And Shostakovich is
Sar-a-to-ga!

SANDOR

What Is Handel?

ALL (*All, suddenly singing to strains from the well-known Handel oratorio:*)

Hialeah! Hialeah!
Oh, what a system!!!

(*The crowd clusters about* SANDOR, *congratulating him on his ingenious system.*)

Curtain

Rehearsal

Seated Center: Judy
Holliday

Right: Sydney
Chaplin

SCENE 4

Susanswerphone. It is early morning. ELLA is sleeping in the chair, in paja-
mas and a robe. The alarm clock on the switchboard sounds. She runs to
turn it off.

ELLA Seven o'clock! All right, Sleeping Prince.

> (*She takes out a mirror, checks her appearance, then starts dialing*
> *JEFF. The TELEPHONE INSTALLATION MAN enters.*)

TELEPHONE MAN Titanic Records?

ELLA Over there.

> (*He starts to connect the Titanic phones as ELLA dials again, a little*
> *disturbed because there is no answer.*)

Why doesn't he answer?

> (*The TELEPHONE MAN trails wires through the door and closes it behind*
> *him.*)

SUE (*Cheerily, as she enters with coffee and bouquet of flowers*) Good morning!

ELLA Good morning.

SUE Brought you some coffee.

ELLA Thank you.

SUE Come on. I'll take over. You've been on long enough.

ELLA (*Uneasily*) I'm just giving someone his call—

SUE (*Glancing at call slip, annoyed*) Jeffrey Moss—*that* one! He takes up more
time than all the other subscribers put together! Okay, Ella! All right, Ella!
Get up!

> (*She pulls out the plug—very impatient with ELLA—and practically*
> *dumps her out of the swivel chair.*)

ELLA (*Rising reluctantly*) Sue, it's a very important wake-up.

> (*Ring.*)

SUE See? Someone else was trying to get him.

> (*She answers as ELLA, hovering near, listens*)

Jeffrey Moss residence. No, Mr. Hastings. Cannot reach Mr. Moss. What is
the message, Mr. Hastings? Yes—(*She writes down message, reading in an*
impersonal manner as she writes) Quote.—If you don't show up at noon
today with outline, will drop *Midas Touch*. Have taken option on another
play. Hope you enjoy trip to Skid Row. Unquote.

ELLA (*Desperately, trying to get to the switchboard*) That's a very important message,
Sue. He's got to get that message! There must be something wrong!

SUE (*Forcefully*) Listen—all this nonsense is over! Just keep remembering one
thing—Inspector Barnes. Now, go out! Have a nice day! He's probably
unplugged his phone again, anyway.

TELEPHONE MAN (*Re-entering*) That's seven dollars and fifty cents for installation.

> (*SUE pays him as ELLA stands there looking helpless and distressed.*
> *Suddenly her face lights up, registering "Eureka!" and she rushes off*

to change into a street dress. SANDOR enters, carrying a bouquet of flowers concealed behind him)

SANDOR Good morning, *Liebchen!*

SUE Oh, Sandor! (*She rises, hiding her bouquet behind her*) Welcome to Susanswer-phone!

SUE & SANDOR (*Extending bouquets simultaneously*) For you!

(They laugh uncomfortably and exchange flowers.)

SANDOR (*Crossing to his table*) Splendid board of directors' meeting last night, Sue. (*One of the new phones rings. He sees them*) Ah, my telephones!

(He answers as SUE sits at the switchboard)

Titanic Records. Good morning. Yes? Fifteen hundred albums of Puccini's Eighth Piccolo Concerto, Opus 1. Right, we'll ship them right out. (*He hangs up. He picks up the other phone, the direct "warehouse" wire*) Hello. Shipping Department? Fifteen hundred albums of Puccini's Eighth Piccolo Concerto, Opus 1, *all three speeds.* (*He hangs up*) See? It's simple. You just pick up the phone, jot down the message, and ring the shipping department on this phone—it's a direct wire—then you give the message just as you got it.

SUE (*Admiringly*) Oh, Sandor—do you know all those pieces of music?

SANDOR (*Modestly*) I studied under the immortal Tsitsinger.

SUE (*Giggling girlishly*) Oh, Sandor, you're a genius!

(His phone rings again.)

SANDOR Your first record order, Sue.

(He watches as she picks up.)

SUE Titanic Records.

(CARL enters with some coffee from the drugstore.)

CARL Good morning.

(He places the order on the table near the door.)

SUE (*She writes*) Thank you. Hello Carl. (*She picks up direct wire phone*) Hello. Shipping Department? Seventy-five albums of Bach's Third Brandenburg Concerto, Opus 5, LP. Right.

SANDOR Splendid!

CARL (*With the avid interest of a record collector*) Hey—Titanic Records. Is that a new label?

SANDOR We have only the finest European recordings.

CARL Oh. Brandenburg No. 3. I have the Fritz Reiner recording. Who's on your label?

(He picks up folder from SANDOR's table. SANDOR slaps it out of his grasp.)

SANDOR (*With enormous authority*) The Dusseldorf Zyder Zee New Light Hanseatic League Symphony—under Karl Flucht!

CARL Flucht! Never heard of him.

SANDOR It's just possible, my dear boy, Flucht never heard of you. Now, please—We are very busy here.

CARL Sure. Sure. Sorry.

> (*He exits. ELLA comes out of the bathroom, dressed to go out.*)

SANDOR 'Morning, Ella.

ELLA (*In a great hurry*) 'Morning.

> (*She picks up her shoes near the switchboard and returns to sit in the big chair as GWYNNE enters.*)

GWYNNE Hi. (*To ELLA*) Where are you going?

> (*ELLA beckons her over for whispered consultation. Ring. SUE answers.*)

SUE Max's Dog and Cat Beauty Shop. Sorry, we don't open till nine o'clock. Thank you.

> (*She busies herself, with SANDOR, over his books.*)

GWYNNE (*Horrified whisper*) Are you out of your mind? Women's Detention Home!

ELLA Shhhh! Someone has to wake him. I'll just do it and leave.

GWYNNE The Inspector said no personal contact.

ELLA It won't be personal. He'll never know who I am.

GWYNNE How are you going to get in?

ELLA (*Breathlessly, about to dash out*) Oh, I'll think of something!

> (*Ring.*)

SUE Ella, take that, please.

ELLA (*Impatiently plugging in—anxious to leave*) Women's Detention Home! I mean, Max's Dog and Cat House!

> (*She looks horrified as she hears what she has said, drops the phone and dashes for the door.*)

Recording session Columbia Records, left to right:

Betty Comden, Goddard Lieberson (Center, President of Columbia Records), Buddy Robbins, Adolph Green, Jule Styne

Quick Curtain

SCENE 5

The street in front of Susanswerphone. INSPECTOR BARNES is waiting outside the door. ELLA, carrying her handbag, comes running out, unaware of him.

BARNES Hello, there!

> *(ELLA stops dead, as if shot, then starts on.)*

Hey!

> *(He dashes over, blocking her way.)*

ELLA (*Overly casual*) Oh, hello, Inspector!

BARNES (*With an evil, suspicious grin*) Sorry about our little misunderstanding last night.

ELLA (*Uneasily, trying to leave*) That's all right. It could happen to anybody.

BARNES (*He again blocks her way*) Where you going?

ELLA Oh—uh—shopping.

BARNES Maybe I ought to come along—

ELLA Oh, that won't be necessary.

BARNES What are you shopping for?

ELLA A—a dress—

BARNES What color?

ELLA Uh—green!

BARNES (*Melting*) Green! Green! My favorite color.

ELLA (*Relieved, thinking she's free*) Mine, too.

BARNES (*Stopping her again*) I don't know what you're up to, but I'm going to keep my eye on you. You seem to be a pretty confused kid.

ELLA (*Realizing she will have to "con" her way out of his clutches, and batting her eyes at him in helpless-ingenue fashion*) Oh, I am—I'm *very* confused. I need advice. I don't mean to be on the wrong side of the law, but sometimes I can't tell right from wrong—I wish you'd help me.

> *(BARNES stands puzzled and transfixed as she gradually wears him down with her naïve and helpless questionings—calculated to wring tears from a stone. She sings)*

> Mother and Dad handed down to me
> A bit of their old philosophy.
> I've stuck to it like an obedient daughter,
> But it always lands me in hot water.
> I'd gladly follow out your suggestions
> If you'd give me the answers
> To these questions.
> Please tell me—
>
> Is it a crime to start each day
> With a laugh and a smile and a song?
> And is it a crime to end each day

With a laugh and a smile and a song?
Is it wrong?

Is it a crime to call the world your valentine?
Is it a crime to grab a lamp post
And then sing "Sweet Adeline"—
I ask you—

Is it a crime to save a wee baby bird
When it falls from its nest?
That little bird should have a chance
To fly like all the rest.

If it's a crime to help old ladies cross the street,
Then put me in jail!
Without bail!
Bread and water from an old tin pail
If that—if that's a crime!
Is it a crime—

Inspector Barnes, I'm puzzled
We're taught two things as we go through life:
    One—Be thy brother's keeper
        and
    Two—Mind your own business.
With a laugh and a smile and a song,

Now, if I knew something—and by telling it to someone in distress,
I could change that someone's life and bring him
The blue bird of happiness—

Is it a crime to tell him?
Or is it a crime not to?
Is it you mustn't
Or—you got to?
Should you say, "Hey, watch out for that banana peel, bud!"?
Or be silent—then laugh as he
Crashes with a thud—

Inspector Barnes, my job is to get messages to people on time—
If I have a job
And I see it through,
And it's just my duty
That I do do do,
Is that—is that—

(He wipes away a furtive tear.)

Inspector Barnes—let's go back a few hundred years.
If there had been answering services—and it had been up to me—
I could have prevented many a famous tragedy—
I could have changed the course of history—with a laugh and a
smile and a song.
Why, every night I lie in bed and my cheeks get soaking wet
When I think what I could have done for
Romeo and Juliet.

(She lifts an imaginary phone.)

Hello. Veronaphone. Oh, yes Mr. Romeo. Juliet Capulet called.
The message is: "To avoid marriage with other fellow am playing
dead. Friar Lawrence gave me great big sleeping pill. When I wake
up, we'll head for border." Oh, don't thank me. It's all in the day's

work—

(She hangs up the imaginary phone and turns to BARNES fiercely.)

See what I could have done?
Maybe I'm right!
Maybe I'm wrong!
But if I'd got that message through on time,
I'm telling you—
THOSE TWO KIDS WOULD BE ALIVE TODAY!
So—

(With a tremendous sob in her voice)

If it's a crime to help old ladies cross the street,
Then I'll confess
I'm just a mess.
Mother and Dad, you were wrong—I guess—

(In tears)

Inspector, were they wrong?

(BARNES is, by now, completely dissolved in tears. He silently pats her shoulder, shaking his head.)

Thank you!

(As the music swells, she turns with a dedicated look and starts walking off solemnly—then looks back at the blubbering BARNES—and dashes madly off stage as the music builds to a big finish.)

BARNES (*Wiping tears*) God bless her! There should be more people in the world like her. (*Still tearful, he calls off to FRANCIS*) Francie—

FRANCIS (*Entering*) Yes, Inspector?

"Hello"
From the MGM Film
Bells Are Ringing

JEFF (Dean Martin),
ELLA (Judy Holliday)

BARNES (*Suddenly very grim*) Francis! Follow that girl!!!

Quick Curtain

JEFF's Apartment. JEFF is still asleep on the sofa with one hand trailing on the floor. The doorbell is ringing—still he sleeps. The door opens and ELLA enters cautiously. She approaches JEFF and studies his face. As she stands happily stunned by his looks, her purse slides to the floor. Collecting herself, she clears her throat to waken him, but he only turns over. Cautiously, she walks over to the typewriter, takes the sheet of paper out of it, sees it is blank and crumples it in impatience. She takes a bottle off the phonograph, looks at it and bangs it down in disgust. The phonograph suddenly blares forth and she crouches out of sight at the end of the sofa. JEFF leaps up wildly, turns off the machine, and then slumps back on the sofa, clutching his head—a dazed, hung-over, nervous wreck.

After a moment ELLA slowly starts to crawl towards the door, past JEFF's sofa, hoping to get by him unnoticed. He sees her out of the corner of his eye and watches transfixed until she collects her purse and starts to creep up the steps to the door. He sits up slowly and taps her on the shoulder. She turns and they stare at each other.

ELLA (*Still crouching, very frightened*) Hello.

JEFF (*Suspiciously*) Hello.

ELLA (*Getting up*) Goodbye.

(*She bolts for the door, but he gets there first and bars the way.*)

JEFF Hey, wait a minute . . .

ELLA I—I must be in the wrong apartment! Well—I—uh—I had this seven o'clock call—I mean an appointment in the wrong apartment. I mean—this isn't 54 Sutton Place South, is it?

JEFF No. This is 64.

ELLA (*Trying to assume it's all settled*) Oh—well—

JEFF Now, wait a minute. I guess I can either call a cop or go back to sleep.

ELLA (*Earnestly*) Oh, don't do that! Please!

JEFF (*Returning to the sofa and curling up*) Never fear—I'm not going to call the police. I give you your freedom.

ELLA I mean—don't go back to sleep. It's past seven o'clock already.

(*She tugs at his ankle.*)

JEFF Look, lady—I don't mind your breaking in here in the middle of the night—Seven o'clock! I told Mom to call me!

(*He springs to the phone.*)

ELLA Excuse me, but your phone's unplugged.

JEFF Oh—oh, yeah. (*He plugs in cord*) I must have pulled this out last night when I was looking for something to hang myself with. (*Ring. He picks up*) Oh, hello, Mom? Oh, you're the other one. Mr. Hastings called? Taken an option on another play? He didn't say who's written it—Shakespeare? Tennessee Williams? Tennessee Ernie? No—never mind. G'bye. (*Hangs up, depressed. Rises*) Well, I might as well go to sleep forever. (*Notices ELLA is still*

BELLS ARE RINGING

there) G'bye, lady. (*He starts to pour himself a drink.*)

ELLA (*A little timidly but determined*) You shouldn't do that.

JEFF What—what did you say???

ELLA I said, you shouldn't do it. You won't be able to do your work.

JEFF (*Losing his temper rapidly, he takes her arm and ushers her to door*) Look, lady—I hope you won't be offended if I point out that my evil little habits are not exactly any concern of yours. Get the hell out of here!

> (*He pushes her out.*)

ELLA You won't do your work!

JEFF Thank you very much! (*He slams the door and comes back into room. Stops, thinks and dashes for door, calling to her*) Miss! (*He opens the door and falls back as ELLA, who has been standing just outside, practically falls into the room*) What work?

ELLA (*Backing him into the room*) Well, if you want to drink at this hour of the morning, there must be some work you're trying to avoid doing. I know from my own experience. When I had to do my homework in high school, I'd do anything to escape sitting down to do it. Mostly I'd sharpen pencils—you know—the yellow kind that say "Ticonderoga" on them? I'd sharpen one down to the Ticonderog—then Ticonder—then Ticon—and Tico and, finally, Ti and T—and then I'd have to start on another pencil. Anything but face that awful blank page.

> (*JEFF glances at his empty typewriter and reaches for a drink. ELLA continues, emphatically*)

Oh, go ahead and drink. Ruin your *last chance!*

JEFF (*Taken aback at her use of the phrase*) Last chance? Last chance to do what?

ELLA Oh—whatever it's your last chance to do. You look desperate to me.

JEFF (*Crumbling*) I'm about to be ill. You don't happen to have a cup of coffee on you, do you?

ELLA (*With a little smile*) Yes, I do.

> (*She takes a large cardboard container of coffee out of her bag, removes the cover, and passes it to JEFF, who takes it in open-mouthed astonishment.*)

JEFF (*Ready for anything*) And a prune Danish, please.

ELLA (*Again reaching into her bag, she produces a piece of cheese Danish*) Cheese.

JEFF (*By now amused and interested*) Listen, Miss—uh—

ELLA (*Improvising swiftly*) Scott—uh—Melisande.

JEFF (*Imitating her rhythm*) Moss—Jefferee. Sit down Miss Scott.

ELLA I can't because I have to go.

> (*She sits down next to him on the sofa.*)

JEFF (*Very much interested*) You know, now that my vision's cleared up and I can make out shapes and colors at six inches, you look pretty good to me. Your appointment doesn't seem very pressing, and I have nothing to do for the next six thousand years or so—

(He has put his arm around her.)

ELLA (*Leaping up*) That's just another way of avoiding your work—girls!! And you *do* have something to do. You have an appointment!

JEFF Who said so?

ELLA Your—your seven o'clock call. You stay up and start writing. You can write alone! You did once!

JEFF (*Rising, more and more amazed*) How do you know I did once?

ELLA Because—because—anyone who's a writer must have written something by himself once.

JEFF Did I say I was a writer?

ELLA No—but—you're not a plumber, are you?

JEFF No.

ELLA (*In a tone that implies "it's obvious"*) Well! But I guess you don't think so yourself or you'd be writing instead of running around all night and coming home at seven in the morning and sleeping all day.

JEFF (*Staring, astonished*) It's uncanny. Are you plugged into me somewhere I don't know about?

ELLA (*Worried*) No!

JEFF Do you know me from someplace!

ELLA No!

JEFF You're psychic!

ELLA (*Relieved, she lights up happily*) Yes! I'm very intuitive. I get feelings about people. I know a lot about you just from listening to you talk—and I get visions and—(*She stares straight ahead as if in a trance, nodding*)

JEFF What's the matter?

ELLA I've got one now! A vision of *you!*

JEFF What am I doing?

ELLA (*Tilting her head, still looking at vision*) Nothing. You're lying face down in the gutter.

JEFF (*Tilts his head to look too*) Stop it! You're scaring the hell out of me!

ELLA I'm sorry. That's what I see and my visions are never wrong—unless you *do* something, unless you act right now—

JEFF (*Rising, very disturbed*) All right. All right! Well, I've tried analysis—why not witchcraft? All right—I go the witchcraft route! We get the dolls, the pins, boil the water, get the drums! (*He does a bit of a drum dance*) You tell me what to do—I do it!

ELLA (*Rising*) Keep your appointment!

JEFF That's no good! I have to turn up with an outline of a whole play!

ELLA (*Forcefully*) Well, do as I say. Sit down at your typewriter!

JEFF (*Under her spell, he goes to the typewriter*) Yeah?

ELLA (*Standing over him*) And now!!

"So that's what you look like—at last I know."

ELLA (Judy Holliday), JEFF (Sydney Chaplin)

Act One

SCENE 1

JEFF (*Eagerly*) And now!!!

ELLA Write it!

JEFF (*Getting up from the typewriter*) I knew there was a catch to it! (*He reaches for his drink.*)

ELLA Oh, stop stalling! You're not so badly off! Why, I know a guy whose father is forcing him to be a dentist when he really wants to be a composer. The poor fellow sits up in his office composing songs on his air hose. No one's keeping *you* from doing what you want—except yourself. You're afraid everyone's going to think, "Oh, it was his partner who was the talented one!" So what! You're afraid what you write won't be important enough, so you don't write anything at all!

JEFF (*Walking away from her, visibly moved by her words*) Boy, do you know me.

ELLA Mr. Moss, you have. to have confidence in yourself. I don't even know you, but *I* have confidence in you.

JEFF (*Looking at her deeply*) You do?

ELLA Yes, I do.

JEFF You're crazy.

ELLA Yes, I know.

> (*They look at each other for a long moment, then he slowly crosses to the desk and sits down at the typewriter.*)

JEFF I'll try.

> (*ELLA picks up her purse and, feeling that her work is done, starts towards the door. He sees that she is going*)

I don't think I can do it unless you're here.

> (*She pauses for a moment, then comes back and sits on the sofa. JEFF types*)

Act Two, Scene One—outline—

> (*He breathes a heavy sigh as someone does who has accomplished a tremendous task. The music begins. He starts typing again, stops, pulls the paper out of the machine, crumples it and reaches for a drink. He looks at her, grins sheepishly, and returns to work. As he types, she watches him intently, then rises to stand behind him. She starts to place her hands on his shoulders, but withdraws them and just leans over, watching him work, with a radiant, loving smile, as the music builds.*)

ELLA (*Standing behind his chair—happily*)

So that's what you like
At last I know

You're better, better than a dream.
What you are is better far than a dream.
I tried to picture your face
But now I see you,
You're out of this world,
You're out of this sphere,
you're out of that outer space.

You're better, better than a dream.
What is real is more ideal than a dream.
To see and hear you,
To be so near you is better,
Better than a dream.

(At the end of her chorus spot dims down on her and comes up on JEFF and as as the musical vamp continues we see him pull the sheet of paper out of the typewriter and read it with a look of mingled pleasure and wonder. He begins to sing the counter melody to "Better Than A Dream." In the course of this chorus he rises and ends up full front and center of stage.)

JEFF

Can this be a dream?
Can I still be asleep on the couch there?
Can this girl be really here?
She seems to know by sheer intuition
How I landed in this condition.
Boy, does she know me—
And the way that I think,
The way that I drink,
The fact that I slept all year.
But it's not a dream
'Cause, look, I've got some words on the paper.
Steady, boy, don't faint or scream.
Don't ask who sent you this angel
It's better, better than a dream.

(As he finishes his chorus, ELLA steps forward and stands next to him, spot picking up both of them with rest of stage in darkness, and third chorus is sung by both.)

(This third chorus is the song and counter melody sung together and is sung most ecstatically while retaining the nature of two separate interior monologues.)

ELLA	**JEFF**
You're better	Can this be a dream?
Better than a dream	Can I still be asleep
	on the couch there?
What you are	Can this girl
Is better far than a dream	Be really here?
I tried to	She really seems to know
Picture your	By sheer intuition
Face,	How I landed in this
	condition
But now I see you,	Boy, does she know me—
You're out of this world,	And the way that I think,
You're out of this sphere,	And the way that I drink,
You're out of that outer space	The fact that I slept
	all year .
You're better,	But it's not a dream 'cause
Better than a dream.	Look, I've got some words
	on the paper
What is real	Steady, boy,
Is more ideal than a dream.	Don't faint or scream.
To see and hear you,	Don't ask who sent you
To be too near you	This angel
Is better	It's better,
Better than a dream	Better than a dream.

Curtain.

SCENE 7

A street. FRANCIS is in a phone booth.

BARNES' VOICE (*Off stage*) Inspector Barnes speaking.

FRANCIS (*Reading excitedly from his report*) Inspector, she's with a man named Moss—Jeffrey Moss.

BARNES' VOICE Moss—let's see. He's a subscriber! No. 37. Francis, we're on the right trail!

FRANCIS 37

BARNES' VOICE What did she do?

FRANCIS She bought a bag of peanuts and threw them at some pigeons. Then she had a Fudgcicle.

BARNES' VOICE Is that all?

FRANCIS No—He came down about an hour later, looking kind of dazed. Then it started to rain—

BARNES' VOICE Cut the weather report! Where are they now?

FRANCIS (*Making it all sound ominous and significant*) Well, he tried to get a cab. She kept saying they'd never get a cab and they should take the subway; he kept saying they'd get a cab, and he ran down the street with her, yelling "Taxi! Taxi!"

> (*The rumble of the subway can be heard, very loud now.*)
>
> *The lights fade.*

SCENE 8

The Subway. JEFF and ELLA are standing, center. JEFF appears dazed. ELLA passes her hand before his face to attract his attention.

ELLA What's the matter?

JEFF He liked it! Larry liked it! I can't believe it!

ELLA Of course he liked it.

JEFF Yeah! Well, he isn't exactly tearing out the front page. He had a couple of criticisms—and he pointed out that it isn't exactly written yet. He made me promise I'd go to the country for a week and work. But by and large, it's something of a miracle.

ELLA It is not a miracle. You did it.

JEFF You know what?

ELLA What?

JEFF (*Turning her toward him and looking into her eyes*) You're the miracle!

> (*The subway lurches to a stop, doors open, people pour in, pushing and jostling. ELLA and JEFF are separated in crowd. They push toward each other until they are again together. JEFF looks around with displeasure.*)

Look—people.

ELLA What did you expect? Herrings?

(Another jolt. A man comes between them.)

JEFF But I feel like celebrating the miracle!

(Turns to her and finds himself face to face with the man. Pushes him aside. ELLA and JEFF exchange looks.)

Do you mind? We ought to be someplace—alone—or at least with some congenial people!

(A man—a real horror with a sour face—turns to face front.)

ELLA We have a car full of them.

JEFF Congenial! This band of cut-throats? Did you ever see such hatred? If I asked any one of them for the time of day, this would turn into a lynch mob.

ELLA *(Laughing)* Everybody wants to be friendly but nobody wants to make the first move. Why don't you say hello to that nice man over there? He'd appreciate it.

(She points to "the horror.")

JEFF Him? That's Dracula's uncle—The Wolf Man. The only thing he'd appreciate would be a nice fresh cup of blood.

ELLA It would be so easy. All you'd have to do would be to say "hello." Watch.

(JEFF shakes his head incredulously at her. She crosses in front of JEFF.)

Hello.

("The horror" turns with a look as though he'd eat her.)

MAN What did you say?

ELLA I only said hello.

MAN *(Amazed, and then starting to sob)* Hello? Hello? Did you say hello? This—this—is the first time anyone said hello to me on the subway in thirty years! Hello!

(Shakes her hand)

My name is Ludwig Smiley.

ELLA How do you do, Mr. Smiley. I'd like you to meet Mr. Moss.

SMILEY (MAN) Hello!

JEFF *(Incredulously)* Hello.

SMILEY *(To another man)* Hello. My name is Ludwig Smiley.

OTHER MAN *(Beaming)* Hello. I'm Charles Bessemer.

(CHARLES BESSEMER, in turn, says hello to the person next to him, and soon everyone is shaking hands with everyone else, happily shouting hello's. Each new person who has his hand shaken reacts suspiciously for a fleeting moment, then, happily delighted at this unexpected outburst of friendship, shakes hands and "hello's" whoever is nearest him. The happy buzz of conversation spreads like wildfire as people start moving about, waving across the car, and making new friends.)

BELLS ARE RINGING

JEFF looks about him, amazed and pleased, as he and ELLA join in the general handshaking and greetings. The occasion suddenly assumes all the aspects of a party as everyone sings a gang song of camaraderie.)

(*ALL sing, still shaking hands with one another*)

Hello, hello there!
Pleased to meet you!
It's a pleasure and a privilege!
Glad to know you!
How are you? Hello!

Hello, hello there!
Pleased to meet you!
It's a pleasure and a privilege!
Glad to know you!
How are you? Hello!

FIRST MAN

Let's have a party
And pour out the wine!

SECOND MAN

I've got salami!

THIRD MAN

So everything's fine!

*"Hello!
Hello There!"*

230

ALL

Let's sing together
And let out a yell
'S always fair weather
When we're singing—

Hello, hello there!
Pleased to meet you!
It's a pleasure and a privilege!
Glad to know you!
How are you? Hello!

(As the party progresses, there are sudden lurches when the train stops and a new batch of strap-hangers enters. They, too, are greeted with hello's and handshakes and quickly join in the fun. The carnival spirit grows—and finally, a group of four men enter and, as they become a part of the party, rapidly rip off their outer clothing, revealing the flamingly colorful costumes of acrobats. They are teeter-board artists. As one of the acrobats prepares to be hurtled off the end of the teeter board and land on a chair that is being held aloft by two of his fellow performers, the train lurches, there is a sudden black-out, and, as the lights go on again, we see that in some mysterious manner, instead of the acrobat, ELLA has been catapulted above into the chair. She graciously acknowledges the cheers of the crowd and the curtain closes on a final rousing chorus of the song.)

Quick Curtain.

SCENE 9

A street. The sun is shining brightly. Many of the people from the subway, including JEFF and ELLA, are emerging into the street. They are still bubbling with high spirits.

JEFF (*Laughing*) That's the best party I've been to in years. Hostess, thank you.

ELLA You're welcome. Drop in any time.

JEFF (*Looking up as if seeing some new cosmic phenomenon*) Hey! The sun! This is the first time I've seen the sun in years. Mom would never believe this! Hey, let's call her!

ELLA (*Transfixed*) Who?

JEFF Mom! That's the little old lady at my answering. service.

ELLA (*Brought back to reality and covering up*) Oh. Oh! I—I—Where are we? Fifty-third Street? I have to go out to Bay Ridge!

JEFF Bay Ridge?

ELLA Yes. I spend a lot of time out there—taking care of my uncle.

JEFF Uncle!

ELLA You don't believe I have an Uncle Gus in Bay Ridge?

JEFF Sure. If you told me the world was flat, I'd believe you. You're the only honest person I ever met in my life.

ELLA (*Troubled*) Honest person.

JEFF (*Looking at her tenderly, deeply*) If I couldn't believe in you—after all this—I'd crumble away like a piece of stale sponge cake.

ELLA (*Very disturbed*) Then believe me—I have to go.

JEFF But I'll be gone for a week. When'll I see you?

ELLA I don't know.

JEFF I'll call you from the country.

ELLA No phone.

JEFF Now wait a minute! You promise I see you a week from today—or I don't go at all. In fact, I tail you to Bay Ridge right now!

(*Agreeing ad libs from interested onlookers.*)

ELLA All right. All right! Your place—next Wednesday—six o'clock.

JEFF Promise?

ELLA Promise.

(*He kisses her cheek. She looks back at him, moved*)

Good-bye.

JEFF Good-bye.

(*She exits. JEFF calls after her:*)

Wednesday—six o'clock. And don't forget to bring the cheese Danish!

(He turns to center stage and, full of exuberance, sings out)

YAHOO!
I met a girl—
A wonderful girl!
She's really got a lot to recommend her for a girl,
A fabulous creature without any doubt.
Hey! What am I getting so excited about?!

She's just a girl
An ev'ry day girl
And yet I guess she's really rather special for a girl,
For once you have seen her the others are out.
Hey! What am I getting so excited about?!

But so what? What has she got others have not?
Two eyes, two lips, a nose—
Most girls have some of those
Yet when she looks up at me, what do I see?
The most enchanting face! My pulse begins to race. Hey!

I met a girl—
A marvelous girl!
She's rarer than uranium and fairer than a pearl.
I found me a treasure and I want to shout!
This is what I'm getting so excited about!
I met a girl and I fell in love today!

(He is carried off aloft by the cheering crowd.)

Recording session

Sydney Chaplin,
Betty Comden, Judy
Holliday, Jule Styne

BELLS ARE RINGING

233

Curtain.

SCENE 10

DR. KITCHELL's office. DR. KITCHELL is a sweet, ineffectual-looking, balding young man with glasses. He is playing a tune on the air hose. Then he sings as he writes it down.

KITCHELL

> I love your sunny teeth—
> Your funny, sunny teeth—
> They're like a pearly wreath
> That hangs over my heart!

ELLA (*Entering*) Hello.

KITCHELL (*Surprised at the strange face*) Hello?

ELLA (*Staring at him, delighted to meet him*) So you're Dr. Kitchell, the dentist!

KITCHELL (*Puzzled*) Yeah, isn't it wonderful! I'm sorry, I forgot we had an appointment. Won't you sit down? What did you say your name is?

ELLA (*Sitting in chair*) It started hurting as I was coming down the hall.

KITCHELL Oh, all rightee—(*Strikes dental mirror on tray, listens as if to a tuning fork and hums an "A"*) Open wide, please.

> (*Looks in her mouth with mirror*)

I don't see anything.

ELLA But it hurts.

KITCHELL (*Suddenly transfixed, sings, soupy-ballad style, staring ecstatically into space*)

> You don't see anything, but it hurts.
> Though you can't see the pain in my heart—
> Oh—oh—how it hu-u-rts!

> (*Returning to reality, he again addresses* ELLA.)

Is it sensitive to hot and cold?

ELLA Ummm-hmmm.

KITCHELL (*Again inspired, sings a rhythmic tune*)

> First you're hot—then you're cold,
> Then you're shy—then you're bold,
> But I'm always sensitive to you-ooooo!

ELLA Gee, those songs are pretty.

KITCHELL (*Excited*) Did you like them?

ELLA Oh, yes!

KITCHELL You're the first one. I lose more patients this way. I'm a terrible dentist. I make up songs all the time—and I can make up songs about anything—anything at all. Just give me a subject—a title—anything. What are you thinking of right now? Right off the top of your head!

ELLA (*JEFF on her mind*) Sponge cake!

KITCHELL Sponge cake?

ELLA No—uh—*The Midas Touch!*

KITCHELL Ah. "The Midas Touch"—about a king—and the gold—and—that's simple.

(*He starts singing:*)

The Mi-das Touch!
The mighty—mighty—mighty Midas Touch!
That Midas wanted gold so much—

ELLA (*Interrupting*) That's brilliant! Well, I guess you'll be there.

KITCHELL Huh? Where?

ELLA Pyramid Club. Friday at ten o'clock. They're auditioning songs.

KITCHELL (*Bursting with excitement*) I'll be there at nine-thirty.

(*FRANCIS has appeared at the transom over the door. He snaps a picture.*)

ELLA You write that down now.

(*As KITCHELL writes, she slips out the door.*)

KITCHELL (*Turning around*) Golly, I don't know how to thank—

(*She has disappeared. He goes to door, opens it, calling:*)

Oh, miss! Oh, miss!

(*Then, suddenly inspired again, he sings*)

Oh, Mississippi steamboat around the bend—
Whooo! Wooo!—

(*He rushes to write it down.*)

Quick Curtain.

SCENE 11

A street. BARNES and FRANCIS enter. BARNES is looking at a picture and checking the subscriber list.

BARNES Let's see—uh-huh—Dr. Kitchell—Number 33—

FRANCIS Inspector, I'm sure she ain't no lady of the evening.

BARNES (*Thinking*) Kitchell. A dentist, huh? I've got it! It's a front for a baby-selling racket. Come on.

FRANCIS She seems such a nice girl—

(*They start off, but turn aside as KITCHELL enters, carrying sheet music—on his way to the audition—and crosses hurriedly, looking for an address. FRANCIS follows him. BARNES exits in the opposite direction.*)

Quick Curtain.

Act
One
SCENE 1

Act One
SCENE 12

"Crazy!"

Left: BARTON (Frank
Aletter)

Right: ELLA
(Judy Holliday)

SCENE 12

A drugstore. Several "Brandos," all dressed alike in jeans and leather jackets, are lounging about, reading Show Business, Variety, *etc. Two of them exchange inarticulate grunts, "Uhhh," while looking at* Variety. *The CLERK is behind the counter. BLAKE BARTON enters, dressed like the others. When he speaks, it is with the hesitant, slurred speech these actors think is an imitation of their idol.*

GUYS Uhnhh—

BARTON Uhnhh—

ONE GUY Hey, Barton, did ya get da part in *The Midas Touch?*

BARTON (*Strokes hair down on his forehead*) Naah. How about you guys?

ALL (*Stroking their hair with the same gesture*) Sssss. Naah!

BARTON (*Going toward the counter. In the "Hey, Stella" delivery*) Hey, Jooeeey—

CLERK (*Wearily*) Yes, sir!

BARTON Gimme—uh—uh chocolit sundae—with the hot fudge action—and look, honey boy!—(*Grasps him by lapels*) no crushed nuts. One crushed nut and, man, I'm steamed—

> (*ELLA, wearing flats and leather jacket and motorcycle cap, enters. All look at her; all scratch their stomachs; ELLA scratches with them, in rhythm.*)

ELLA (*Speaking like the rest of them*) Whose motorcycle 'sat out there?

ONE GUY 'At's Barton's.

BARTON Crazy, ain't it?

ELLA (*Snaps fingers and kicks*) Cuckoo—

ALL (*Same gesture*) Cuckoo.

ELLA (*To the CLERK*) Hey, Fellaaaa! Gimme unhh double banana split—two scoops with plenny the jazz-anna extra saucer for my marbles. (*Takes several marbles from her mouth and deposits them in saucer which the CLERK holds out to her*) So you're Barton, huh? Havin' any luck?

BARTON (*He takes from his pocket a white woolen mitten and pulls it on while speaking*) Naah—thought I had a chance at that new show, *The Midas Touch.* I coulda been a contender—but—I—I—dunno—

GUYS (*Doing the same with mittens*) Uhhh—I dunno—

ELLA D'j' ever try wearing a suit?

> (*All freeze, shocked.*)

BARTON What? I can't do that! What d'ya take me for? A traitor? We gotta name for actors dat wear suits. I ain't turnin' Walter Pidgeon for nobody.

ELLA Sure! Be a punk imitation the rest of your life! I'm tellin' ya! If you want da job, you gotta cut da blue jeans action! Look around ya! You're a glut on the market. You're *nothin'!*

> (*BARTON looks around at the others, realizing the truth in this. At this point, FRANCIS appears, snaps a picture and exits, unnoticed.*)

BARTON Okay! You're right! I'll do it!

ELLA (*Happily, resuming her own speaking voice*) Brooks Brothers! Forty-fourth and and Sponge Cake!—*Madison!*

BARTON Cuckoo!

ELLA Cuckoo!

> (*She exits.*)

BARTON All right, come on fellas! On to Brooks Brothers! (*They turn from him as from a leper*) Okay! I'm not afraid of you. I'm going all the way! (*In a strong British accent*) Tennis, anyone?

> (*He does royal ballet leap and flies out the door.*)

> *Curtain.*

Act One
SCENE 13

SCENE 13

A street. BARNES and FRANCIS enter. BARNES is checking the subscriber list.

BARNES Number 52. Blake Barton. We got an actor, a dentist—I got it! She's probably pushin' dope! It's a dope ring!

FRANCIS But she seems like such a nice girl.

(*They start off, but turn aside as BARTON enters and crosses hurriedly with a Brooks Brothers box under his arm. FRANCIS follows him off. BARNES exits in the opposite direction.*)

Curtain.

SCENE 14

Susanswerphone. It is one week later. SANDOR is talking on the Titanic phone; GWYNNE is at the switchboard; SUE is seated at the table near the center door.

GWYNNE No, this is not Telanswerphone. This is Susanswerphone.

SANDOR Yes. Yes, that's fifteen hundred copies of Beethoven's Tenth Symphony, Opus 6, all speeds. Yes. Yes, that makes five thousand three hundred orders in all today on Beethoven's Tenth. Yes, we've had a splendid week.

(*He hangs up and goes toward the door.*)

SUE (*Stopping him*) Sandor—

SANDOR I was just on my way to watch them run off the Beethoven pressings at the Long Island plant. See you at dinner, *Liebchen. Aufwiedersehen!*

SUE Bye, bye!

(*SANDOR steps aside to let ELLA enter, then goes out. ELLA looks worried*)

Hi, Ella.

ELLA (*Subdued*) Hi. I'll take over, Gwynne.

GWYNNE (*Rises. ELLA sits at the switchboard. GWYNNE sits in the big chair*) What's the matter, Ella?

ELLA Oh—nothing.

SUE Well, see you later, girls. I'm off to the bank. *Aufwiedersehen!*

(*She exits. Ring.*)

ELLA (*Plugging in*) Mr. Linden's residence.

VOICE Hello. This is Miss Penny. Did he leave a message? For me?

ELLA Yes, Miss Penny. Mr. Linden will pick you up at twelve-thirty. He said to wear something high-priced and low-cut. It's a small party at the Gilbert Millers' for Ali Khan, Betty Kean and Harry Cohn.

VOICE Thank you. Good night.

ELLA Good night.

(*ELLA unplugs. The Titanic phone rings; she picks it up as CARL enters with an order and places it on table*)

Titanic Records.

GWYNNE Hi, Carl.

CARL Hi.

ELLA Yes? (*Writing*) Three hundred copies of Beethoven's Tenth Symphony, Opus 6, LP. Thank you.

GWYNNE Boy, is that a popular piece.

CARL Hey, there must be a mistake in that order. Beethoven only wrote nine symphonies.

ELLA Really?

GWYNNE But there have been so many orders for Beethoven's Tenth today.

CARL They gotta mean the Ninth. Tchaikovsky—six, Brahms—four, and Beethoven—nine.

ELLA Well, you sure know your music. I better tell the shipping department, huh?

> (*She dials. GWYNNE pays CARL.*)

Hello, shipping? I have an order for three hundred albums of Beethoven's *Ninth* Symphony, Opus 6, LP. Yes—and, look—change all the other orders you have for Beethoven's Tenth to Beethoven's Ninth. Sure I'm sure—

> (*Looks at CARL, who makes a reassuring gesture.*)

—absolutely sure. Thank you. (*She hangs up*) Thanks, Carl.

CARL Any time.

> (*He exits.*)

GWYNNE Well now, who's on the outpatient list for today?

ELLA Nobody!

GWYNNE I know what's bothering you. This is Wednesday, six o'clock—the return of George Bernard Moss.

ELLA (*Trying to cover her feelings*) Nothing is bothering me. I'm never going to see him again.

GWYNNE But you made a date with him for tonight.

ELLA But I'm not going to keep it. He thinks I'm the most honest person who ever lived. He never believed in anybody before. I *can't* tell him the truth. I can't! I'm not going to crumble the sponge cake!

GWYNNE The what?

ELLA (*Trying to assume a light air*) I got a good look at him—got him to work— Mission accomplished. I'm going to forget him. Never going to see him again—couldn't care less.

> (*Ring. ELLA answers*)

Susanswerphone.

JEFF'S VOICE Hello. Mom?

> (*At the sound of his voice, ELLA crumbles inside. She holds out the headpiece to GWYNNE, then snatches it back. GWYNNE leans on the switchboard.*)

ELLA (*Controlling herself. In Mom's voice*) Yes, Mr. Moss?

JEFF'S VOICE (*Bright and exuberant*) Listen, Mom—I've only got a minute—I'm unpacking, but I wanted to call you to thank you for the insane faith you've had in me. I have a chance of coming through for you after all. Got nearly two acts done. Don't know if they're any good, but they're there.

ELLA That's good, Mr. Moss.

JEFF'S VOICE Say, Mom—have there been any messages from a Melisande Scott?

ELLA (*Controlled*) No, Mr. Moss. Absolutely none.

JEFF'S VOICE Oh, well! I have a date with her for this evening.

OLGA'S VOICE Hello, Jeffrey.

(*ELLA freezes and gasps.*)

JEFF'S VOICE Olga—how did you get in here?

OLGA'S VOICE Oh darling I've been waiting for you. Oh Sweetheart—Oh Jeffrey!

JEFF'S VOICE (*Hurriedly*) Well—I—uh—call you back, Mom!

(*He hangs up. ELLA unplugs, jumps up, snatches her purse, and dashes for the door. Suddenly she stops and almost sits on a chair. She starts and stops several time—hesitating, frantic.*)

GWYNNE What's the matter?

ELLA (*Very offhand*) Nothing.

(*Suddenly ELLA lets out a hoarse animal scream, reminiscent of Sir Laurence Olivier's famous anguished cry in* Oedipus Rex, *and dashes out.*)

(*As the music comes up strong, the set revolves to JEFF's apartment.*)

SCENE 15

JEFF's apartment. OLGA, a flashy brunette, is with JEFF. He carries bags to a closet and puts them inside. He looks healthy, businesslike and well organized.

OLGA Oh, don't be a pill, Jeffrey. You can work some other time. They're waiting for us downstairs.

JEFF (*Impatiently*) Look, Olga. I'm not going to the trotting races in Yonkers. I have a business appointment here.

OLGA Business appointment—Ha!

JEFF And I'm going to work!

OLGA Look—if you think you're going to get rid of me that easily—

(*ELLA enters, slamming the door.*)

JEFF (*Happy*) Mel!

ELLA (*Breathless*) Hello, Mr. Moss!

OLGA Business appointment! Ha!

ELLA (*A demon*) I'm Mr. Moss's secretary.

(*Crosses to OLGA and backs her towards the door, imitating OLGA's screechy voice.*)

Listen, Mr. Moss has work to do. You're not going to waste his time dragging him to the races. Get somebody else to take you to the races.

(*OLGA flops back on the steps, dumbfounded.*)

Now, where were we, Mr. Moss? (*Goes to typewriter and sits down, very businesslike*) Act Twelve, Scene Nine, wasn't it?

JEFF (*Going along with it*) Yes, Act Twelve, Scene Nine—

(*OLGA, stunned, stares open-mouthed. JEFF helps her up.*)

You see, I really do have to work, Olga. Good-bye. Call you some time.

(*He sees her out. He looks at ELLA.*)

Hey, how'd you know about her—and the races?

ELLA (*Contemptuously*) It was written all over her face. She even looks a little like a horse.

JEFF I can't believe it. You're really here.

ELLA (*Gets up from typewriter uneasily, suddenly conscious of where she is*) I can't believe it, either.

JEFF (*Also a little uneasy*) Well, now that she's out of the way—let's take it from the top. You come in the door and I say, "How are you, Mel?"

ELLA I'm fine, thank you. How are you?

(*They are standing, somewhat uncomfortably, in the middle of the room.*)

JEFF *I'm* fine, thank you.

(*They shake hands.*)

ELLA (*Formally*) How did your work go?

JEFF Well, I didn't quite do five million pages. I rewrote the first act—and finished more than half the second—and only threw up forty or fifty times a

BELLS ARE RINGING

day. It went quite well, actually.

(She looks troubled.)

What's the matter?

ELLA Nothing

(He starts toward her.)

JEFF Oh—Mel—

ELLA (Avoiding him) Oh, no!

JEFF What is this! What did you come back for, anyway?!

ELLA I thought you needed a secretary.

JEFF A secretary!

ELLA You're pretty well fixed for girls.—But I guess you don't really need me so—so—I'll—

(She tries to get her purse from the sofa. He blocks her path.)

JEFF (Brusquely) All right—if you're here as a secretary—then get to the type-writer! What do you charge?

ELLA Nothing!

JEFF Come on!

ELLA (Angry and tense) Oh—a thousand dollars an hour!

JEFF (Looking at her, saying the first thing that comes to him) That sounds reasonable enough—and don't worry—I'll keep my grimy paws off you. Sit down!

(She sits, tentatively. He paces restlessly.)

Where were we? Act Twelve, Scene Nine. Señor Mendoza's Hacienda in Iceland. Old faithful Rodriguez is kneeling by his bedside. Never mind that—(Stops and begins again tenderly) Would you take down this message, please? It's to a girl—"Dearest"—that's the beginning of the message—

(He sings:)

Dearest—Dearest—
One thing I know—
Everything I feel for you
Started many years ago.

Long before I knew you—
Long before I met you—
I was sure I'd find you
Some day, some how.
I pictured someone who'd walk and talk and smile as you do,
Who'd make me feel as you do right now!

But that was long before I held you

(He crosses to stand behind her.)

Long before I kissed you,
Long before I touched you and felt this glow;

(Places hands on her shoulders)

But now you really are here and now at last I know

> That long before I knew you,
> I loved you so.

ELLA Is that all?

JEFF But you didn't write anything down.

ELLA I didn't have to—

(*She sings:*)

> Long before I knew you—
> Long before I met you—
> I was sure I'd find you
> Some day, some how.
> I pictured someone who'd walk and talk and smile as you do
> Who'd make me feel as you do right now!

(*He touches her cheek. She gets up, agitatedly, picks up her purse and starts for door. She speaks.*)

I really have to go!

JEFF Mel, you can't! You dropped into my life like a miracle! You saved me when I was drowning! You can't throw me back to the sharks! (*Simply*) Mel—I love you.

(*She hesitates, then dashes out. He sinks to the sofa, dejected. Suddenly, the door opens and ELLA returns—*)

ELLA (*Looking like the Statue of Liberty holding the beacon aloft*) If it's a crime to help old ladies cross the street—

(*She throws down her purse and leaps into JEFF's arms. They kiss passionately and happily as FRANCIS slips in the door, snaps picture, and exits.*)

Curtain.

Rehearsal picture "You see, I really do have to work, Olga. Good-bye."

ELLA (Judy Holliday), JEFF (Sydney Chaplin)

Act Two

SCENE 1

Susanswerphone. The following night. ELLA *is seated at the switchboard in a resplendent ball gown. It contrasts ludicrously with the drabness of her surroundings, as does her regal bearing and proud, queenly smile. The gown looks a little too theatrical for any normal surroundings. It clearly suggests grand opera and is, in fact,* MADAME GRIMALDI's *ball gown from La Traviata.* GWYNNE, *seated at stage left, is eyeing it dubiously as the phone rings.*

ELLA (*Picks up and speaks in a haughty British accent*) The Duchess of Windsor's residence.

VOICE Is the Duchess in?

ELLA The Duchess won't be back till after Labor Day.

VOICE Thank you.

ELLA Not at all!

> (*She unplugs the phone, rises and twirls about the stage, humming an air from* Traviata *as* SUE *enters.*)

SUE Oh, Ella! You look absolutely radiant! Like something out of *Traviata!* (ELLA *is deflated for an instant*) Something's happened to you since yesterday. You got in real late last night, didn't you?

ELLA I'm sorry—

SUE Oh, I'm tickled! If you found a fella you like—well, that's wonderful! (*Giggling*) I should know! (*To* GWYNNE) Well—I'll be back a little later to relieve you, Gwynne. (*To* ELLA) Have a good time, honey!

> (*Kisses finger and places in on* ELLA's *cheek.*)

ELLA You, too.

> (*Returns kiss.* SUE *exits.*)

GWYNNE Yesterday it was "man overboard." What's your excuse for seeing him tonight?

ELLA Woman overboard! And—besides—I can't let Madame Grimaldi's gown go to waste.

GWYNNE And he still doesn't know you're the dear little old lady of the switchboard?

ELLA (*Suddenly troubled*) No. I—I meant to tell him last night. But somehow I forgot. But I'll tell him tonight. I'll find the right moment and I'll just tell him. It shouldn't be so hard to do, should it, Gwynne? Should it?

GWYNNE (*Dubiously*) Good luck, honey.

> (*Steps on* ELLA's *dress and it rips when* ELLA *moves*)

Dandy. Here, we better shorten that.

> (*She helps* ELLA *up on the chair and rips off the lower ruffle.* CARL *enters with two sinister-looking men. They are the* HENCHMEN *of the Covello mob, the racing syndicate for which* SANDOR *works.*)

CARL (*To the* HENCHMEN) Is this the place you mean?

HENCHMAN Is Sandor around?

ELLA He's at the Crying Gypsy Café.

HENCHMAN Let's go.

"The Duchess of Windsor's residence!"

ELLA (Judy Holliday)

*"Oh, Ella, you
look absolutely
radiant!"*

ELLA (Judy
Holliday),
SUE (Jean
Stapleton)

(The men exit.)

CARL (*Looking at* ELLA) Wow!

ELLA Thanks.

CARL (*Yelling up to the street*) Hey, Pedro! Get a load of Ella!

> *(Down come several neighborhood characters who look at* ELLA. *They
> ad lib, indicating excitement and approval.)*

BOY Hey! Where ya goin'? That's some dress!

GIRL Oh, Ella! You look beautiful! Goin' to some big fancy society ball?

ELLA (*Charmingly offhand*) No, just a friend and myself. Just the two of us—El
Morocco, Pyramid Club—who knows?

CAROL (*One of the neighborhood girls, enters, carrying an evening purse*) Hey, Ella—
here it is! Does it go with it all right?

ELLA (*Taking the purse, delighted*) Perfect! Thanks, Carol.

ANOTHER BOY (*Entering with a red handkerchief*) Here's the handkerchief. My ma
just finished ironing it.

GWYNNE And don't lose this. It's copied from a very good copy.

> *(She puts a bracelet on* ELLA'S *wrist.)*

CARL (*Chagrined*) And I got nothing to give you. Hey! Maybe you could use a cha-cha lesson. You can't go dancing unless you know the cha-cha!

ELLA (*Defiantly*) I can mambo!

CAROL Not the same thing!

CARL You're dead if you can't cha-cha! Free lesson! Look!

> (*CARL and CAROL beat out the rhythm with their hands; ELLA picks it up.*)

ELLA What about my feet?

> (*They teach her the basic steps. At one point they do a more intricate step. She stops.*)

Sneaks!

> (*They all resume the simpler routine.*)

I've got it! I've got it!

"Me-cha cha? Senor, si-si cha cha."

ELLA (Judy Holliday)

(They lead her to a chair.)

BOY Now you're at the Pyramid Club.

ELLA I'm at the Pyramid Club.

GIRL And Carl's going to be there and he'll ask you to dance.

ELLA Oh, you're going to be there, Carl?

GIRL No—It's a game.

ELLA Oh, it's a game and I'm at the Pyramid Club and Carl's going to ask me to dance. O.K.

> *(CARL has removed his jacket, revealing a gaily colored shirt, and has picked up a straw hat. He seems suddenly transformed into a slinky, Latin-type male.)*

CARL (*Sings*)

    Aye, yi, yi, yi, yi!

ELLA

    Aye, yi, yi, yi, yi!

CARL (*Insinuatingly*)

    Mu-cha-cha, tell me, do you cha-cha?

ELLA (*In a coy, high squeak*)

    Me-cha-cha? Señor, si-si cha-cha.

CARL

    Now, cha-cha, please show me how cha-cha.

ELLA

    I got-cha—you watch-a cha-cha.

    (*She rises and they dance during the following.*)

CARL

    Hey, cha-cha, is this the way cha-cha?

BELLS ARE RINGING

ELLA

Si! Oh, cha-cha, away we go cha-cha.

CARL

Ay, cha-cha; I'm feeling high cha-cha.

BOTH

Oh, such a
hot-cha-cha
Cha-cha

ELLA

Come a little closer, then a little closer,
Then you turn and walk away.
Ay yi!

BOTH

Ta ta tum ta ta ta ta ta ti-ga ti-ga
Tum ta ta ta ta ta tiga-tiga
Tum ta ta ta ta ta ti-ga tiga
Tum ta ta ta ta ta ti-ga ti-ga.

""Mu-cha-cha!"
Center: CARL (Peter
Gennaro), CAROL
(Ellen Ray)

CARL

> Come a little closer, then a little closer.
> Don't go way, my little mu-chacha—
> The dance is through, cha-cha.

ELLA

> Now, cha-cha, let's have some chow, cha-cha.

CARL

> Then, cha-cha, we'll dance again, cha-cha.

BOTH

> Closer and closer
> And closer and closer
> And closer and closer to you
> Mu-cha-cha!

(ELLA exits, cha-cha-ing madly, to the cheers of her friends, who, caught up in the spirit of the rhythm they have created, continue their dancing, temporarily turning Susanswerphone into a Cuban dance hall.)

BELLS ARE RINGING

SCENE 2

A street bordering the park. At night. In the background are trees and a vista of the New York skyline. JEFF, in evening attire, is seated on a bench, waiting for ELLA. A man crosses. JEFF, with sudden happy inspiration, sings, "Hello, hello there!" as the man passes. The latter turns and looks at him with disbelief and extreme suspicion, then dashes off. JEFF shrugs and laughs, amused. At this point ELLA comes on—an unusual sight in her red ball gown, especially since she is still determinedly executing the cha-cha and muttering the steps to herself. JEFF rises, a trifle taken aback.

ELLA *(Breathlessly)* Hello. One—two—cha-cha-cha.

JEFF Hello.

> *(She continues to dance)*

Hey, wait a second!

ELLA I've just learned this. I don't want to lose it.

JEFF *(Laughing)* Don't you want to hear the news? Larry liked all the stuff!

ELLA *(In cha-cha rhythm)* Good! Good! Good, good, good! *(She sits, but continues the steps with her feet)*

JEFF And Paul Arnold, our star, is here from Hollywood.

ELLA Oh, good!

JEFF And Larry's giving a big party for Paul tonight.

ELLA Good! I hope they all have a swell time.

JEFF And we have to go—

ELLA *(Stopping suddenly)* Oh, no!

JEFF I have to, darling. Paul Arnold's the star of my show.

ELLA *(Uneasy)* But—but I don't know any of those famous people—

JEFF So you'll meet them.

ELLA I don't want to. *(She rises and starts dancing again)*

JEFF Hey, I met all *your* friends on the subway. Don't be such a snob!

> *(She stops, laughs.)*

ELLA *(Referring to her dress)* But—is *this* all right?

JEFF It's magnificent—like something out of *Traviata*.

> *(Seeing her look suddenly crestfallen, he kisses her.)*

You look lovely.

ELLA But I thought we were going to go dancing—just the two of us.

JEFF All right, let's dance.

ELLA Where?

JEFF Right here.

ELLA In the park?

JEFF What's the matter? No guts?

*"My partner.
Miss Twinkletoes
Scott!"*

ELLA (Judy
Holliday), JEFF
(Sydney Chaplin)

(He starts dancing her madly across the stage.)

ELLA (*Laughingly protesting*) Stop it!

JEFF Don't you like dancing?

ELLA I love it!

(She snuggles close and they dance a few steps quietly.)

JEFF Actually, it's all *your* fault we have to go to a party! If I hadn't found you crawling around my floor I wouldn't have been invited anyplace. I could have been resting comfortably, face down in the gutter—remember? (*JEFF sings*)

> Just in time
> I found you just in time
> Before you came, my time was running low.
> I was lost,
> The losing dice were tossed,
> My bridges all were crossed—
> Nowhere to go.
> Now you're here
> And now I know just where I'm going;
> No more doubt or fear—
> I've found my way.
> For love came just in time;
> You found me just in time
> And changed my lonely life that lovely day.

(Several people have entered and are watching with interest.)

MAN (*Applauding*) Hey, you guys must be professionals.

JEFF (*Satirically*) Why, you rascal, you've been peeking. (*To ELLA*) Shall we do that little number we used to do in Chicago?

ELLA Where?

JEFF The stockyards. Are you ready, partner?

ELLA (*Falling into the spirit of the thing*) Let's slaughter 'em!

JEFF (*He dances a few steps, à la Astaire-Kelly, then indicates ELLA with a "take-it-away" gesture*) My partner. Miss Twinkletoes Scott!

ELLA (*Dancing toward him*) Nothing at all!

(She takes his hand and dances around him.)

JEFF Easy on the arm. It only bends one way—

(They continue a corny little song and dance routine, made up of scraps of old vaudeville and musical movie turns.)

BOTH (*Facing each other*) Tea for two and two for tea. One—two—three—four.

(JEFF dances away from her.)

ELLA Where are you going?

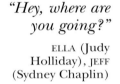

"Hey, where are you going?"
ELLA (Judy Holliday), JEFF (Sydney Chaplin)

JEFF Over here on one leg.

ELLA Wait for me!

> *(They continue dancing. As the dance reaches a "torrid" climax, ELLA almost delivers a "bump.")*

JEFF Hey, wait a minute! Don't give them everything.

> *(Ad libs from the crowd, wanting more. JEFF gets down on one knee. ELLA sits on his other knee. JEFF sings)*

> Just in time.

ELLA

> Do de do do do de do

JEFF

> I found you just in time

ELLA

> Do de do de do de do de

> *(She lets her handkerchief trail over his face)*

JEFF

> Before you came, my time—

ELLA

> Do do—

"Do de do de do de do …"

JEFF (Sydney Chaplin), ELLA (Judy Holliday)

Next page

"Just in Time"

ELLA (Judy Holliday), JEFF (Sydney Chaplin)

JEFF

Was running—

(ELLA rises and singing in a high-pitched, babyish voice.)

This act could play the Palladium
Or even the Yankee Stadium!

JEFF *(Rising)*

I was lost.

ELLA

He was lost.

JEFF

The losing dice were tossed.

ELLA

They were tossed.

JEFF

My bridges all were crossed.

ELLA

They were crossed.

JEFF

Nowhere to go

(JEFF and ELLA "conduct" the assembled citizens in two separate groups.)

CROWD *(Sings)*

Now you're here
And now I know just where I'm going;
Never a doubt or fear—
I've found my way.

(JEFF's and ELLA's eyes meet, and they suddenly forget the people and their vaudeville routine as they join each other center stage and kiss tenderly.)

JEFF *(Sings)*

For love came just in time;
You found me just in time

BOTH

And changed my lonely life that lovely day.

(They stroll off slowly, arm in arm, completely wrapped up in each other, turning for just a moment to wave fondly at the people, who wave back smilingly as they disperse.)

The lights fade.

SCENE 3

LARRY HASTINGS' penthouse apartment. A spacious, elegant living room, chic and tastefully modern, with large French doors in back opening onto a terrace. In the background are the twinkling lights of the city at night.

A large party is in progress—the men in evening clothes and the women in elegant sheaths, mainly of pastel shades.

As the curtain rises, the guests are grouped around the piano, applauding some smart bit of patter, no doubt. JEFF and ELLA enter happily. Several people turn to greet them. ELLA's vivid red ball gown creates a rather "fish-out-of-water" contrast to the modern elegance of the assembled ladies. The guests ad-lib greetings.

JEFF Hey, listen, everyone. This is Melisande Scott. Mr. and Mrs. Trent, Lenny Wendell, Dan Zachary, Mr. and Mrs. Courtney, Veronica Smith, and—

>   *(ELLA is saying how-do-you-do's, very much aware of how the girls are dressed and feeling them sizing her up.)*

PAUL ARNOLD (*A tall, good-looking chap*) Hello, Jeff!

JEFF Paul Arnold! Paul, this is Melisande Scott.

PAUL How do you do.

ELLA How do you do. I've admired your work in the movies—

PAUL Thank you, dear. (*To JEFF*) Listen, I read the script. I agree with Larry. I think it's coming along swell.

JEFF Thanks, Paul.

PAUL And we both liked that kid we auditioned today—Blake Barton. Okay to sign him for the part of the young dentist?

JEFF Blake Barton? Sure.

>   *(ELLA perks up happily upon hearing this bit of information.)*

PAUL Miss Scott, I hope you won't think I'm rude but I've got to drag Jeff off for about five minutes—a business talk with Larry.

JEFF I was afraid something like this would happen. (*He looks around and spots a friend*) Oh, Michelle!

MICHELLE (*A very, very chic and poised young lady*) Jeff, darling!

JEFF Michelle, will you look after Mel? She doesn't know the gang yet.

MICHELLE (*Looking her over*) I'd be delighted.

JEFF (*To ELLA*) Five minutes—that's all.

ELLA Oh, sure, I'll be fine,

>   *(JEFF and PAUL exit.)*

MICHELLE Oh, what a pity, darling. You just missed seeing Josh!

ELLA Ohhhhhh. Josh who?

MICHELLE Josh Logan!

ELLA (*Dubiously*) Oh.

(A small group passes by, talking animatedly.)

MAN I tell you it was dear diary night. Mary and Ethel sang for hours around the fireplace—

(To ELLA, who has, somehow, joined them.)

Oh, hello.

ELLA Hello. Mary and Ethel who?

FELLOW Mary Martin and Ethel Merman.

ELLA *(Feeling idiotic)* Oh.

(Another group drifts by.)

ANOTHER MAN Well, it was a pretty memorable gathering. All those wonderful people who'd been in the Theatre fifty years or more—Mary and Ethel and—

ELLA *(Eagerly, with great confidence)* Mary Martin and Ethel Merman!

MAN No. Mary Pickford and Ethel Barrymore.

ELLA *(Really confused)* Oh.

BUTLER *(He has been watching and notes ELLA's confusion and discomfort)* Don't be flustered, miss. Just do what the others do. Just drop a name.

(The following names are tossed out in rapid succession by the group, and a number develops between ELLA and the other guests—a sort of ritual, in which ELLA is the discordant note.)

Ed!
Murrow!
Noel!
Coward!
Sammy!
Davis!
Bennett!
Cerf!
Somerset!
Maugham!
Jennifer!
Jones!

Jose Ferrer and Janet Blair and Fred Astaire and Vincent Minelli
Daniel Mann and Lynn Fontanne, Elia Kazan, the former Grace Kelly
Louie Shurr and Courtney Burr and Irving Lazar
Anthony Quinn—

ELLA *(Triumphantly)*
And Rin-Tin-Tin!

ALL
Doris Day and Barry Gray and Edna Best
Arthur Loew and Vaughn Monroe, Rebecca West
Irwin Shaw and Evelyn Waugh, Errol Flynn
Rory Calhoun—

ELLA
And Rin-Tin-Toon!

ALL
> Barney Baruch and King Farouk, Alistair Cooke and Debbie and Eddie
> Lucille Ball and Lauren Bacall, Hedy Lamarr, Roz Russell and Freddie
> Carol Reed and Sammy Snead and Deborah Kerr
> Anna May Wong

ELLA
> And Rong-Tong-Tong!

MAN
> Luncheon was fun at Twenty One,
> Then I had to run for drinks at the Plaza.

GIRL
> Dined with Jean, Le Pavillon,
> Then flew right on to St. Mark's Piazza.

SECOND MAN
> Took a group for onion soup at dawn to Les Halles—
> It never shuts—

ELLA
> Like Chock-Full-O'-Nuts!

GIRL
> My Christian Dior I wore then tore,
> Got fitted for a new Balenciaga.
> Then to Jacques Fath for just one hat—
> Got something that will drive you ga-ga—

SECOND GIRL
> Valentina's where I've been; I just adore Val—

THIRD GIRL
> Things with *good* lines—

ELLA
> Like things from Klein's!
>
> *(There is a shocked silence, then ELLA continues grandly.)*
>
> I do all my shopping there with Mary and Ethel.

THIRD GIRL
> Mary and Ethel who?

ELLA (*Very flatly*)
> Mary Schwartz and Ethel Hotchkiss.

ALL
> Errol Flynn!

ELLA
> Rin-Tin-Tin!

ALL
> Edmond Gwenn!

ELLA
> Ren-Ten-Ten!

ALL
> Ali Kahn!

ELLA
> Rahn-Tahn-Tahn!

ALL
Raymond Massey!

ELLA (*Almost stopped, but coming through*)
Lassie!

ALL
THAT'S the way you play the game.
Drop that name!

(*ELLA, slightly stunned by her ordeal, stands with hand extended over head in the last gesture of the number until the group has drifted away into groups of threes and fours. She lowers her hand as JEFF enters.*)

JEFF Mel!

ELLA (*With hysterical alacrity*) Mel Ferrer!

JEFF Are you all right?

ELLA (*Taking his arm*) Oh—yes—

JEFF Sorry I took so long, darling—but, as a matter of fact, I spent most of the time talking about you.

ELLA About me?

JEFF And this is *the* Larry Hastings.

ELLA (*Highly interested. It is another subscriber*) So you're Larry Hastings!

LARRY So you're the wonder girl!

ELLA (*A little uneasy*) Jeff, what did you say about me?

LARRY Listen, if one-tenth of what this maniac says about you is true, you're fantastic! How did you do it? He claims you're the most brilliant woman since Madame Curie, and when I see the change in Jeff I think you're the greatest magician since Houdini! Thank you.

(*The guests begin crowding around her and, during the following, ELLA progresses from uneasiness to discomfort to embarassed despair.*)

MICHELLE My dear, I hear that you can tell all about people the second you meet them. It's spooky!

PAUL (*Entering*) Hey, Miss Scott, I've got to get a better look at you! Jeff's been singing your praises. From his description I pictured you in a turban with a crystal ball. He said you have the most fabulous intuition, the greatest intelligence, the deepest understanding and insight—

JEFF (*Putting his arm around ELLA*) It's all true—and not only that, she's a great deal prettier than Sigmund Freud.

MICHELLE May I come around some time for a character reading?

MAN Show us how you do it, Miss Scott. Do we have to turn out lights and all hold hands or what?

WOMAN Oh, I just love séances. Is that what she does?

JEFF (*Sensing that she is highly uncomfortable*) Oh, come on, gang—that's enough.

LARRY Let's all have some supper. Jeff, bring Miss Scott and come along—

(*All start towards the terrace.*)

ELLA (*Holding back, tensely*) Jeff.

JEFF (*To others*) We'll be with you in a minute.

ELLA (*Desperately*) Jeff, I want to talk to you. All those things you told them about me. I'm not really like that. I'm nothing like that.

JEFF What are you talking about? You're wonderful!

ELLA But you said I had "the most fabulous intuition," "the deepest insight"—I—

JEFF Well, it's true. You do—

ELLA (*Searching for the right words*) But, Jeff—suppose I didn't? Suppose I really weren't like that at all? Would it matter a lot to you? I mean, how would you feel about me? I mean, suppose—

JEFF What's all this supposing? That's what you are. That's why I fell in love with you.

> (*ELLA crumples visibly. He senses something is wrong.*)

Look—let's cut out of here. I'll say good night to Larry.

> (*He exits to terrace.* ELLA *looks after him. She is now standing alone.*)

ELLA (*Sings with a sort of trancelike resignation*)
He's in love with Melisande Scott,
A girl who doesn't exist.
He's in love with someone you're not,
And so, remember, it was never you he kissed.

The party's over—
It's time to call it a day—
No matter how you pretend
You knew it would end this way.
It's time to wind up the masquerade—
Just make your mind up—
The piper must be paid.
The party's over—
The candles flicker and dim—
You danced and dreamed through the night—
It seemed to be right, just being with him.
Now you must wake up—
All dreams must end—
Take off your make-up—
The party's over—
It's all over, my friend.

> (*With sad determination, she hurriedly writes a note to* JEFF, *leaves it on the couch and exits as—*)

The curtains close.

SCENE 4

Crying Gypsy Café. An East Side, sort of Yorkville-Mittel-Europa spot with a seedy mural depicting Emperor Franz Joseph surrounded by assorted danc-ing Bavarian natives in Tyrolean garb.

SUE is seated at a table; SANDOR is pacing hysterically; and the two Corvello HENCHMEN stand nearby—calm but menacing.

SANDOR But— it's impossible! A wrong order! Impossible! I must think—!

SUE Sandor, who are those gentleman?

SANDOR (*Wryly*) Two musicians from the Chicago Symphony Orchestra.

HENCHMAN Look, Sandor—you switched the orders. We're stuck with the wrong shipment, and Maestro Corvello says you'll have to cover the cost to the tune of five thousand, six hundred albums.

SANDOR Five thousand, six hundred albums! Gentleman! I am innocent—and I refuse!

HENCHMAN Well, in that case, Sandor, we may find it necessary to take you across the river for a recording session.

SANDOR A recording session—!?

HENCHMAN Yes. Maestro Corvello is waiting to record Siegfried's Rhine Journey and Funeral March.

　　　　(*SANDOR groans.*)

SUE (*Sweetly*) Sandor, don't let little business worries upset you. You'll get ulcers.

HENCHMAN Yeah. Perforated ulcers! We'll be back. You got two hours.

　　　　(*They exit.*)

SUE 'Bye, 'bye!

　　　　(*SANDOR groans and sits heavily, his face buried in his hands.*)

You've just got to learn to relax! You know, you need someone to look after you and keep you from driving yourself— Well—a woman.

SANDOR (*He leaps up and kneels beside her, taking her hand*) Sue—your saying so sweet thoughts makes it possible for me to speak. You see, Titanic Records is now affiliated with one of the biggest rackets—*record* combines—my English!—which in turn means more eventual expansion for Susanswer-phone. (*He is quite beside himself*) Sue—how much money have you got?? You must trust me. I am talking to you as someone who *may* love you

　　　　(*He kisses her hand.*)

SUE I have about sixty-five hundred dollars. It's at my apartment in a little blue sock.

SANDOR (*Simply*) Sue, I love you.

SUE (*Sings, ecstatically*)
　　　　You said it! You said it!
　　　　I heard you say it! Oh, Sandor!

SANDOR (*With gypsy passion*)
　　　　Sue, Sue, Sue, I love you, honey.
　　　　Sue, Sue, Sue, give me your money.
　　　　With your life savings in the little blue sock.

SUE

> We will have enough to keep us out of hock.

SANDOR

> We'll fly together to a place I know
> Where we oh so happy will be.

SUE

> Oh, where, oh where is this place of mystery?

SANDOR

> Where? Oh—
>
> *(Improvising quickly)*
>
> In Salzburg by the sea
> Where love and laughter live eternally
> In Salzburg by the hill
> Where gondolas go gliding by the mill.

SUE

> What a thrill, darling!

SANDOR

> Tropical nights!

SUE

> Festival lights.

SANDOR

> Strudel for two at the midnight bullfights!
>
> *(He spins her.)*

SUE (*In mad abandonment*)
> Arriba!

SANDOR

> In Salzburg, lovely Salzburg
> Where the flying fishes play—
> Where the schnitzel is high as an elephant's eye
> And the skies are not cloudy all day.
> Come to Salzburg with me—*Leibchen!* By the sea. *Olé!*
>
> *(He starts dragging her off the stage.)*

Come on, Sue.

SUE (*Thrilled and delighted*) Oh, Sandor, tell me more!

SANDOR You want more? *(Looks at watch, mops his brow and then reluctantly continues)*

> In Salzburg by the sea—
> Where all the world's in love with Gay Paree!

SUE

> You said you love me!

SANDOR

> In Salzburg on the shore—

SUE

> He loves me!

SANDOR

> Where Geisha girls keep coming back for more.

SUE

Sandor!

SANDOR

Liebchen!

SUE

We'll live in style—

SANDOR

Gold by the pile—

BOTH

Goulash for two as we barge down the Nile!
In, Salzburg, lovely Salzburg—

SANDOR

Where the corn and 'taters grow.

SUE

In our sweet home sweet home
All the roads lead to Rome—

SANDOR

So, my darling, let's hurry and go!

BOTH

Come to Salzburg with me—*Liebchen!* By the sea! *Olé!*

(He finally manges to get her off.)

Curtain.

Recording session

Left to right: Sydney
Chaplin, Adolph
Green, Betty Com-
den

SCENE 5

The Pyramid Club. A lush, gaudy café executed in the style of an Egyptian sarcophagus. It is hideous. JEFF and LARRY are at a table near the bar. JEFF is in a state of total dejection.

LARRY (*Rising*) Jeff, it's no use. We've covered every place in town. Come on back to the party.

JEFF She and I had a plan to go dancing here. I don't know the first thing about her—where she lives—how to reach her—

LARRY Jeff, let's go—

JEFF No, Larry, don't worry about *The Midas Touch*. I'll keep working.

LARRY Good.

> (*LARRY exits. BLAKE BARTON, the actor, now conservatively dressed in Brooks Brothers style, enters and goes to the bar.*)

BARTON Hey, daddio—gimme a double Old Rarity on the rocks.

> (*He spots JEFF and comes over to the table.*)

Say, Mr. Moss—

JEFF Yeah?

BARTON (*Eagerly*) Don't you know me? I'm Blake Barton. Gee, I love the part they set me for in your play today. You know—this young dentist—wantsa be a composer. It's a very interesting part. Where do you writers get an idea like that from? I mean where do you get 'em from?

JEFF (*With sudden fury*) Aaah, shut up, will ya!

BARTON (*Offended, starting to leave*) Excuse me, Mr. Moss.

JEFF (*Grabbing his arm, very sorry*) I'm sorry, Barton. I—uh—I feel rotten. Well, let's put it this way—I wish I were dead.

BARTON (*Seating himself*) Gee, Mr. Moss—I know how you feel. A couple of weeks ago I was lower than a duck's behind—hadn't worked in months— then, a miracle happened.

JEFF Please—no miracles. I got miracles of my own to worry about.

> (*FRANCIS and BARNES have appeared on the other side of the club.*)

BARNES (*Seeing JEFF and BARTON*) There's two of her sidekicks now. The third one must be around here some place. Francis, we're going to close in tonight.

FRANCIS Are you sure?

BARNES Positive. No one but me know she's Miss Big. It's a ring of counterfeiters. Come on.

> (*They duck off as fanfare sounds and the MASTER OF CEREMONIES enters and dashes to the center of the dance floor.*)

MASTER OF CEREMONIES And now folks, the Pyramid Club presents its new all-summer review, featuring music and lyrics by Joe Kitchell!

> (*Four DANCING GIRLS enter, dressed in brief attire. A corny number ensues, made up of all the bits we have heard DR. KITCHELL composing on the air hose in his office. The number is about on a par with the general decor of the club.*)

GIRLS (*Sing, in terrible voices*)
>> Oh,
>> First you're hot and then you're cold;
>> Then you're shy and then you're bold,
>> But I'm always sensitive to you.
>> First you fill my heart with pain,
>> Then your kiss is novacaine
>> But I'm always sensitive to you—

(As girls exit, an Elvis Presley-type SINGER comes to the microphone and sings as an adagio team performs, with the girl being hurled about in the customary fashion.)

SINGER
>> You don't see anything—
>> But it hurts!
>> 'Though you can't see the pain in my heart!
>> Oh—oh—how it hurts!

(Adagio dancers exit as four DANCING BOYS in gold jackets enter and sing and dance in rock-and-roll fashion)

BOYS (*Sing*)
>> The Midas touch, the mighty, mighty, mighty, mighty Midas touch!
>> The Midas touch, the mighty, mighty, mighty, mighty Midas touch!
>> The Midas touch! The mighty, mighty, Midas touch!
>> Gold in the morning; gold in the evening;
>> Gold in the summer; gold in the winter.

(DANCING GIRLS return in abbreviated gold costumes.)

GIRLS
>> Dr. Midas said to me,
>> "Be sure you take your vitamins G-O-L-D."
>> And that's what he said to me.
>> Hey!

(As the BOYS and GIRLS dance, they scatter great handfuls of gold dust on themselves and the customers. The Elvis Presley SINGER returns to conclude the number with the microphone turned up to a deafeningly loud pitch.)

SINGER
>> Gold in all its glory—
>> And that's the story
>> Of the Midas touch!

(As all the performers take their final tableau, a mighty shower of gold dust is released upon them from above. During the "Midas Touch" portion of the number, JEFF has been listening in growing bewilderment. As the applause dies down, DR. KITCHELL, now in street clothes, can be seen walking up and down among the tables in a state of happy excitement.)

KITCHELL (*Applauding*) Wonderful, wonderful—I wrote those songs. Great, wasn't it? I wrote those songs!

JEFF (*Stopping him*) You wrote that *last* song? "The Midas Touch?"

KITCHELL Yeah. Great title, isn't it?

JEFF I always thought so. Won't you join us?

KITCHELL (*Sitting, very pleased*) Thanks. My name is Joe Kitchell.

JEFF How do you do. Jeffrey Moss. Blake Barton.

> (*They shake hands.*)

Tell me, Mr. Kitchell—

KITCHELL It's *Dr.* Kitchell. Actually, I'm a dentist.

JEFF A dentist?!

BARTON A dentist?!

KITCHELL Sure.

BARTON That's *funny.* I'm a *dentist.*

KITCHELL You're a dentist?

BARTON No, I mean, I play a dentist in a play.

KITCHELL (*Rather surprised*) That's funny. Well, I'm not a dentist any more. I'm a composer now. My father didn't want me to be a composer, so he sent me to dental—

BARTON (*Disbelieving*) *My* father doesn't want *me* to be a composer—

KITCHELL He doesn't?

BARTON My father in the play.

KITCHELL (*A little staggered*) That's funny.

BARTON Very interesting part. Real funny and sad. You know—I make up these tunes on the air hose.

KITCHELL (*Totally stunned*) I wrote "The Midas Touch" on the air hose.

JEFF (*Who has been listening in quiet amazement*) So that's what's holding up the play. I was using paper.

KITCHELL What play?

BARTON The play we're talking about. He wrote it.

KITCHELL (*To JEFF*) You wrote the play?

JEFF Yeah. It's called *The Midas Touch.*

KITCHELL (*Filled with awe in the presence of the occult*) That's the name of my song!

JEFF Yeah, I know.

KITCHELL That's funny.

> (*They all stare at each other with wild surmise. They think they are going mad. Complete silence.*)

KITCHELL Oh, I remember now—I got that title from that girl.

JEFF What girl?

KITCHELL The girl that said she was thinking of "The Midas Touch" that day.

JEFF What day?

KITCHELL Oh, the day that changed my whole life. I was feeling lower than low—hopeless—and suddenly a miracle happened.

JEFF A miracle?

BARTON *He's* got a miracle, too.

KITCHELL This girl—she wasn't in the office more than a coupla minutes—tipped me off on this job—and I got it. She was blonde, pretty, about five-feet-six, big brown eyes—

JEFF & BARTON (*Both grab KITCHELL*) Wait! Wait a second!

BARTON Listen, Mr. Moss, that's how I got the chance at the part in your play! Some girl comes up to me in the drug store. She tipped me off about myself. I get the part. She changed my life! What I'm working up to is—she's blonde, five-feet-six, pretty, big brown eyes—

JEFF (*Leaping up, wild eyed*) Melisande!

BARTON & KITCHELL Who?

JEFF Melisande Scott! Where is she?

BARTON (*Rushing off, followed by KITCHELL*) He's flippin! Let's get outta here!

JEFF (*Catching them*) No—no—wait! This girl you're talking about is the same girl who dropped into my life.

KITCHELL (*Befuddled*) Same girl?

JEFF Yeah. When did you see her last?

KITCHELL She was in the office a couple minutes and disappeared. I never saw her again.

"A miracle?"
"He's got a miracle, too!"

JEFF (Sydney Chaplin), DR. KLITCHELL (Bernie West), BARTON (Frank Aletter)

BELLS ARE RINGING

BARTON Same with me.

JEFF (*Highly excited*) Look, you guys—I'm going to get to the bottom of this. I've got to find her. I'm in love with her. Where can I call you later?

BARTON I don't know where I'll be.

KITCHELL I don't know where I am.

BARTON (*Writing on match cover*) Look—I'll give you my phone number.

KITCHELL (*Taking card from his pocket*) I'll give you my phone number, too.

JEFF Thanks! (*He takes the matches and card and starts off.*)

BARTON Where ya goin'?

JEFF Bay Ridge! (*He is gone.*)

BARTON Good luck! Bay Ridge. Seems like a logical move.

KITCHELL When in doubt, I *always* go to Bay Ridge.

(*BARNES, FRANCIS, and the COPS enter.*)

BARNES Okay, you two! Come along.

(*KITCHELL and BARTON are grabbed in viselike grips by a COP.*)

KITCHELL Wait a minute! What *is* this?

BARNES You're coming to the station for some questioning.

BARTON Would this have anything to do with a blonde girl?

BARNES (*With big grin*) You said it!

KITCHELL & BARTON That's funny!

(*The COPS start to pull them off.*)

KITCHELL Wait!

(*They stop. He starts to sing.*)

That's funny—that you love me like you do!

(*The COPS pull them off as he continues to sing.*)

Quick Curtain.

SCENE 6

A subway platform. A sign reads Bay Ridge. A MAN *is in phone booth.* JEFF *is frantically looking through the phone directory. The* MAN *comes out of the booth.*

JEFF Excuse me—do you know anybody around here named Melisande Scott?

MAN You must be from out of town.

> *(He exits.* JEFF *throws down phone book and stands, discouraged, thinking of* ELLA.)

JEFF (*Sings, sadly, to himself*)
> I pictured someone who'd walk and talk and smile as you do—
> Who'd make me feel as you do right now!
> But that was long before I held you,
> Long before I kissed you,
> Long before I touched you and felt this glow;
> But now you really are here and now at last I know
> That long before I knew you, I love you so.

> *(He stands there for a moment, defeated. Then:)*

Kitchell. *(He takes the card from his pocket, enters phone booth and dials the number on it)*

SUE'S VOICE Dr. Kitchell's Dental Clinic.

JEFF Where can I reach the doctor?

SUE'S VOICE Dr. Kitchell left no message.

JEFF Is this—Susanswerphone?

SUE'S VOICE That is correct. Who's calling?

JEFF Never mind. *(He hangs up, puzzled)* Susanswerphone. *(He takes out the match cover and dials)*

SUE'S VOICE Blake Barton's residence.

JEFF *(More puzzled)* Susanswerphone?

SUE'S VOICE Yes . . .

> *(*JEFF *hangs up, steps out of booth.)*

JEFF *(Now extremely puzzled)* That's funny. Kitchell, Barton and me—all Susanswerphone. That was the other one I talked to—Mom—Melisande—(*A look of dawning realization comes over his face. Then, incredulously, softly*) Mom? (*Louder, convinced, Eureka-time*) Mom! (*Then yelling as if the sound could reach all the way to New York*) M—O—O—M!!!

> *(He dashes off.)*

> *Quick Curtain.*

SCENE 7

Susansweprhone. SUE is at the switchboard, looking troubled. ELLA, in street clothes, is finishing packing a suitcase, collecting belongings around the place.

SUE Well, I admit what you did was kind of extreme—but I know you were only trying to help. Please don't go, Ella.

ELLA I have to, Sue. I couldn't bear to hear his voice day after day.

SUE Ella, if you feel the way you do about him, you should tell him.

ELLA Oh, Sue, I can't. I don't want him to know it was all a trick. I've been walking and thinking for hours and suddenly it hit me. I'm not real. I've spent half my life tuning in on other people's lives, playing all kinds of imaginary characters—even with someone I fell in love with—and when the make-believe love became *real*, it had no place to go—because *I* wasn't real. Actually, it's what you've been telling me all along. I don't really know my subscribers—they don't really care about me.

SUE That's not true! Only today Mrs. Mallet called twice about her little son, Junior. He wanted to talk to Santa Claus. They always ask for you. They call me the *other* one.

ELLA The trouble is, I don't really know myself who I am. (*She sings*)

> I know you; your name is Sue.
> But who am I?
> I've gotta find out.
> At least—I'm gonna try.
>
> I'm going back
> Where I can be me
> At the Bonjour Tristesse Brassière Company
> They've got a great big switchboard there
> Where it's just "hello—goodbye—"
> It may be dull, but there I can be
> Just me, myself and I—
> A little modeling on the side—
> Yes, that's where I'll be—
> At the Bonjour Tristesse Brassière Company.
> And if anybody asks for Ella, Mella, or Mom
> Tell them that I'm going back where I came from—
> To the B. T. Brassière Company.

(*With exaggerated "blues" mannerisms:*)

> Goodbye, everybody—Goodbye, Madame Grimaldi—
> Goodbye, Junior Mallet—Santa Claus is hittin' the road—
> Listen to your mama, mama, mama.
> Eat your spinach, baby—Eat your spinach, baby, by the load—

(*Changing to French chanteuse style*)

> La Petite Bergère Restaurant—*adieu,*
> *Je ne reviendrai jamais—jamais—jamais*
> *C'est tous fini—Adieu*—to you.

(*In all-out "Mammy" style:*)

> I'm going back
> Where I can be me—
> To the Bonjour Tristesse Brassière Company—
> And while I'm sitting there, I hope that I'll find out

Just what Ella Peterson is all about
In that Shangri-la of lacy lingerie—
A little modeling on the side—
At the Bonjour Tristesse Brassière Company.

Send me my mail there!
To the Bonjour Tristesse Brassière Company.

(She exits with her suitcase but returns immediately.)

I forgot my canary.

(SANDOR enters, followed by the two CORVELLO HENCHMEN.)

HENCHMAN Come on Sandor! The money!

SANDOR (*Going to his books, checking the accounts*) In a minute! But first I must find out who changed those orders for Beethoven's Tenth to Beethoven's Ninth? Who could have done that?

ELLA Oh, I did. You know, Beethoven only wrote nine symphonies.

SANDOR (*Exploding*) You idiot! You put all the money on the wrong horse! I was almost bumped off for this by the Corvello mob!

HENCHMAN Shut up!

SANDOR To think my simple little bookie system could be loused up by this dumb broad!

ELLA Horses!

SUE Bookies! Sandor—is *that* what I gave you all that money for?

ELLA Sue, you didn't!

HENCHMAN That's swell, loud mouth! Now these dames know all about it!

SANDOR What's the difference! They can't talk! They're as much in this as we are. One peep out of them and the cops put them in jail and close up Susanswerphone!

SUE Oh, no!

HENCHMAN The money! Let's go!

SUE My life savings! Ella, please!

HENCHMAN Shut up!

ELLA (*Laughs wildly*) They don't get it!

SUE Get what?

ELLA (*To SUE, picking up the exact tone and manner of the HENCHMAN*) Shut up! (*To SANDOR*) Inspector Barnes!

SANDOR Barnes?

ELLA Barnz! B-A-R-N-Z!

SANDOR Z?

ELLA Z!! The whole thing was a trap. He was after you the whole time.

SANDOR But—it's impossible!

MEN (*Grabbing girls*) Then you're both coming along—to Corvello's!

ELLA (*Laughs again, improvising rapidly*) It won't do any good to rub us out because—because you've all been spillin' your guts into a tape recorder!

MEN Where is it?!

ELLA Where is it? Think we're kids? Where is it! Where is it?? Why, it's hooked up to the police station! As a matter of fact, Barnes should be here any minute!

BARNES (*Entering, followed by policeman.* FRANCIS *and another policeman enter from door stage right*) Awright!!

ELLA (*Screams*) Ohhh! Inspector Barnes! Am I glad to see you!

(*She falls against him, relieved.*)

BARNES All right, Miss Peterson. Get your tooth brush. Come along.

ELLA My toothbrush? Ohh, Inspector, we can drop the act now. I've got the whole bookie ring here. Just take 'em away!

SANDOR (*Running to* BARNES) Inspector Barnes—I surrender happily! These are two of Corvello's henchmen!

BARNES Huh?!

SANDOR I want to congratulate you for having such a brilliant ally—

(*Cowering behind* ELLA.)

Working with you to uncover the Corvello gang! Me—I am nothing!! Small potatoes! Corvello's the head of everything. We only work for him.

BARNES (*Flabbergasted*) What!

ELLA Inspector Barnes—don't you get the picture?!! Titanic Records is a bookie operation. Take 'em away.

BARNES (*Befuddled*) Take 'em away!

(*The cops remove the men.* SANDOR *hangs back.* FRANCIS *beckons.*)

SANDOR (*To* SUE, *as he goes*) Farewell, my *Liebchen!*

SUE Oh, Sandor!

SANDOR We could have made beautiful music together.

(*He tosses her the blue sock containing her money*)

Aufwiedersehen!

FRANCIS You'll get a promotion for this, Inspector Barnes!

BARNES But I didn't *do* anything.

FRANCIS I told you she was a nice girl.

(*He waves his fingers to* ELLA *and exits.*)

BARNES (*Warmly*) Is it a crime for a man to have made a human mistake? I misjudged you.

(*He and* ELLA *shake hands; he starts out, then comes back as though suddenly remembering something.*)

You know, those two kids might have been alive today. (*To* SUE) Would you come to the station with me? I might need your help.

SUE I'll be glad to. Now, Ella, promise you won't leave.

ELLA I'll watch the board till you get back.

(Ring.)

SUE *(Plugs in)* I'll take it. Susanswerphone. What? . . . Who? . . . Talk slower . . . Nobody by that name here . . . Well, it won't do you any good; there's nobody here by that name.

ELLA *(Wearily)* Hang up on him!

SUE *(Unplugs)* Crackpot!

BARNES Come along, please.

(BARNES exits; SUE starts to follow.)

ELLA *(In sudden panic)* Sue! What was that?

SUE Somebody looking for somebody. I said there was nobody here by that name.

ELLA By what name?

SUE Melanie or Melisande. Said he was coming down here.

ELLA *(Terrified)* No! Sue! I can't stay here!

SUE Watch the board!

(She is gone.)

ELLA *(Phone buzzes)* Oh, no! I can't stay here!

(Starts out with bird cage and her suitcase as the ringing continues. She plugs in and speaks hastily.)

Max's Dog and Cat Beauty Shop. Nobody home!

(She unplugs the connection and starts to dash out as JEFF's voice suddenly sounds off stage.)

JEFF'S VOICE Keep the change.

ELLA *(In tremendous hysteria, weeping)* Oh, no!

JEFF Is Susanswerphone in this block?

CARL Right here.

JEFF No, no. It must be an office building.

CARL This is it.

JEFF Are you sure?

CARL Yes.

JEFF Thanks.

(During this, ELLA has rapidly picked up the afghan from the back of the armchair, has flung it about her shoulders, detached a mop and placed it on her head, and has found a pair of SANDOR's glasses and put them on. She can hardly see. She staggers to the switchboard, an insane sight, and sits hunched over like an old woman. JEFF enters excitedly, then stares around the office in amazement)

Hey, what kind of place is this? It's right out of Oliver Twist!

(He sees ELLA and is thunderstruck at the weird sight.)

What?

"Keep away,
young man."

JEFF (Sydney
Chaplin), ELLA
(Judy Holliday)

"We girls aren't
allowed to be
familiar with the
customers. Get
out!"

JEFF (Sydney
Chaplin), ELLA
(Judy Holliday)

"*Get the picture—it's* me!"

JEFF (Sydney Chaplin), ELLA (Judy Holliday)

ELLA (*In exaggerated toothless old lady's voice*) Keep away, young man! You have no right to be here! Now—we girls aren't allowed to be familiar with the customers. *Get out!*

JEFF (*Realizing it is she, but playing along with it, amused. He kneels beside her*) Mom, don't you know me? Don't you know your li'l ole telephonic Sonny Boy?

ELLA (*Turns and peers at him*) Mr. Moss—oh, yes! (*Turning away immediately*) Now, get out!!

(*The mop falls off. He picks it up and replaces it on her head. She bursts into tears, pulls it off, and leaps up*)

Oh, all right! Get the picture—it's *me!*

JEFF (*Lovingly*) Melisande!

ELLA (*Escaping from him*) No—ME! ELLA—Ella Peterson! There is no Melisande. I just made her up!

JEFF (*Following her*) All right—Mel—Ella—Mom—whatever your name is. I love you!

ELLA But you can't! I tricked you!

JEFF Pretty shabby trick—saving a man's life!

ELLA But—all that intuition stuff. I was just telling you what you told Mom. I'm nothing.

JEFF (*Very tenderly*) Don't you call Mom "nothing." I loved talking to her. She was warm, sympathetic, understanding, wise. I thought she was a little old lady. Isn't it a nice surprise to find out she's a beautiful blonde who can cha-cha!

(*He removes her glasses.*)

ELLA You've got to let me explain what I did to you!

JEFF (*Taking afghan from her shoulders*) Never mind. I've got you pretty well figured out. I had a long trip from Bay Ridge to work on it—

(*ELLA crosses to the switchboard with a moan.*)

Kitchell, Barton, me—

(*She sits on the stool, moaning again. JEFF kneels beside her.*)

Mel—Ella—Ella! You do things like that just the way you say hello to people on the subway. You're a girl with a lot of love to give. Instead of spreading it around all over the place, give it to me. I need it. I want it.

(*He kisses her hands. Then lifts her to her feet and places her arms about his neck. They kiss. Ring. ELLA reaches behind her, turns off the board and goes back into embrace. SUE, BARNES, and GWYNNE enter.*)

SUE Oh—!

ELLA (*Breaking out of the embrace and presenting JEFF*) Sue, this is Plaza O-double four, double three.

SUE How do you do?

BARNES (*Shaking hands*) How are you?

GWYNNE Hi!

(*JEFF acknowledges the introductions.*)

BARNES (*To ELLA*) And here are some people who want to see you.

(*He stands at door and announces, like a butler*)

Butterfield 8-9971

(*KITCHELL enters.*)

ELLA Dr. Kitchell!

KITCHELL How can I ever thank you!

ELLA Don't thank me—

KITCHELL (*Inspired again, singing*)

Don't thank me—but let me thank you—

(He goes to one side, writing it on paper.)

BARNES Murray Hill 3-9970!

(BARTON enters.)

ELLA Blake Barton!

BARTON Listen, girl—you gave my life a crazy switcheroo.

ELLA Cuckoo!

Judy Holliday with
Sydney Chaplin and
other cast members

BARTON Cuckoo!

BARNES Plaza 8-4099!

HASTINGS Where is that wonder girl?

> *(All of the subscribers enter through all of the available doors to greet ELLA. They mill about as JEFF and ELLA, oblivious to all, embrace center stage.)*

> *Curtain.*

COMDEN AND GREEN

DISCOGRAPHY

ON THE TOWN

ON THE TOWN 1945 studio production. **MUSIC:** Leonard Bernstein. **WORDS:** Betty Comden, Adolph Green. **CONDUCTOR:** Lyn Murray, Tutti Camarata, Leonard Joy. **CAST:** Nancy Walker, Betty Comden, and Adolph Green of the original cast; Mary Martin.
(78/Dec album 416; Dec 8030, with Lute Song. More complete: CD/MCA MCAD-10280, with Fancy Free.)

ON THE TOWN 1960 studio production. **CONDUCTOR:** Leonard Bernstein. **CAST:** Nancy Walker, Betty Comden, Adolph Green and Chris Alexander of the original cast; John Reardon, George Gaynes, Leonard Bernstein ("Randel Striboneen").
(Col OS-2028. More complete: CD/Col CK-2038.)

ON THE TOWN 1963 London production. **CONDUCTOR:** Lawrence Leonard. **CAST:** Elliott Gould, Don McKay, Franklin Kiser, Carol Arthur, Gillian Lewis, Meg Walter. (CBS(E) APG-60005)

ON THE TOWN 1949 film soundtrack, with additional songs by Roger Edens, Betty Comden and Adolph Green. **ORCHESTRATION:** Conrad Salinger. **CONDUCTOR:** Lennie Hayton. **CAST:** Frank Sinatra, Gene Kelly, Jules Munshin, Ann Miller, Betty Garrett, Vera-Ellen, Alice Pearce. (Caliban 6023, with Dancing Co-Ed. Incomplete: Show Biz 5603.)

ON THE TOWN 1959 studio production, including songs of the 1949 film production.
CONDUCTOR: Geoff Love. **CAST:** Fred Lucas, Dennis Lotis, Lionel Blair, Shane Rimmer, Noele Gordon, Stella Tanner.
(Col(E) SCX-3281; Stet DS-15029.)

ON THE TOWN 1992. London Symphony Orchestra. **CONDUCTOR:** Michael Tilson Thomas. **CAST:** Frederica von Stade, Thomas Hampson, Samuel Ramey, Cleo Laine, David Garrison, Kurt Ollmann, Evelyn Lear, Marie McLaughlin, and Tyne Daly as "Hildy."
CD, Deutsche Grammophon 437-516-2
VIDEO: 4400722973 VHS. Same cast, 1993.

WONDERFUL TOWN

WONDERFUL TOWN original production. **MUSIC:** Leonard Bernstein. **WORDS:** Betty Comden, Adolph Green. **ORCHESTRATION:** Don Walker. **CONDUCTOR:** Lehman Engel. **CAST:** Rosalind Russell, George Gaynes, Edith Adams, Delbert Anderson, Warren Galjour, Albert Linville, Jordan Bentley, Cris Alexander. (Dec 9010; CD/MCA MCAD-10050).

WONDERFUL TOWN 1958 TV production. **CONDUCTOR:** Lehman Engel (of original production). **CAST:** Rosalind Russell, Jordan Bentley and Cris Alexander of original production; Sydney Chaplin, Jacquelyn McKeever, Sam Kirkham. (Col OS-2008).

WONDERFUL TOWN 1955 records by members of 1955 London production. **CONDUCTOR:** Cyril Ornadel. Pat Kirkwood: "Swing!," "One Hundred Easy Ways" (78/Col(E) DB-3569) Kirkwood, Shani Wallis: "Ohio," "The Wrong Note Rag" (78/Col(E) DB-3568) Wallis: "A Little Bit in Love" Dennis Bowen: "A Quiet Girl/It's Love" (78/Col(E) DB-3570)

WONDERFUL TOWN 1961 Los Angeles production. **CONDUCTOR:** Homer R. Hummel. **CAST:** Veronica Lehner, Jerry Lanning, Phyllis Newman. (Location 1261-368)

WONDERFUL TOWN contemporary album. **CONDUCTOR:** Norman Leyden. **VOCALS:** Sandy Stewart, Frank Murphy. "Ohio," "A Quiet Girl," "A Little Bit In Love," "It's Love." (45/Epic album EG-7001)

WONDERFUL TOWN 1986 London production. **ORCHESTRATION:** Michael Reed. **CONDUCTOR:** David Steadman. **CAST:** Maureen Lipman, Ray Lonnen, Emily Morgan, Michael Fitzpatrick, Nicolas Colicos, Roy Durbin, Daniel Coll. (CD/First Night(E) 618260-2)

BELLS ARE RINGING

BELLS ARE RINGING original production. **MUSIC:** Jule Styne. **WORDS:** Betty Comden, Adolph Green. **ORCHESTRATION:** Robert Russell Bennett. **CONDUCTOR:** Milton Rosenstock. **CAST:** Judy Holliday, Sydney Chaplin, Jean Stapleton, Eddie Lawrence, Peter Gennaro, George S. Irving. (Col OS-2006; CD/Col CK-2006.)

BELLS ARE RINGING 1960 film soundtrack with two new Styne-Comden-Green songs. **ORCHESTRATION:** Alexander Courage, Pete King. **CONDUCTOR:** Andre Previn. **CAST:** Judy Holliday, Dean Martin, Eddie Foy Jr., Hal Linden. (Cap SW-1435, Stet DS-15011, CD/Cap CDP-792060.)

COMPILATION DISK

A PARTY WITH BETTY COMDEN AND ADOLPH GREEN 1977 production, with some new material, recorded live in Washington. **PIANO:** Paul Trueblood. **CAST:** Betty Comden, Adolph Green. (Stet S2L-5177 (LP-489); CD/DRG Records CD-2-5177.)

Acknowledgments & Photo Credits

The authors and the publisher are pleased to acknowledge the cooperation of The New York Public Library for the Performing Arts and especially Brian E. O'Connell, Preservation Librarian who together with Bob Taylor, Curator, and Kevin Winkler, Asst. Curator, were especially valiant in their assistance to our project.

Photo Credits

Bells are Ringing: The Friedman-Abels Collection, The Billy Rose Theatre Collection, New York Public Library for the Performing Arts

On The Town/Wonderful Town: The Van Damm Collection, The Billy Rose Theatre Collection, New York Public Library for the Performing Arts

Additional Photos: Whitestone Photo p.3, Chris Alexander p.4, Bob Golby p.25

THE MUSICAL

A LOOK AT THE AMERICAN MUSICAL THEATER
by Richard Kislan

New, Revised, Expanded Edition

Richard Kislan examines the history, the creators, and the vital components that make up a musical and demonstrates as never before how musicals are made.

From its beginnings in colonial America, the musical theater has matured into an impressive art and business, one that has brought millions the experience that director-choreographer Bob Fosse describes as when "everybody has a good time even in the crying scenes."

Kislan traces the musical's evolution through the colorful eras of minstrels, vaudeville, burlesque, revue, and comic opera up to the present day. You'll learn about the lives, techniques, and contributions of such great 20th-century composers and lyricists as Jerome Kern, Rodgers an d Hammerstein, Stephen Sondheim and others. Kislan explains all the basic principles, materials and techniques that go into the major elements of a musical production—the book, lyrics, score, dance and set design.

Richard Kislan's acclaimed study of America's musical theatre has been updated to bring it up to the cutting edge of today's musicals. A new section entitled: Recent Musical Theater: Issues and Problems includes chapters on **The British Invasion • Competition from the Electronic Media • Escalating Costs • The Power of the Critics • The Depletion of Creative Forces • Multiculturalism • The Decline of the Broadway Neighborhood*** **Stephen Sondheim** and his influence on the present day musical theater.

Paper $16.95 • ISBN 1-55783-217-X

THE LONGEST LINE

BROADWAY'S MOST SINGULAR SENSATION: A CHORUS LINE

BY GARY STEVENS AND ALAN GEORGE

Relive the glory of A Chorus Line from behind the scenes, as told by one hundred twenty five artists and professionals who made it happen — cast and management; costume, lighting and sound designers; musicians, carpenters, box office and crew; advertising execs and press agents.

Here is the final authoritative record and celebration of Broadway's "Most Singular Sensation." But it is also the most detailed, in-depth portrait of any musical in Broadway history.

More than 300 photos
Cloth $45.00 ISBN: 1-55783-221-8

A CHORUS LINE

THE BOOK OF THE MUSICAL

The Complete Book and Lyrics of the Longest Running Show in Broadway History

"*A Chorus Line* is purely and simply **MAGNIFICENT, CAPTURING THE VERY SOUL OF OUR MUSICAL THEATER.**"   Martin Gottfried

Photos from the original production
Cloth $24.95 ISBN: 1-55783-131-9

ON SINGING ONSTAGE
New, Completely Revised Edition
by David Craig

Other than Stanislavski's own published work, the most widely read interpretation of his techniques remains Sonia Moore's pioneering study, The Stanislavski System. Sonia Moore is on the frontier again now as she reveals the subtle tissue of ideas behind what Stanislavski regarded as his "major breakthrough," the Method of Physical Actions. Moore has devoted the last decade in her world-famous studio to an investigation of Stanislavski's final technique. The result is the first detailed discussion of Moore's own theory of psychophysical unity which she has based on her intensive practical meditation on Stanislavski's consummate conclusions about acting.

Demolishing the popular notion that his methods depend on private—self-centered—expression, Moore now reveals Stanislavski as the advocate of deliberate, controlled, conscious technique—internal and external at the same time—a technique that makes tremendous demands on actors but that rewards them with the priceless gift of creative life.

PAPER: $12.95 • ISBN: 1-55783-103-3

A PERFORMER PREPARES
A Guide to Song Preparation for Actors, Singers, and Dancers
by David Craig

"David Craig knows more about singing in the musical theatre than anyone in this country—which probably means the world. Time and time again his advice and training have resulted in actors moving from non-musical theatre into musicals with ease and expertise."
—Harold Prince

"Studying with David Craig means infinitely more than learning how to perform a song. I find myself drawing upon this unique man's totally original techniques in all the arenas of my work. If mediocrity ever enters his studio, it is never allowed to depart."
—Lee Remick

"For those of us who were still terrified of singing, David Craig's class was the Second Coming... He is a master at creating exercises and tasks that release that talent, tasks that are measurable."
—Lee Grant

A Performer Prepares is a class act magically transformed to the printed page. It's a thirteen-part master-class on how to perform, on any stage from bleak rehearsal room to the Palace Theater. The class will cover the basic Broadway song numbers, from Show Ballad to Showstopper. With precise, logical steps and dynamic and entertaining dialogues between himself and his students, Craig takes anyone with the desire to shine from an audition to final curtain call, recreating the magic of his New York and L.A. coaching sessions.

CLOTH: $21.95• ISBN: 1-55783-133-5

THE COLLECTED WORKS OF PADDY CHAYEFSKY

This four volume collection includes Chayefsky's finest work for the stage, screen and television. Available individually or as a boxed set.

THE STAGE PLAYS include:
GIDEON • MIDDLE OF THE NIGHT • THE LATENT HETEROSEXUAL • THE TENTH MAN • THE PASSION OF JOSEF D.

$12.95 • PAPER • ISBN 1-55783-192-0

THE TELEVISION PLAYS include:
MARTY • THE MOTHER • PRINTER'S MEASURE • HOLIDAY SONG • THE BIG DEAL • BACHELOR PARTY

$12.95 • PAPER • ISBN 1-55783-191-2

THE SCREEN PLAYS VOL I include:
NETWORK • THE AMERICANIZATION OF EMILY • THE GODDESS

$14.95 • PAPER • ISBN 1-55783-193-9

THE SCREEN PLAYS VOL II include:
MARTY • HOSPITAL • ALTERED STATES

$14.95 • PAPER • ISBN 1-55783-194-7

$59.80 The Deluxe Boxed Set • ISBN 1-55783-195-5

 APPLAUSE

THE COLLECTED WORKS OF HAROLD CLURMAN

Six Decades of Commentary on Theatre, Dance, Music, Film, Arts, Letters and Politics

edited by Marjorie Loggia and Glenn Young

"...RUSH OUT AND BUY *THE COLLECTED WORKS OF HAROLD CLURMAN*...Editors Marjorie Loggia and Glenn Young have assembled a monumental helping of his work...THIS IS A BOOK TO LIVE WITH; picking it up at random is like going to the theater with Clurman and then sitting down with him in a good bistro for some exhilarating talk. This is a very big book, but Clurman was a very big figure."

JACK KROLL, *Newsweek*

"THE BOOK SWEEPS ACROSS THE 20TH CENTURY, offering a panoply of theater in Clurman's time...IT RESONATES WITH PASSION."

MEL GUSSOW, *The New York Times*

For six decades, Harold Clurman illuminated our artistic, social and political awareness in thousands of reviews, essays and lectures. In 1930 he began a series of lectures at Steinway Hall that would lead to the creation of the Group Theater. His work appeared indefatigably in Tomorrow, The New Republic, The London Observer, The New York Times, The Nation, Stagebill, Show, Theatre Arts and New York Magazine.

This chronological epic offers the most comprehensive view of American theatre seen through the eyes of our most extraordinary critic–the largest collection of criticism by a dramatic critic ever published in the English language.

CLOTH $49.95 •ISBN 1-55783-132-7 PAPER $27.95 • ISBN 1-55783-264-1

CITY OF ANGELS
Book by Larry Gelbart
Lyrics by David Zippel

"There's a miracle on Broadway, an *American* musical, with American wisecracks and an original American script. . . It's smart, swinging, sexy and funny. Wit is all over the stage."

—Jack Kroll, *Newsweek*

"Larry Gelbart's book is so brilliantly original, so chills-up-your-spine inventive. . . The jokes snap, the dialogue crackles, the story pops. . . *Angels* put me on Cloud 9."

—Joel Siegel, ABC-TV

"How long has it been since a musical was brought to a halt by riotous jokes? One would have to travel back to the 1960s to find a musical as flat out funny as *City of Angels*."

—Frank Rich, *The New York Times*

"One of the most innovative, brilliant, perfect, breathtaking, entertaining pieces of theatre I have ever seen. The lyrics by David Zippel. . . are bright and diamond hard. . ."

—Liz Smith, *New York Daily News*

cloth $19.95 ISBN: 1-55783-081-9 • paper $9.95 ISBN: 1-55783-080-0

THE FANTASTICKS
Music by Harvey Schmidt
Words by Tom Jones

"An entertaining look at the world's longest-running musical:Richly illustrated, it is **IDEAL FOR FANS OF THE SHOW, AS WELL AS ADMIRERS OF MUSICAL THEATRE...**"

—Variety

"Anybody who has seen the show (who hasn't?) should read the book..."

—Entertainment Today

"A THEATRICAL WONDER"

—Life

cloth $19.95 ISBN: 1-55783-074-6 • paper $7.95 ISBN: 1-55783-141-6

APPLAUSE

A LITTLE NIGHT MUSIC

Music and Lyrics by Stephen Sondheim, Book by Hugh Wheeler

"**Heady, civilized, sophisticated and enchanting.** Good God! An adult musical."
—Clive Barnes, The New York Times

Cloth $19.95 ISBN: 1-55783-070-3 • Paper $9.95 ISBN: 1-55783-069-X

A FUNNY THING HAPPENED ON THE WAY TO THE FORUM

Music & Lyrics by Stephen Sondheim, Book by Burt Shevelove & Larry Gelbart

"**A good, clean, dirty show! Bring back the belly laughs**"   —Time
"**It's funny, true nonsense! A merry good time!**"   —Walter Kerr, Herald Tribune

Cloth $19.95 ISBN: 1-55783-064-9 • Paper $9.95 ISBN: 1-55783-063-0

SUNDAY IN THE PARK WITH GEORGE

Music and Lyrics by Stephen Sondheim, Book by James Lapine

"*Sunday* is itself a modernist creation, perhaps the first truly modernist work of musical theatre that Broadway has produced."
—Frank Rich, The New York Times

Cloth $19.95 ISBN: 1-55783-068-1 • Paper $9.95 ISBN: 1-55783-067-3

SWEENEY TODD

Music and Lyrics by Stephen Sondheim, Book by Hugh Wheeler

"**There is more artistic energy, creative personality, and plain excitement than in a dozen average musicals.**"   —Richard Eder, The New York Times

Cloth $19.95 ISBN: 1-55783-066-5 • Paper $9.95 ISBN: 1-55783-065-7